THE ROOTS OF MORAL EVIL

Dietrich von Hildebrand

THE ROOTS OF MORAL EVIL

Dietrich von Hildebrand

Edited by Martin Cajthaml

HILDEBRAND
PROJECT

First Edition
Published 2024 by Hildebrand Press
1235 University Blvd., Steubenville, Ohio 43952

Copyright © 2024 Dietrich von Hildebrand Legacy Project
All rights reserved

The research manifested in this book was supported by a three-year research grant of the Czech Science Foundation no. 18-06856S *Value and Teleology: Toward a More Fruitful Intellectual Encounter Between Material Value Ethics and Traditional Ethics.*

Publisher's Cataloging-in-Publication Data

Names: Von Hildebrand, Dietrich, 1889–1977, author. | Cajthaml, Martin, 1971–, author. | Crosby, John F., 1944–, author.
Title: The Roots of Moral Evil / by Dietrich von Hildebrand ; edited and introduction by Martin Cajthaml ; preface by John F. Crosby.
Description: Includes bibliographical references and index. | Steubenville, OH: Hildebrand Press, 2024.
Subjects: LCSH Ethics. | Christian ethics—Catholic authors. | Phenomenology. | Christianity—Philosophy. | Conduct of life. | BISAC PHILOSOPHY / Ethics & Moral Philosophy | PHILOSOPHY / Movements / Phenomenology | PHILOSOPHY / Movements / Realism. | RELIGION / Christian Theology / Ethics
Classification: LCC BJ1249 .V6 2019 | DDC 171.1—dc23
ISBN: 978-1-939773-21-0

Set in Adobe Caslon
Typeset by Kachergis Book Design

Cover Design by Marylouise McGraw George

Cover Image: The Garden of Eden with the Fall of Man, by Peter Paul Rubens and Jan Brueghel the Elder, housed in the Mauritshuis art museum in The Hague, Netherlands. Image source: Wikimedia Commons.

Front Cover Font: Circular Bold by Laurenz Brunner

Produced by Christopher T. Haley

www.hildebrandproject.org

Contents

Foreword by John F. Crosby xiii

Introductory Study by Martin Cajthaml xix

I. Introduction 1
    I.i. Moral Disvalues as Polar Opposites of Moral Values 1
    I.ii. Erroneous Accounts of Immoral Actions 2
    I.iii. The Roots of Immorality: Pride and Concupiscence 11

II. Concupiscence 17
    II.i. Nature of Concupiscence 17
    II.ii. Three Main Concupiscent Types 20
    II.iii. The Subjectively Satisfying as Appealing to Concupiscence 23
    II.iv. Bodily Pain 36
    II.v. Bodily Displeasures 52
    II.vi. The Subjectively Satisfying in the Psychic Sphere 56
    II.vii. Money 69
    II.viii. The Sphere of Pure Concupiscence: Sadism and Curiosity 77
    II.ix. Concupiscence in the Realm of the Objective Goods for the Person 82
    II.x. Property 86
    II.xi. Laziness 90

III. Pride   101
    III.i. Satanic Pride   102
    III.ii. Pride of Self-Glorification   104
    III.iii. Vanity   107
    III.iv. Pride of Exterior Lordship   108
    III.v. Haughtiness   110
    III.vi. The Role of Pride in the Different Spheres of Life   112
    III.vii. The Character of Pride Depends on the Values That Are the Object of Pride   114
    III.viii. Static and Dynamic Pride   129
    III.ix. Conceit   132
    III.x. The Pharisee   133
    III.xi. Pride Referring to Non-Values   135
    III.xii. Pride Referring to the Absence of One's Personal Values   139
    III.xiii. Pride Referring to Exterior Goods   145
    III.xiv. Pride Referring to Wealth and Money   149
    III.xv. The Reaction of Pride to Being Loved   153

IV. Hatred   157
    IV.i. Hatred as the Attitude Rooted not Just in Concupiscence and Pride but Also in Certain Particular Situations and Experiences   157
    IV.ii. Hatred as the Antithesis to Love   159
    IV.iii. The Relation between Pride and Hatred   160
    IV.iv. Hatred That Is Not Based on Pride; and Its Roots, Revenge   164
    IV.v. The Center of Irascibility and Its Reactions to Offenses   168
    IV.vi. Two Stages of Hatred   178
    IV.vii. Fanaticism   179
    IV.viii. The Hatred Directed to the Enemy of God   182
    IV.ix. The Nature of the Due Response to Moral Depravity   189

V. Overall Conclusion   193

VI. Immanent Logic   195

Index   213

Dietrich von Hildebrand

Dietrich von Hildebrand was born in Florence in 1889, and studied philosophy under Adolf Reinach, Max Scheler, and Edmund Husserl. He was received into the Catholic Church in 1914. He distinguished himself with many publications in moral philosophy, in social philosophy, in the philosophy of the interpersonal, and in aesthetics. He taught in Munich, Vienna, and New York. In the 1930s, he was one of the strongest voices in Europe against Nazism. He died in New Rochelle, NY in 1977.

Hildebrand Project

WE ADVANCE THE RICH TRADITION of Christian personalism, especially as developed by Dietrich von Hildebrand and Karol Wojtyla (Pope St. John Paul II), in the service of intellectual and cultural renewal.

Our publications, academic programs, and public events introduce the great personalist thinkers and witnesses of the twentieth century. Animated by a heightened sense of the mystery and dignity of the human person, they developed a personalism that sheds new light on freedom and conscience, the religious transcendence of the person, the relationship between individual and community, the love between man and woman, and the life-giving power of beauty. We connect their vision of the human person with the great traditions of Western and Christian thought, and draw from their personalism in addressing the deepest needs and aspirations of our contemporaries. For more information, please visit: www.Hildebrandproject.org

Editorial Board

General Editor: John F. Crosby*
Franciscan University of Steubenville

Rémi Brague
*University of Paris, Sorbonne, Emeritus
Romano Guardini Chair of Philosophy,
Ludwig Maximilian University of Munich, Emeritus*

Rocco Buttiglione
*John Paul II Chair for Philosophy and History of European Institutions
Pontifical Lateran University*

Antonio Calcagno
King's University College at The University of Western Ontario

Hanna-Barbara Gerl-Falkovitz
Technische Universität Dresden, Emerita Hochschule Heiligenkreuz

* Student of Dietrich von Hildebrand

Dana Gioia
Judge Widney Professor of Poetry and Public Culture
University of Southern California

John Haldane
University of St. Andrews
Baylor University

Alice von Hildebrand*†
Widow of Dietrich von Hildebrand

Joseph Koterski, SJ †
Fordham University

Sir Roger Scruton †
Writer and Philosopher

Josef Seifert*
Edith Stein Institute of Philosophy, Granada, Spain

D. C. Schindler
Pontifical John Paul II Institute for Studies on Marriage and Family
Washington, DC

Christoph Cardinal Schönborn
Archbishop of Vienna

Fritz Wenisch*†
University of Rhode Island

* Student of Dietrich von Hildebrand
† Deceased

Foreword

by John F. Crosby

AT THE CENTER OF THE ETHICS of Dietrich von Hildebrand is the concept of value, by which he means the intrinsic worth or dignity or excellence or splendor of a being. Everything of value merits an appropriate response, it calls for some appreciation that is proportioned to its value. Thus for example a person is owed a certain measure of respect in virtue of his or her value as a person. Hildebrand tries to explain morally good acts and actions in terms of value-response, that is, in terms of giving things of value their due. But important as the concept of value is in the Hildebrandian ethics, almost equally important is that which he contrasts with value, namely the importance of the merely subjectively satisfying. This contrast not only serves to focus the concept of value, it also gives Dietrich von Hildebrand what he needs to undertake a major work of re-thinking the structure of morally evil acts and actions.

It is not that he thinks that every act or action motivated by the merely subjectively satisfying is morally bad; after all, he acknowledges a morally legitimate interest in the merely subjectively satisfying, such as our interest in enjoying a good meal. But he thinks that the appeal of the subjectively satisfying commonly inhibits and skews our efforts to give things of value their due, as when I procure a fine meal for myself while ignoring my starving children. If the subjectively satisfying does not remain subordinate to the world of value, if we pursue it without any reference to a higher law, then we go wrong in the moral life. He further thinks that this disordered interest in the merely subjectively satisfying takes on two basic forms in human nature: the form of concupiscence and the form of pride. Thus all morally bad acts and actions derive their badness from concupiscence or from pride, or from some combination of both. But how does this concept of disordered subjective satisfaction, and its two kinds, enable Dietrich von Hildebrand to do a major work of re-thinking moral evil, as I just claimed?

In order to understand the full originality of Hildebrand we have to pay close attention to *the strong essential contrast* that he affirms between value and the merely subjectively satisfying. He does not think that the merely subjectively satisfying is itself a form of value and differs from value only by being a small measure of value. In other words, he does not think that my interest in enjoying a good meal is a value-response, one that differs from other value-responses by being a response to a lower value. He does not think that the badness of procuring a fine meal for myself while letting my children starve comes from preferring a lower value to a higher value. He rather thinks that it comes from completely stepping out of the motivation of value-response altogether; it comes from being motivated by the merely subjectively satisfying *instead of* by value.

Hildebrand would put it like this: conscientiously providing for my children appeals to one center in my moral being—he calls it the "reverent, value-responding center"—while selfishly neglecting them in the pursuit of my own subjective satisfaction appeals to an entirely different center in my moral being—the concupiscent center. These centers are fundamentally incommensurable with each other. When I choose to exit the reverent center and to live out of the concupiscent center, I exercise my most fundamental moral freedom, and I do so in such a way as to become morally bad.

Hardly any previous moral philosopher has explained this incommensurability as ably as Hildebrand has explained it. As a result, hardly any previous moral philosopher has defeated as decisively as he has the ethical intellectualism that comes to us from the Greeks according to which we go wrong in the moral life only by committing some error about what is good and what is bad. Hildebrand does not trivialize moral evil by explaining it in terms of error. He does full justice to it by explaining it in terms of a will that is not only drawn to value but is also vulnerable to the siren song of the merely subjectively satisfying—a will in which we choose between giving ourselves to the call of value, and trampling on value to the extent that it inhibits our subjective satisfaction.

Here is a remarkable fact about Hildebrand's ethics. On the one hand, he fiercely defends the objectivity of value against the subjectivists and relativists; but on the other hand, he resists the idea that the will is always motivated by value, or by an apparent value. He thinks that the human will is often motivated by something that lacks any and every aspect of value, and that this is exactly what happens insofar as the will is motivated by the merely subjectively satisfying. He thinks that we cannot make sense of moral evil without taking account of this abandonment of value-response.

Now all of these ideas of Hildebrand have already appeared in print, especially in his *Ethics* in the chapters on moral evil, chapters 30–35. Many of us have thought that these chapters give us the whole of his thought on moral evil. Martin Cajthaml has performed for us the service of showing that this is not the case, and that there are in fact many pages in Hildebrand's *Nachlass* that add significantly to those chapters. Cajthaml has collected these pages into the present volume. The result is as if a dialogue of Plato, long thought to be lost, has been found. We find in this volume many significant developments and amplifications of Hildebrand's published thought on moral evil.

For example, we find in this volume a nuanced discussion of laziness as a form of concupiscence and as a source of morally bad attitudes and actions. Hildebrand examines not only the obvious case of physical laziness, such as the natural resistance we feel to performing some arduous labor that is required of us; he also considers the psychic and spiritual laziness that makes us unwilling to live at a deep level of existence. He is thinking of people who would have to be deeply recollected in order to be ready for an important encounter with another person, but who are unwilling to make the spiritual effort of recollecting themselves. They find it easier to remain on the periphery of their being, as he puts it, and to manage the encounter in a more superficial way. Or perhaps someone deals superficially with a great work of art or philosophy, shrinking from the spiritual *élan* of entering deeply into the mystery of the work. Von Hildebrand observes that sometimes a person whose moral life is undermined by spiritual laziness may be hard-working and productive; indeed, sometimes the productivity and efficiency of a worker may serve him as an escape from the spiritual exertion that he is called to by the depth and significance of his work. We are reminded here of the famous passage in Kierkegaard's *The Sickness unto Death,* in which he focuses on the extravagance of God's love for each human person. Each is called by name and is loved by God as if the only human person. Kierkegaard says that, in the face of such extravagant love, we are tempted to turn away saying, "that is too much for me, it takes me too far out of my comfort zone, I am content to live among the relativities of finite being without the stress of encountering ultimate being." A perfect specimen of the spiritual laziness of which Hildebrand speaks! One sees that he brings to light many aspects of this laziness that are easily overlooked.

One more example. In many places throughout his corpus Hildebrand warns against getting stuck in the "immanent logic" of an activity. In the newly published papers of the present volume he gives a fuller account of this danger than he gives in any of his previously published writings. For example, the generals in charge of waging a war may become so absorbed in the process of waging and winning the war that they lose sight of the larger question whether the war is still worth waging. They may not notice that the reasons they had for going to war are no longer good reasons for continuing it. They are in danger of being kept in the war for no compelling reason but only because of the immanent logic of waging war. Hildebrand shows that it is a combination of both pride and concupiscence that lock us into the immanent logic of some activity, when we should have the freedom of spirit to soar above it. In this way he brings to light a source of moral evil that has received little attention from philosophers.

Hildebrand has already published major contributions to our understanding of moral evil. The typescripts and manuscripts published here for the first time show that his contributions extend even further than we had thought.

Introductory Study

by Martin Cajthaml

I. *The Aim of the Present Volume*

THE AIM OF THIS VOLUME is to make accessible, for the first time, a representative selection of hitherto unpublished texts of Dietrich von Hildebrand on moral evil. These texts are part of Hildebrand's *Nachlass* (literary remains) preserved at the Bavarian State Library (BSB) in Munich.[1]

The purpose for which these texts were written is not entirely clear. But it is possible they were written in connection with writing the fourth section of Hildebrand's *Ethics* that is entitled "Roots of Moral Evil." There are three reasons for assuming so. First, the headline of many of the manuscripts and typescripts belonging to this group reads "The Roots of Moral Evil. Chapter VIII." Second, there are several references in these materials to various parts of *Ethics*. Third, some—although not many—of the unpublished materials have word-for-word counterparts in the fourth part of *Ethics*.[2]

---

1. Bayerische Staatsbibliothek.
2. There are three editions of Hildebrand's *Ethics*. The first was published as *Christian Ethics*

The sheer extent of the material, the detail of elaboration, and the richness of the themes far surpass what we find in the corresponding sections of *Ethics*. It is unclear why Hildebrand eventually decided not to publish them as a part of his *magnum opus*. Perhaps, after writing them, he realized (or was made to realize by his editor) that the material was too extensive to be incorporated in the already voluminous book. He may subsequently have decided to add only a fraction of the material to *Ethics*, hoping to publish all of it later as a separate volume. The following remark from *Ethics* would seem to indicate as much: "In a later work, to which we have had occasion to refer several times, a thorough analysis of all the ramifications of concupiscence and pride will be offered."[3] Unfortunately, that never came to pass. The material would remain unedited and only later, following Hildebrand's death, included in the *Nachlass* deposited at the BSB.

Since the material assembled in the present edition clearly relates to the final chapters of *Ethics*, the question arises whether it is just a continuation of the inquiry commenced in *Ethics* or whether it brings something genuinely new to the three main themes discussed in the edited materials: concupiscence, pride, and hatred. The largest part of the section on concupiscence in the newly edited materials consists of a detailed analysis of different forms of concupiscence. The same forms are mentioned also in *Ethics*[4] but they are merely listed there, with the already mentioned remark that, in a later work, a thorough analysis of all the ramifications of concupiscence will be offered. This is exactly what we find in the edited material. Hence, we may conclude that, regarding concupiscence, what we find in *Ethics* is related to the edited materials as a promise is related to its fulfilment.

Regarding pride, the new aspect with respect to *Ethics* is the discussion of various problems and points arising from the analysis of pride in

---

by David McKey, New York, 1953. The second edition with the same pagination was published by Franciscan Herald, Chicago, 1972. The third and definitive edition was published by Hildebrand Press, 2020. I quote according to the pagination of the third edition with the pagination of the previous editions in parentheses. For the overlapping passages, see Hildebrand, *Ethics*, 455–457, 462–464, 465–476 (431–433, 437–440, 441–452).

3. Hildebrand, *Ethics*, 459 (435).
4. Ibid., 458–459 (434–435).

Ethics. One of these points is, for example, the apparent paradox arising with the pride of self-glorification analyzed in *Ethics*, namely that the more we are responsible for having certain values the worse it is, morally speaking, to take pride in them. Another such question, related to the same form of pride, not discussed in *Ethics* but considered in the edited material, is pride taken in disvalues, pride in non-existent values, or pride wounded by the absence of certain values. In general one may say that, both regarding concupiscence and pride, the novelty of the edited material with respect to *Ethics* lies mainly in offering explications and further developments of themes mentioned or implied in *Ethics* rather than in presenting something entirely new.

The most substantial new idea to be found in the newly edited material with respect to *Ethics* is the theme of hatred. In *Ethics*, hatred is mentioned as one of the evil responses rooted in pride.[5] But it is only in the edited materials that it is given proper attention and is analyzed in its various forms and its complex relationships not just to pride but also to concupiscence and revenge.

II. *The Contents of the* Nachlass *and Editorial Policy*

The material used for this volume consists of almost four hundred pages of manuscripts and nearly two hundred pages of typescripts, all of which belong to section 14 of the *Nachlass*, entitled "Roots of Moral Evil." Photocopies of the manuscripts were transcribed to a Word document by hand, while photocopies of the typescripts were converted to a Word document and subsequently corrected manually. All of the edited material existed first as hand-written manuscripts. Extended sections of these manuscripts were subsequently converted by Hildebrand into typescripts. In terms of grammar and style, the typescripts are clearly superior to the manuscripts. Although the person who made the transcripts is not known, we can safely assume it was not Hildebrand himself.[6] Some

---

5. Ibid., 476 (451).
6. It is possible that the typescripts were made by Alice M. Jourdain, later Alice von Hildebrand, Hildebrand's second wife. Some may have been made by Donald A. Drennen, Dr. William

of the typescripts include additional handwritten notes by Hildebrand. Given that the quality of the typescripts far surpasses the manuscripts, a decision was made to base the present volume on the typescripts wherever possible. For precise details on the use of typescripts and manuscripts, the editor's notes to the text should be consulted.

Since English was not Hildebrand's mother tongue, it was necessary to make more grammatical and stylistic changes to the text than could be accommodated by the usual system of editorial marks; thus, for readability, editorial marks have not been included in the present volume. Nevertheless, the changes were made very sensitively and only where either grammatically necessary or for the clarity of Hildebrand's ideas. Since this is a critical edition and not the author's approved final version of the text, I ask the reader's indulgence for certain stylistic imperfections which, for the reason just given, could not be, nor should be, removed.

Hundreds of hours of work by a number of people, whose names should be mentioned, are behind the final form of the edited material now before the reader. Elizabeth Shaw, Susanna Spencer, D. T. Sheffler, Mark Spencer, Sarah Blanchard, and last but not least Dr. John F. Crosby worked extensively on the final form of the text, and Justin Keena provided the index. It is hoped that this notable effort will make the final version of the text more readable.

III. *Moral Evil*

The starting point of reflection on the roots of moral evil in our philosophical tradition is the famous view ascribed to Socrates, namely that the origin of all moral evil is the ignorance of the good. Despite the merit of Socrates' insight that the knowledge of the good is the foundation of all virtue, already Plato noted that the claim "No one does wrong knowingly" must be rectified. His theory of the tripartite soul, developed conceptually in *Republic* IV and echoed in the allegory of the chariot in

---

A. Marra, Madeleine Froelicher, and Bernard B. Gilligan. In the Preface to *Ethics*, Hildebrand acknowledges the assistance of all of the above, but gives particular mention to Jourdain.

Phaedrus, served both these aims, that is, to defend the Socratic insight into the fundamental role of moral knowledge for the moral life, and also to explain how acting against one's better knowledge is possible. Plato's account of four basic virtues, later called "cardinal," is inseparably linked with the theory of the tripartite soul. The tripartite soul is *just* when each of its part fulfils its proper task. It is *wise* when the rational part succeeds in acquiring the knowledge of the good. It is *courageous* when the spirited part supports effectively the rational part in its occasional struggles with the appetitive part. And it is *moderate* when the appetitive part follows the orders of the rational part. Note that, unlike in Socrates, on this Platonic account, there is, next to the ignorance of the good, a second root of moral evil: man's occasional incapacity to choose effectively what he knows to be the best for him. This incapacity is due to the desires of the appetitive part of the soul which sometimes push against the rational desire to do what one knows to be the best for him.

Aristotle's division of the soul in rational, sensitive, and nutritive makes for a different starting point in conceptualizing moral virtue in comparison to Plato. However, both thinkers share the basic view that moral excellence cannot be acquired just by the exercise of the intellect. Famously, Aristotle teaches that moral virtues are acquired by habituation, not by instruction. In basic agreement with Plato's concept of the formation of the spirited part of the soul, Aristotle sees habituation as the process in which practical rationality transforms gradually what in the beginning is just a natural temperament into a moral character. Although Aristotle puts in the foreground the concept of virtuous activity, not that of the harmony of the soul, both thinkers, in agreement with Socrates, teach that genuine happiness is possible only on the basis of moral virtue and finds its ultimate fulfilment in intellectual excellence. Aristotle also shares, to a significant extent, Plato's view regarding the ultimate roots of moral evil. He holds that the ultimate root of moral evil is man's incapacity to know the good. But he also acknowledges that one can occasionally act against one's better knowledge. He goes far beyond Plato in analyzing, in the *Nicomachean Ethics* VII, the phenomenon of *akrasia*. Sometimes this term is rendered as "weakness of will." This is, however, misleading, because Aristotle, similarly as Plato in *Republic* IV, does not consider *akrasia* to be morally reproachable willing (*proairesis* or *būlēsis*) but a mental state in which strong emotions or appetites temporarily obscure one's capacity for practical reasoning.[7] It is only in late Antiquity that Augustine, drawing on the Stoics, locates moral evil in evil will.

It is intriguing to note that all the three philosophical masters of classical Antiquity tend to see evil as some lack of the (due) good. Socrates sees it as the lack of the knowledge of the good which man should not be lacking, wherefore he summons his fellow citizens to care for their souls. Plato sees evil as the lack of the due order of the tripartite soul. Aristotle, in his doctrine of moral virtue, sees evil as the lack of the right measure, the too much or too little with respect to the mean found by man's practical reason. Also his understanding of a morally bad life as a life which fails to hit its proper target, namely true eudaimonia, tends to see evil as a lack of the (due) good. It seems that the tendency to see moral evil as a privation of the good is tied to the proclivity of some ancient philosophers to ground moral evil in a metaphysical concept of evil as (ontological, epistemological, and axiological) imperfection.[8] In late Antiquity, this trend is most outspoken in Neoplatonism. Augustine takes the doctrine of evil as privation of the good from this source and gives it a specifically Christian note and theological interpretation. It is through Augustine, and later through Aquinas, that the account of evil as privation of the good became the dominant perspective of Christian theologians and philosophers in approaching the mysterious reality of evil.

---

7. Martin Cajthaml. *The Moral Philosophy of Dietrich von Hildebrand*, Washington: Catholic University of America Press, 2019, 115–119.

8. Cf. the so-called indefinite Dyad in Plato's "unwritten doctrines," prime matter in Aristotle, the matter in Plotinus, etc.

IV. *Hildebrand's Account of Moral Evil*

It may seem when reading von Hildebrand's *Ethics* and the texts brought together in the present volume that their author questions the traditional doctrine of evil as privation of the good. For both in *Ethics* and in the edited material, he presents good and evil as *polar opposites*. However, Hildebrand, in presenting good and evil as opposites, has always in mind *moral* good and evil, not the metaphysical or ontological one. His argument for seeing moral good and evil as polar opposites is simple. Moral evil, as a personal attitude, does not present itself in lived experience as a mere lack of moral good. For example, hatred is not a mere lack of love. A mere lack of love is indifference. By hatred, we mean an outspokenly negative attitude toward another person. Nature, forms, and relations of this attitude to other phenomena, say, pride, are open to philosophical inquiry and can be investigated in their own right, without bringing in the presupposition of the metaphysical meaning of evil as privation. This is the approach Hildebrand takes in the texts collected in this edition. It is only at the very end of his investigation of pride and concupiscence, that he raises the metaphysical question. He writes:

> This analysis of the roots of moral evil has disclosed to us that pride and concupiscence are always at the basis of all moral evil. The metaphysical question arises: how do these two morally negative centers enter into the human person? It is obvious that they do not come from God, that they are not something issuing from God's hand in creating man. Every creature of God is positive, possessing value, reflecting in some way His infinite goodness. "Nothing is evil, but the perversion of our will," says St. Augustine.[9]
>
> Are they a result of the fall of man? Many symptoms of concupiscence and pride are certainly the sad heritage of original sin, such as the tendency of our nature to abandon the attitude of *religio* when we are confronted with the subjectively satisfying, the rebellion of our instincts against our spirit, the immanent logic

---

9. [Possibly a paraphrase of *Confessions* 7.16.22. Editor.]

of our nature: the continuous tendency of our nature to infect our good intentions by pride and many other symptoms of the mysterious rupture and disharmony in our fallen nature that, notwithstanding its negative character, has such a tremendous reality.

But is not the original sin due to pride and concupiscence? One may answer: pride and concupiscence are but a privation and nothing positively existing. This may be true, but it does not explain the mystery. The question arises: where does this privation come from?

We do not pretend to be able to answer this question and to explain the mysterious temptation to pride—potentially connected to the priceless privilege of free will. We restrict ourselves to stating the following two fundamental facts. Firstly, God can never be the cause of pride and concupiscence. Secondly, pride and concupiscence exist in fallen man and are the roots of all moral evil.[10]

From this passage it is obvious that while Hildebrand does not provide (and does not aim to do so) a speculative answer to the question of metaphysical evil, he does not embrace an account of evil which would compromise, not to say contradict, divine omnipotence or the basic metaphysical truth shared by both Christians and Platonists that God cannot be the cause of any evil. For him, as already for Augustine, whom he quotes, the ultimate root of evil is not God's will but the disordered will of His creatures. It is important to point out Hildebrand's rootedness in the tradition regarding this fundamental point. However, in order to grasp the philosophical originality of his account of moral evil, it is even more important to show how he interprets and develops this Augustinian insight that the evil will is the ultimate source of moral evil.

(1) He does so, first, in the context of his highly original and, arguably, groundbreaking explanation of how one is able to act against one's better knowledge.[11] Hence the problem of evil appears here in the form of the question how one's will can become emancipated from the guid-

---

10. See 193–194 below.
11. Cajthaml, *The Moral Philosophy of Dietrich von Hildebrand*, 120–122.

ance of moral reasoning, commanding actions at odds with what one knows to be the best course of action in the given situation. The cornerstone of his explanation is the distinction between the so-called merely subjectively satisfying and the important-in-itself (value), the two "categories of importance," as he calls them. This distinction, developed in chapter 3 of his *Ethics*, can be explained briefly by stating that while the important-in-itself is the importance of the intrinsic value of some being, the merely subjectively satisfying is an entirely subjective type of importance that persons, things, or events acquire in human experience as a result of causing subjective satisfaction or dissatisfaction in us. This total divorce in principle of the merely subjectively satisfying as a category of motivation from the objective structure of a given being makes it incommensurable to the motivation rooted in the intrinsic worth of things and persons around us. This brings Hildebrand to say that there is no "common denominator" between these two categories of importance. That means, for example, that by intensifying the mere subjective satisfaction we are not coming closer to the viewpoint of the intrinsically important. It means also that it is impossible to consider the merely subjectively satisfying as a lower type of intrinsically important, or to consider it as retaining a *ratio boni*. Despite the approach in Aristotelian tradition to use the term "good" analogously, traditional approaches often tend to order all goods on one and the same scale. Even Max Scheler who discovered the notion of value in the sense of intrinsically important held the agreeable for a lower type of value. The originality and philosophical merit of Hildebrand lies in his breaking with this tendency and in acknowledging and highlighting the absolute incommensurability of the intrinsically important with respect to the merely subjectively satisfying.

It is this insight that enabled Hildebrand to explain acratic action differently from his predecessors. In Plato and Aristotle, as has been mentioned, acting against one's better knowledge is explained not by a morally reprehensible volition but by emotions or desires interfering with one's capacity for practical reasoning. Ever since Augustine, the decisive factor in explaining the possibility of acting against one's better knowledge became the will. But the explanation how such willing is possible was often given in terms of the distinction between true and apparent good. I choose what is worse by preferring what appears to me to be the higher good while in fact it is lower. Such a choice, however, does not really represent acting against one's better knowledge. Rather, it is an example of acting on one's (culpable or inculpable) ignorance of what, in the given situation, is the higher good. As such, it is rather a variant of the Socratic claim that no one errs knowingly than an explanation of how one's will can go against one's knowledge of the best. Hildebrand's explanation of how this is possible is simple, elegant, and profound.

One chooses to act against one's better knowledge by giving in, in a particular situation, to the attraction of the merely subjectively satisfying at the expense of the appeal of the intrinsically important. For example, I choose to go to the party which promises a lot of pleasure instead of assisting my needy friend. The reason for this morally reprehensible decision is not my (culpable) ignorance of what is the higher good in the given situation. I know well that, from the viewpoint of the intrinsically important, it is better to assist my needy friend than going to the party. I know also that, from the perspective of mere subjective satisfaction, going to the party is preferable to the other alternative. So the moral decision is here ultimately a choice between two incommensurable viewpoints: the appeal of the intrinsically important versus the attraction by the merely subjectively satisfying. This explanation makes it fully understandable why our decisions (and actions based on them) are sometimes at odds with our knowledge of the best.

This explanation also shows that the mystery of evil will lies on a deeper level than the will commanding particular actions. For whether, in a concrete situation, we withstand the temptation to choose the merely subjectively satisfying at the expense of the intrinsically important, depends on our deeper attitudes towards these two opposing motivational viewpoints. Ultimately, it depends on whether we are, on a deeper level, firmly committed to the call of values, whether our fundamental moral attitude is imperfect, or whether it is just lacking altogether.

(2) This brings us to the second point where Hildebrand goes well beyond the tradition in explaining how human will is the cause of

moral evil. He addresses this deeper level by analyzing what the tradition called moral virtues and vices. Hildebrand interprets moral virtue as value-response, one of his most important and original concepts. More precisely, he defines moral virtue as a general superactual value-response.[12] It means, first, that the virtuous person does not only respond to values of individual beings but to whole value domains. Second, it means that moral virtues are value-responses which exist in the human person, as it were, underneath the stream of present conscious life. They are realities in the human person which pervade and form our conscious experiences, including our moral choices in particular situations. Hildebrand thus develops a singular account of the nature of moral virtue distinct from the Aristotelian notion of moral virtue as a habit and the mean between two extremes.

In chapter 31 of his *Ethics*, he develops this idea of moral virtue as a general superactual value response into the account of three "centers" in the human person: the free, loving, value-responding "center" and the "centers" of pride and concupiscence. On this basis, he develops, in chapter 32, an intriguing account of five basic types of morally deficient characters. It is based on the observation that although the value-responding center in the human person is antithetical to the centers of pride and concupiscence, it nevertheless coexists with them in most human beings in several basic ways. Sometimes this coexistence has the character of an open fight between the antithetical centers as in the upright but still morally struggling man. Sometimes the value-responding center is merely juxtaposed to the centers of pride and concupiscence as in the morally unconscious man. Sometimes, again, a compromise is struck between the antithetical centers, as in the third type, etc. This chapter of *Ethics* presents a theoretical background for the detailed discussion of pride and concupiscence contained in the present volume. It reveals the importance of the striving for moral goodness which is of volitional nature but lies deeper than volitions governing particular actions. Together with the preceding two chapters, it should be read before one starts reading the present edition.

The effort to develop one's fundamental value-responding attitude is,

---

12. Hildebrand, *Ethics*, 376–398 (357–378).

for Hildebrand, the deepest dimension of human freedom. In its readiness to submit unconditionally to the demand of moral and morally relevant values, it is a volitional act. To the extent it involves what Hildebrand calls moral consciousness, it is also an act of practical reason. And in its capacity to transform affective responses by means of the so-called cooperative freedom, it stretches even into the sphere of affective life of the human person. In the edited material of this volume, this fundamental value responding attitude is sometimes called *religio,* or reverence. Hildebrand's account of moral goodness developed on the level of the fundamental moral attitudes allows him to pinpoint the deeper roots of moral evil. As he shows time and again in the newly edited material, the ultimate roots of moral evil are not decisions leading to morally reprehensible actions but the centers of pride and concupiscence hindering one to develop one's fundamental value-responding attitude.

(3) Hildebrand's third major contribution to the analysis of evil will as the ultimate root of moral evil concerns the epistemic effects of pride and concupiscence: they render us incapable of perceiving certain values. Hildebrand calls this incapacity value blindness and analyzes its forms and roots in *Sittlichkeit und ethische Werterkenntnis* and later in *Graven Images*.[13] In contrast to Socrates, who identifies virtue with moral knowledge, Hildebrand, through minute analysis of different ways in which morally problematic attitudes, especially one's unconscious proclivity to pleasure, cause value blindness, uncovers a reciprocal relationship between the two. On one hand, moral virtue, as it is perfected, leads to a deeper moral knowledge. On the other hand, moral knowledge, as it grows deeper, leads to greater moral virtue. That means, however, that even though value blindness is a specifically cognitive dysfunction, it is rooted in the moral sphere. It is not an incapacity that exists independently of free stances and actions of the value-blind person. Therefore, it is subject to moral accountability. Since we are responsible for our basic moral attitudes we are also, indirectly, responsible for our value knowledge and our value blindness, given that these are rooted in those.

---

13. For both a summary presentation of Hildebrand's theory of value blindness, see Cajthaml, *The Moral Philosophy of Dietrich von Hildebrand*, 123–152.

Thus the three ways in which Hildebrand develops creatively the traditional account of evil will as the cause of moral evil are (1) his account of acratic action which explains how one's will can oppose one's knowledge of the best in the given situation, (2) his account of moral virtue as a superactual general value-response antithetical to pride and concupiscence, and (3) his analysis of value blindness as a cognitive defect rooted in the deeper strata of the affective and volitional life of the person. After situating Hildebrand's account of moral evil in the broader context of philosophical views about evil, we are now in the position to understand better his account of pride and concupiscence as two ultimate sources of moral evil.

V. *Concupiscence*

In his treatment of concupiscence, Hildebrand elaborates upon its nature and main types. He describes concupiscence as "the turning to the merely subjectively satisfying as the one exclusive measure of our life—implying an outspoken indifference toward the reign of morally relevant values and any value or importance-in-itself."[14] Since, however, this

---

14. See 20 below. "The idea of the morally relevant values is inspired by Scheler's insight that the end at which the intention of the agent aims must never be the realization of a moral value itself but rather the realization of a nonmoral (material) value. Presupposing this distinction, Hildebrand proposes to distinguish further between those values the realization of which is a source of a genuine moral value in the strict sense of the term, on the side of the realizing act/agent, and those the realization of which is not the source of such a value. The same distinction he draws also in the sphere of responses and attitudes: there are responses and attitudes to values and disvalues that are morally good or evil, in the strict sense of the term, and those that, however genuinely valuable, are not morally good or evil in this sense. If, for example, I fall asleep during a masterful performance of Beethoven's *Eroica*, I surely do not give a proper response to the aesthetic value of this composition in general or to the value of this actual performance in particular. By this 'omission,' however, I do not become morally bad in the strict sense of the term. If, however, I fail to save the drowning child I could have easily saved, my omission bears a disvalue of a strictly moral nature. According to Hildebrand, the reason for this difference in evaluation of our actions, responses, and attitudes is that only in the latter case was a call for an adequate response to a morally relevant value (the value of human person) ignored, while in the former case, the violated value (the aesthetic value of a musical composition) was not a morally relevant one. Note that, according to Hildebrand, moral values can become morally relevant ones. An example could be my effort to persuade my friend to do something morally good. This effort is itself morally good. And it is such precisely because it contributes to the realization of a moral value in my friend. In this example, the moral value is, at the same time, a morally relevant one." Cajthaml, *The Moral Philosophy of Dietrich von Hildebrand*, 29–30.

characterization is also applicable to pride, his subsequent analysis aims at elaborating upon the form of the merely subjectively satisfying specific to concupiscence.

One of the most interesting aspects of Hildebrand's approach to concupiscence is that he resists the overly restricted understanding of concupiscence as, ultimately, the passionate craving for carnal pleasures. While acknowledging that this is the classical articulation of concupiscence, Hildebrand describes in considerable detail two typologically distinct concupiscent types. In the first of them, the agreeable is not an object of fierce, impetuous desire as in the passionate type, but rather of a phlegmatic, lazy, bovine-like "consummation" of the agreeable. Despite the quite stark difference between impetuous, dynamic craving for and phlegmatic, passive consumption of pleasurable goods, these two concupiscent types have in common a certain "hardness" displayed in the unscrupulous brutality with which they would push aside any obstacle to the gratification of their desires. This makes them clearly different from the third, "soft" concupiscent type. This type, when confronted with pain, or some other disagreeable experience, responds not with brutality but with inflated self-pity. This type of person, think of Nero from Sienkiewicz's *Quo vadis*, enjoys the soft and friendly atmosphere, he desires to be petted, caressed, and cherished. Despite the brutality of the first two types, and the soft, hypersensitive reactions of the third type, all three have in common total egocentrism and absence of charity.

Following on this basic typology, Hildebrand distinguishes many subspecies of concupiscence. The most basic dividing line runs between concupiscence related to an object that may but need not appeal to concupiscence, and "pure" concupiscence, which pertains to an object that exclusively relates to concupiscence but never to a morally licit attitude. Intriguingly, Hildebrand's examples of pure concupiscence are sadism and curiosity in the sense of sensationalism. It is hard to imagine two apparently more heterogeneous phenomena than these two. And yet, as Hildebrand shows, both have in common that the pleasure which makes them attractive has never a morally licit form. This is more obvious in the case of sadism. The physical suffering of another person can never be a source of pleasure for the legitimate center to which normal types of subjectively satisfying, for example bodily pleasure, appeal. It can only be the object of a concupiscent attitude. This means that this type of subjective satisfaction is evil in itself and cannot, therefore, under any circumstances become morally good or neutral. The same holds true for curiosity even though it is morally much more innocuous. Curiosity means in this context the eagerness to know the minutest details of another person's life, particularly private affairs. The subjective satisfaction derived from such indelicacy is by its very nature morally bad.

All forms of pleasure, with the exception of those featuring pure concupiscence, may have both a morally legitimate and a morally illegitimate (concupiscent) form. Hence an intriguing question arises: When and why does a licit desire for a given pleasure become illicit (concupiscent)? As a response to this question, Hildebrand distinguishes different attitudes toward pleasure: the attitude of the saint, the attitude of the noble pagan such as Socrates, the morally unobjectionable attitude, the morally imperfect attitude, and the morally evil attitude. It is in the morally imperfect attitude, he contends, that we observe the transition of the legitimate center to which the agreeable appeals to a concupiscent attitude. In the morally evil attitude, we are confronted with concupiscence in its fully developed state.

As the next step, Hildebrand distinguishes many types of this potentially concupiscent attitude to the agreeable starting with physical pleasure. He distinguishes various forms of bodily pleasures, bodily displeasures, and physical pains. One particularly interesting point in this discussion is the following asymmetry between bodily pleasures and displeasures, particularly bodily pain: while the immanent tendency of striving for bodily pleasure is always fraught with the danger of abandoning reverence and of consuming such pleasure in a concupiscent way, the effort to avoid intense bodily pain is, in itself, morally legitimate. In contrast, striving for bodily pleasure is, as such, neither morally legitimate nor illegitimate. It becomes morally legitimate only when subservient to *religio* and morally illicit when detached from it. From this, it follows that trying to avoid bodily pain becomes morally illegitimate only when an *extraordinary* moral obligation requires its endurance as, for example, in the case of someone being tortured in order to give false witness about an innocent person. By contrast, striving for bodily pleasure can be immoral even if there is no such *extraordinary* obligation forbidding it. However, from the fact that the tendency to avoid intense bodily pain is morally legitimate, it does not follow that there could be no concupiscent attitude to bodily pain.

Another intriguing point in this discussion are different types of reactions to bodily pain by the different concupiscent types: hard (passionate or lazy) and soft. The attitude of the hard types to inevitable bodily pain is an impotent rebellion. Expressed through cursing, this state is accompanied by a brutal and entirely self-centered approach to anyone who might try to help alleviate that suffering. The attitude of the soft concupiscent type to bodily pain is characterized by a propensity to exaggerate subjective bodily pain.

Turning to the role of concupiscence in the psychic sphere, Hildebrand explores such various phenomena as games, superficial forms of socializing, light literature, movies, pop music, and even concupiscence which can be detected in the satisfaction of one's psychic urges and in the unloading of one's mental energies. Particularly interesting is Hildebrand's analysis of the second mentioned phenomenon: superficial forms of socializing. He distinguishes three variations of concupiscence that we encounter in this sphere. The first is the desire to "let oneself go," to enjoy an atmosphere of wild abandon in which responsibility is suspended. The second is the concupiscence of the "elegant man," who, unlike the first type, prefers the superficial, polite ambience of the salon. In this instance, the inclination to replace the value-response attitude with conventional forms of politeness and elegance is both unconscious and concealed in the illusion of appearing well-mannered. The third variation of concupiscence in this sphere relates to a superficial form of socializing that is not desired purely for enjoyment's sake. Rather, it is pursued in the hope of forgetting, of escaping the burdensome awareness of one's own troubles. Such a tendency is also a fruit of concupiscence, argues Hildebrand, because the tendency to flee from oppressive reality contradicts the value-response attitude.

Intriguing is also Hildebrand's discussion of concupiscence related to the unloading of psychic energies, as with, for example, giving expression to one's gifts and talents. Hildebrand notes that concupiscence becomes an issue here only when the subjective satisfaction arising from the appeasement of these urges becomes thematic as a motive for action, as it is, for example, in the case with a person whose primary motive in having a "friend" is being able to satisfy an urge to talk. Or consider the physicist whose primary aim in carrying out scientific research is to expend mental energy. In the former case, the "friend" is reduced to a mere conduit for one's own subjective satisfaction, an object of appeasement for a psychic urge. In the latter, the search for knowledge, which is the natural goal of scientific activity, is subordinated to the search for pleasure, which is solely associated with discharging mental energy. This perversion is especially palpable in cases where the activity in question relates to morally relevant values. "To nurse a sick person," writes Hildebrand, "primarily in order to display motherly instincts or to relish our skill, instead of being motivated by our interest in the sick person, in mitigating her sufferings, in serving her, is repugnant and frustrates the moral value of this action."[15] The origin of this type of perversion, which often goes unnoticed by morally unconscious types, is a specific form of concupiscence.

Hildebrand's inquiry into concupiscence in this edition concludes with two short typescripts. The theme of the first is property. In this context, the concupiscent attitude does not relate to our attainment of goods merely on account of their offering pleasure but on account of their belonging to us. There is an elementary satisfaction to be gained from the mere possession of a good, which differs from any other satisfaction the good can provide. Although Hildebrand highlights the absolutely legitimate desire of a human being to own goods, the satisfaction derived from the simple act of ownership can itself become an object of

---

15. See 67 below.

concupiscence. As in most other cases, concupiscence is revealed when the attitude to the ownership of the goods becomes detached from the value-response attitude.

The second short typescript deals with the theme of laziness, a typical outgrowth of concupiscence. Hildebrand distinguishes laziness proper from a more general phlegmatic temperamental disposition which is of no obstacle to the value-response attitude. The most typical form, laziness proper, is embodied in a type of concupiscent person who craves neither for the appeasement of passions nor for pleasure as such. What satisfies her is a state of dumb, vegetative rhythm of life, sinking in the automatism of the bodily life. A particularly intriguing point in this discussion is Hildebrand's contention that inertia is also an expression of concupiscence. This observation corrects the above-mentioned tendency to think of concupiscence simply in terms of a passionate craving for (carnal) pleasures. Hildebrand also distinguishes laziness in the sense of an unwillingness to work, whether manually or intellectually, from spiritual laziness. In this context, he makes an interesting observation that even "The most assiduous man, efficient in his work, endowed with a great potential for activity and agility, whom we would contrast with the inert and lazy man, the man who could not live without work, who relishes business, who is reliable, punctual, self-controlled, may still be typically lazy in the sense of spiritual laziness."[16]

VI. *Pride*

Following this rich, complex, yet systematically elaborate account of concupiscence, Hildebrand turns to the other main root of moral evil: pride. The feature that pride and concupiscence share is the detachment of the striving for the merely subjectively satisfying from the attitude of reverence. The basic difference between pride and concupiscence is that whereas the concupiscent person "plunges into subjectively satisfying goods and throws himself away on them," the proud individual "is char-

---

16. See 96 below.

acterized by a reflexive gazing at himself."[17] Therefore, the relation between the subjective satisfaction and the *ego* (self) differs significantly in each case. Using Hildebrand's metaphor, in concupiscence "man renounces his birthright for a mess of pottage." In pride man assigns himself a right that is above him; he exalts himself in an illegitimate way.

Like concupiscence, pride has many forms. Hildebrand distinguishes in his *Ethics* four basic types of pride, and in the manuscripts and typescripts of the present volume he distinguishes five. The first, also the rarest and most radical, is satanic pride. Essentially metaphysical, satanic pride aspires to "metaphysical lordship" or "metaphysical grandeur." Precisely because of this aspiration, satanic pride revolts in hatred against every value and most of all against God.

The second basic form of pride is the pride of self-glorification. Like satanic pride, it is directed at the values in oneself; however, it does not aim at "dethroning" them. Rather, the person dominated by this form of pride uses values as the means for self-glorification, as the "source of one's grandeur." The pride of self-glorification is further divided into sub-types, each of which relates to the set of values exploited. The morally worst of all, according to Hildebrand, is the Pharisaic attempt to seek self-glorification in religious and moral values. Less abhorrent is seeking self-glorification in intellectual values, actual or alleged. Less objectionable still is taking pride in one's good looks, bodily strength, and so on.

The third basic type of pride is vanity. Like the pride of self-glorification, it refers to its own perfection. However, unlike the pride of self-glorification, which can be both static and dynamic, vanity is essentially static. It consists in relishing the possession of real or alleged perfections. More importantly still, vanity does not feature the perverted attitude to values we find in both satanic pride and the pride of self-glorification. The vain person may have a certain understanding of values and a readiness to conform to their call. In addition, vanity can be restricted to certain value-spheres. One may, for example, be satisfied with one's good looks but at the same time remain indifferent to other

---

17. See 101 below.

perfections, say, intellectual brilliance or moral stature, even if these are objectively superior.

The fourth basic type of pride places value on external goods, such as political power or exceptional social status. Hildebrand calls it the pride of exterior lordship. Similar to the pride of self-glorification, this pride does not operate on a metaphysical level. The perversion of values that characterizes this type of pride is different from the perversion we find in satanic pride and pride of self-glorification. It downplays or entirely overlooks the actual significance of moral and religious values, particularly their normative force. These values are regarded as an unimportant obstacle for attaining exterior lordship. The hostility implied in the pride of exterior lordship is directed at whatever presents itself as a tangible force in the outside world. For only that force can rival such ambition. Specifically, the pride of exterior lordship only takes moral or religious values seriously when they appear as exterior forces, such as those unleashed in social and political movements. Essentially dynamic, this pride is typically revealed in persons of ambition.

The fifth basic type of pride Hildebrand lists is haughtiness. Like vanity, haughtiness is partially compatible with a value-response attitude because it does not imply a hatred of values. In this type of pride, values are not used as a means of self-glorification. The haughty individual recognizes and can indeed heed a whole range of value-spheres, acknowledge that moral obligations are grounded in values, and, occasionally, come to respect legitimate authority. However, such a person is incapable of displaying emotions such as contrition, compassion, or gratitude: contrition, because haughtiness does not permit the admission of personal moral failures, even to oneself; compassion, because it is based on the idol of pseudo-virility; and gratitude, because it refuses to recognize one's indebtedness to another person. Equally, haughtiness abhors any reduction of personal strength and independence, because it erroneously associates this with weakness, fragility, or guilt. Haughtiness recognizes only one evil: weakness.

While elaborating upon the second mentioned type of pride, that is, the pride of self-glorification, Hildebrand makes three notable points:

(1) Pride is not always based on values one actually possesses. One can take pride also in *non-existent* values. For example, a conceited person may base her pride on misconceptions about her own intelligence, abilities, or physical appearance. Her conceit thus may be based on merely imagined values. Unlike conceit which can be based both on really existent and merely imagined values, Pharisaic pride can exist only with respect to non-existent values. This is because it concerns one's own moral excellence and piety and the actual possession of these values precludes one from being proud of them. This claim is not based on an empirical improbability of a person taking pride in her actual moral values but in the essential incompatibility of the value-response attitude with a prideful fundamental moral attitude. This incompatibility does not mean that both attitudes cannot coexist in the same person in one way or another. It means that both attitudes exclude each other similarly as, according to Plato's theory of Forms, largeness can never admit of smallness even though the same entity can be both large and small at different times and in different respects.

(2) Hildebrand realizes that the pride of self-glorification can also be taken in moral *disvalues* even though this possibility does not, as such, make for a separate type of pride. In some cases, say, when a thief is proud of his thievery, he is not dominated by pride of self-glorification. His motivation for stealing is his concupiscence, not his pride. The glorifying moment is here more accidental. By contrast, when somebody glorifies himself because of an evil idol, say, the idol of a pseudo-virility, the idol itself is already an outgrowth of pride. In this case, the glorifying moment is dominant.

(3) Hildebrand also analyzes pride wounded by the awareness of *not* possessing certain values. This pride, similar to pride taken in the possession of certain values, naturally depends on the type of values concerned. If one's pride is hurt by not having, say, a beautiful appearance, it is much more innocuous and superficial than the wounded pride of acknowledging oneself insufficiently clever or artistically skilled. However, the nature of this pride depends also on one's response to admitting deficiency in respective values. There are two different ways the proud person can re-

spond: "The first is a desperate effort to acquire the perfections he lacks and a hostile attitude toward those people who appear to him to be his superior."[18] This attitude is the source for envy, jealousy, and hatred of anyone deemed superior. The second type of response is still worse: *ressentiment*.[19] This phenomenon is described as "the attempt to overcome one's own inferiority by minimizing or devaluing the values that one's fellow man possesses and that one does not possess."[20] So, although there is an acceptance that another person may possess a certain value, this does not stop the victim of *ressentiment* from denigrating and calling into question the value itself. And while this attitude avoids expression of the open hatred, jealousy, and envy characteristic of the first response, the price of that concealment is very high. Much like satanic pride, the person corrupted by *ressentiment* harbors a sneaking, half-conscious hatred of the value coveted. But unlike satanic pride, the desire to discredit a given value is not simply due to the value itself, but because one cannot stand the superiority of the person in possession of it.

VII. *Hatred*

As already mentioned, Hildebrand sees hatred as a unique embodiment of moral wickedness, as a polar opposite to love. However, hatred is not opposed to love in the same sense in which indignation is opposed to enthusiasm, sorrow is opposed to joy, or contempt is opposed to esteem. These types of opposition are paradoxically rooted in an essential similarity of intention: not only do both positions express a value-responding attitude, they also issue from the same center in the human being. The opposition between them stems from the object to which they respond: indignation is a due response to a disvalue, while esteem is a due response to a value; sorrow is a response to a disvalue, while joy is a response to a value, and so on. Hatred, by contrast, is not an expression of a

---

18. See 142 below.
19. Hildebrand draws here on Scheler's famous analysis of *ressentiment*. Cf., for example, the freely accessible English translation of Scheler's *Das Ressentiment im Aufbau der Moralen* at https://hscif.org/wp-content/uploads/2018/04/Max-Scheler-Ressentiment.pdf
20. See 143 below.

value-responding attitude differing from love only in that it refers to an object the importance of which is in polar opposition to the importance of the object of love. "Hatred in the strict sense," Hildebrand contends, "is never a value-response attitude. Its venomous, dark character is qualitatively the very antithesis to the victorious intrinsic goodness of charity."[21] This means that love and hatred issue from two opposite centers in a human being. While love is an expression of the value-responding center, hate is an expression of the center of pride and also, occasionally, of concupiscence.

The worst sort of hatred is hatred of God. "Satanic pride," Hildebrand writes, "is the incarnate ultimate hatred, and it extends itself, as we saw before, to every value reflecting God and to every human person."[22] While satanic pride involves necessarily this type of hatred, other forms of pride are not necessarily connected with hatred. Thus, for example, the pride of the Pharisee need not involve hatred, at least not the hatred of every value or even of every morally relevant value. In the other ramifications of the pride of self-glorification, Hildebrand observes, the mutual relationship between pride and hatred is even more contingent. The decisive difference here hinges on whether a person takes pride in qualities firmly believed to be in one's possession *or* feels inferior knowing the qualities desired are out of reach. In the first case, the person will experience hatred only accidentally, that is, only upon discovering that the possession of the qualities one prides oneself on is rivaled or surpassed in someone else. Far worse, in the second case, the person will fall victim to *ressentiment*, a condition that poisons all relations with other people. All things considered, this is a much more pervasive and morally sinister type of hatred.

Hildebrand explores further the link between hatred and other types of pride. In haughtiness, vanity, and exterior lordship, the ties between pride and hatred are rather contingent. However, in cases of dynamic pride, for instance, where an ambitious person is repeatedly humiliated, embitterment gives rise to *ressentiment*, the worst type of hatred. Curi-

---

21. See 159 below.
22. See 160 below.

ously, vanity displays the least potential for hatred, Hildebrand notes, since it is essentially a static form of pride.

Hildebrand also shows that some types of hatred are rooted neither in pride nor in concupiscence. One of them is hatred associated with revenge. Another one is hatred emanating from different forms of enmity, such as that between clans and families. Still different roots are found in the hatred of people believed to profess improper or evil ideas, a hatred typical of religious fanaticism. And there is also hatred provoked by indignation over the moral meanness or depravity of a person.

VIII. *Immanent Logic*

The edition concludes with a typescript dealing with absorption in the immanent logic of an activity as a root of moral evil. What is "immanent logic" in this context? Every action or situation requires that one proceeds in certain ways in order to be effective. To construct a machine, one must heed the laws of mechanics; to escape a burning building, one must act according to the inner logic of the situation; to learn how to play a musical instrument, one must practice in the right way. The immanent logic implied in all of these cases is, by itself, morally neutral. Also, the activities guided by this inner logic are good or bad dependent on the *telos* at which they aim. The negative moral relevance of the given activity, that is, independently of the importance of its telos, arises only when we become *enslaved* by its immanent logic. Not only is this enslavement itself morally negative, it is also the source of other types of moral evil.

The phenomenon of enslavement (or absorption) by the inner logic of a situation is well illustrated by the following simple example: I want to write the next page of my paper. I know that I have notes I want to use in my desk drawer. I reach for them but discover that the drawer is stuck. I try to open the drawer repeatedly but without success. But I become so absorbed in my struggle with the drawer that I forget I can also write without the aid of notes; simply retrieve the contents from memory. Instead of seeking an alternative course of action, time and energy are wasted.

What is the cause of this patently unreasonable behavior? Hildebrand responds: I become so absorbed by the effort of reaching the intermediate *telos* of my action that I forget I might reach my final aim by taking an alternative course of action. There are three characteristics of this "becoming captive" to the immanent logic of an activity. (1) The means becomes detached from its end, meaning what originally was a means becomes an end of its own. (2) The teleology of my activity assumes a character of automatism whereby I lose the necessary distance to it. I am no longer the master of the situation. I am dominated by this immanent teleology which pushes me forward according to its immanent logic. (3) What originally was a means acquires, through my yielding to the immanent logic of the given subordinated activity, an illegitimate importance to which I, governed against my better judgment, become captive.

In the "drawer" example, becoming captive to the immanent logic of an activity is more unreasonable than immoral. But in other cases, Hildebrand points out, it can become a root of at least three types of moral evil. (1) Imprisoning oneself in the automatism of the given activity itself. (2) Where I isolate the subordinate end while ignoring the superior end to which the subordinate end is a means, I risk becoming instrumental to a potentially immoral end. For instance, a military general, who, having grown so wholly absorbed by the immanent logic of battle, no longer cares whether the war is just or not. (3) Entrapping myself in the immanent logic of an activity can blind me to the moral significance of the means used to attain my end. For example, I become embroiled in discussion with an opponent on an important issue. Having become so caught up in the immanent logic of winning the argument, I resort to insults in an expression of hate and thus lose the whole debate.

In some cases, pride is the ultimate root of this absorption, argues Hildebrand. For instance, returning to "the drawer example," the frustration I feel in not being able to exercise "masterly sovereignty" over a physical object wounds my pride. In many other cases, the most important cause of the absorption is the relegation of the reverence to the world of values in favor of fulfilling the task at hand. The failure to stay spiritually alert to the call of values, particularly the morally relevant ones, that is, the failure to live a life of moral virtue, leads to becoming captive to the immanent logic of one's activity—to the point of not caring whether what one does is, ultimately, moral or immoral. This attitude, notes Hildebrand, is a fruit of spiritual laziness, a theme already discussed in connection with concupiscence. Hence, in many cases, the ultimate root of the absorption in the immanent logic of a situation is concupiscence.

IX. *Manuscripts and Typescripts Used*

Concerning the materials from the *Nachlass*, reference is made to the signature of the *Nachlass* at the Bavarian State Library (BSB) in Munich (Ana 544). The ensuing Roman numeral refers to the overall thematic group. All typescripts and manuscripts used in this edition are from group "VI"—that is, *Ethics*. The first Arabic numeral (14) used indicates the specific thematic group; in this case, "The Roots of Moral Evil." The second Arabic numeral references the number of the folder. Example: Ana 544, VI, 14, 8.

For those intending to consult the BSB manuscripts or typescripts used in this edition, note that previous numbers were assigned to folders by Prof. Ave-Lallemant, who first sorted the materials. For example, in folder 1 of thematic group 14 ("The Roots of Moral Evil"), the numbers read 131, 151, 161. Since, however, these numbers do not feature on the shelf markings, they have been omitted. Note also that the numbers on the folders in the *Nachlass* are assigned as follows: "M 1/8" and not "8." Following is the list of all used manuscripts and typescripts:

MANUSCRIPTS
1. The Roots of Immorality, 137 pp., Ana 544, VI, 14, 1.
2. Laziness, 35 pp., Ana 544, VI, 14, 1.
3. Eigengesetzlichkeit, 35 pp., Ana 544, VI, 14, 1.
4. Pride, 22 pp., Ana 544, VI, 14, 1.
5. Pride (continuation), 89 pp., Ana 544, VI, 14, 2.
6. Hatred, 48 pp., Ana 544, VI, 14, 2.

TYPESCRIPTS

1. The Roots of Moral Evil (Concupiscence), c. 100 pp., Ana 544, VI, 14, 4.
2. The Roots of Moral Evil (Concupiscence), 104 pp., Ana 544, VI, 14, 5.
3. The Evil Fruits of Pride and Concupiscence (Hatred), 17 pp., Ana 544, VI, 14, 5.
4. Laziness, 26 pp., Ana 544, VI, 14, 9.
5. Immanent Law, 26 pp., Ana 544, VI, 14, 5.
6. Property, 6 pp., Ana 544, VI, 14, 5.

This Introductory Study is based on the article: Martin Cajthaml. "Von Hildebrand on the Roots of Moral Evil." *Religions* 14: 843 (2023). https://doi.org/10.3390/rel14070843

THE ROOTS OF MORAL EVIL

I

Introduction[1]

I.i. *Moral Disvalues as Polar Opposites of Moral Values*

MORALLY NEGATIVE VALUES AND MORAL BADNESS are found in certain human attitudes, responses, and actions, just as much as morally positive values and moral goodness are.

The moral depravity of the action of a murderer slaying a human being in order to get his money or to take revenge is obvious. The morally negative value is clearly given to us in contemplating this action. Analogously, we clearly grasp the negative value of the hard-heartedness of a man who remains completely indifferent in seeing his fellow man in great misery and refusing any help, even when he could help him without sacrificing anything of his own. We cannot see the violent hatred of someone without grasping also the moral wickedness of this attitude. In reading of Cain and Abel, the horrible character of Cain's deed strikes us.

It is not the absence of something positive that is given to us, but the

---

1. [Ana 544, VI, 14, 1. Editor.]

presence of something that seems to be the outspoken antithesis to the moral goodness, that is, a reality contrasting with the morally good in a manner analogous to how bodily pain contrasts with bodily pleasure.

A metaphysical analysis may reveal that this morally negative value is nothing but a privation on the grounds that every evil is a privation of being and is not something that possesses being analogous to the real existence of the good. But for our immediate experience the morally negative values are a reality, really given to us as an intense quality characterizing certain human attitudes. They present themselves to us in a way completely different from the mere absence of something positive.

The great ethical problem, which is here at stake, is the question which elements make a human attitude morally bad. What are the conditions that make for a morally negative value? If we had to deal before with the problem of what is presupposed for a human attitude to be morally good, which features are required in a human act in order to endow it with moral values, we have now to pose the same question with respect to moral badness. Upon which factors does the immoral character of a human attitude depend?

We shall first examine this problem in the sphere of actions, then in the sphere of the affective responses, and finally in the sphere of the superactual attitudes or habits, that is to say, with respect to vices.

I.ii. *Erroneous Accounts of Immoral Actions*

The Immorality of Actions Not Due to Ignorance

We have seen in the former analysis that there exist three essentially different categories of importance: the important-in-itself, or value; the objective good for the person; and the merely subjectively satisfying.[2]

The typical morally good action presupposes that our will has the character of a value-response and, moreover, that the value motivating our will is a morally relevant one.

---

2. [See Hildebrand, *Ethics*, chaps. 1–3, where he gives the fullest account of the three categories of importance. Editor.]

In the morally bad action, on the contrary, our will ignores in one way or another a good possessing a morally relevant value; it consents to destroy or to injure this good. As the positive interest in the morally relevant value, that is, respect for the call of this value, is the source of the moral goodness of an action, so the disrespect for the morally relevant value is the source of the moral badness of an action. But the difficulty which immediately arises is the question of how it may occur that someone disrespects a morally relevant value. Why does a man not respond to the call of the morally relevant value, why does he assent to destroy or injure a good having such a value? There must be some reason or motive for this unreasonable attitude.

Different answers have been given to this question. The famous thesis of Socrates is well known: ignorance is the reason for this attitude. Nobody would act wrongly if he possessed a perfect knowledge of the good in question. Or as it is formulated generally, no one does wrong knowingly. The morally wrong action is thus, according to this Socratic conception, exclusively conditioned by ignorance. Because someone has no clear notion of the value of a good, he disrespects it.[3] As soon as he would know it, he would conform to the value, he would no longer disrespect it. A thief would no longer steal, if he grasped the value of property, the rights of his fellow man, and the call of justice. Nobody would commit adultery, if he grasped the value of marriage or the value of purity. Only because he is ignorant of it, can he act so.

This theory is untenable for many reasons, and it has even been already corrected and restricted by Plato in the *Republic*, and Aristotle has refuted it in the *Nicomachean Ethics*.[4] Above all St. Paul has said: "I do not understand what I do. For what I want to do I do not do, but what I hate I do."[5] We shall restrict ourselves here to point out briefly the different reasons that reveal the impossibility of reducing immorality to ignorance, that is to say, to an error concerning the good in question.

---

3. [In Hildebrand's terminology, "a good," like the German "Gut," stands for an entity endowed with a value, not for the value itself. Editor.]

4. [Plato discusses this problem in *Republic*, bk. 4, Aristotle in *Nicomachean Ethics*, bk. 7. Editor.]

5. [The reference is missing in the manuscript, but presumably Hildebrand has in mind Romans 7:15. Editor.]

In all cases where a struggle precedes an action, where the person experiences a conflict between the voice of conscience and the temptation, ignorance concerning the value of the good is out of question. She may even be fully aware that she does morally wrong in yielding finally to the temptation. It is obviously not because she is ignorant of the value of the good that she shrinks back from the right action until she ultimately yields to the temptation. The basic error is rather in overlooking the essential difference between the categories of importance that can motivate our will, nay, even the existence of different categories. *Bonum* is supposed to be a univocal instead of an analogous concept, and thus the choice of something that has a negative value cannot be admitted. The silent presupposition is that there exists only one possible motivation of our will, namely, the *bonum* in a univocal sense. Thus the acceptance of a morally relevant evil is conceived as a result of ignorance, of an imperfect understanding. The drama that in our moral life results from the two different categories of importance—the subjectively satisfying and that of value—is completely ignored in this thesis. Just consider how we see this drama in the thief who is tempted by the subjectively satisfying aspect of money and fails to respect the value that is inherent to the property. The struggle between the voice of conscience and the subjectively satisfying would be impossible if the thesis of Socrates were right. And nobody can deny that such a struggle exists in reality.

Secondly, it must be said that in the cases where ignorance of the morally relevant values is really found, this blindness to the values is not just a mere intellectual failure like, for example, the ignorance concerning physical or chemical facts. Already Plato points out that the passions darken our capacity for true knowledge of the good. And Aristotle shows that the understanding of what is good and morally right depends upon the right disposition of our will.

There is no doubt that a blindness concerning morally relevant and moral values exists. If Raskolnikov, in the novel of Dostoevsky, believes that he does something courageous and grand in killing an old, mean woman, a usurer, and in robbing her, he is obviously blind to the value of a human life as such, blind to the dignity that all human beings possess independently of their moral character, that is to say, that they possess independently of their moral meanness and of the fact that their life is a nuisance for human society.

But obviously this blind spot in his conscience cannot be put on the same level with the ignorance of a man who believes that thunder is the voice of a mighty ghost or that the earth is flat.

Moral blindness is, on the contrary, always a result of the misdirection of our will. The man who has given himself over more or less to his pride or concupiscence, who looks at being from the point of view of satisfying his pride or concupiscence, becomes blind to the important-in-itself, to values. He shuts his spiritual ears to the voice of morally relevant values and to the voice of his conscience. He cripples himself, though not by an outspoken intention to become blind and deaf, through the direction of his will, by the enslavement of pride and concupiscence that he permits to dominate him. He is thus more or less responsible for his moral blindness.

This clearly reveals that in saying ignorance is the source of the immoral action, the diagnosis concerning those cases where moral blindness is in play limits itself to stating certain symptoms without exploring the causes of these symptoms.

Now is not the time to enter into a detailed analysis of the nature of moral blindness, which is itself a very important and difficult task. It will suffice to say for now that the real root of any immoral action is not merely lack of knowledge.[6]

Hence we can summarize: firstly, it cannot be denied that there exist immoral actions where a knowledge of the morally relevant value is given; and secondly, where an ignorance of the morally relevant value is really found, the ignorance itself is merely a symptom of the real root of immorality, namely the general misdirection of our will.

---

6. [A detailed analysis of value blindness is not contained in this manuscript or elsewhere in the manuscripts and typescripts from this thematic circle. Hildebrand deals with it in both his early work, *Sittlichkeit und ethische Werterkenntnis,* and his later work, *Graven Images.* For a synthetic and critical presentation of his doctrine of value blindness, see Cajthaml, *The Moral Philosophy of Dietrich von Hildebrand*, Ch. 4. Editor.]

The Immorality of Actions Not Due to Preferring a Lower Value to a Higher One

Another attempt to explain the roots of immoral action is the thesis that disrespect for the morally relevant good is caused by preferring a lower value to a higher one. According to this conception, the thief steals because he prefers the value of money to the value of property, notwithstanding the fact that the value of property ranks objectively higher than the value of money.

This theory again overlooks the essential difference between the different categories of importance, that is to say, it turns a specimen of the merely subjectively satisfying into something important-in-itself. It presupposes that our will is always exclusively motivated by the important-in-itself. Or, as we may put it: it reduces the essential difference between the subjectively satisfying and the value to a mere difference of degree in the realm of values.

We saw in the beginning that this reduction is impossible.[7] We do not need to explain again that the difference between these two categories is an essential one and not one of degree.

In the case where a thief disrespects the value of the property of his fellow man in order to obtain money for himself, it is obvious that no preference in the strict sense is found.

If he is a habitual thief, he is indifferent to the question of whether something has a morally relevant value or not. He is concerned only with getting money, which obviously interests him not as something important-in-itself but only as something subjectively satisfying. A preference for obtaining money over respecting the value of property is thus out of the question. The value of property plays no role at all in his decision; he is completely indifferent to it. Thus he cannot prefer something to it.

He simply follows his desire and assents to the violation of the property of his fellow man as something neutral. The only possible obstacle

---

7. [The passage to which Hildebrand refers is not part of the manuscript, but is found in Hildebrand, *Ethics*, Ch. 3. On the irreducibility of the merely subjectively satisfying to a lower value, see Cajthaml, *The Moral Philosophy of Dietrich von Hildebrand*, 62–71. Editor.]

that he could weigh in his decision is the fear of being discovered and of enduring hardships. He may at some time find the risk of unpleasant consequences too great and thus abstain from stealing. One may speak of a preference only insofar as it is clear that he compares the benefit of money with the danger of being imprisoned, and ultimately prefers avoiding the danger over gaining money.

But obviously he compares here only something subjectively satisfying and something subjectively disagreeable. He remains thus exclusively in the frame of the category of the subjectively satisfying, and the category of the important-in-itself does not enter into his consideration. But the reason for disrespecting a morally relevant value is obviously not preference, because even in abstaining from stealing he is not acting out of respect for the morally relevant value. The preference here remains exclusively in the frame of the subjectively satisfying and is thus of no interest for the moral character of his action.

If, on the contrary, the thief is not a habitual one and steals because he has succumbed to a particular, isolated temptation, a struggle between the voice of his conscience and the temptation to steal may precede his act. Thus the value of the property plays a role in this case, but the final decision to steal has in no way the character of a preference. The struggle between the voice of his conscience and the temptation has the character of being drawn in two completely different directions. Two different worlds fight for the soul of this man; two completely different points of view are at stake, two essentially different categories of importance that exclude any comparison on the basis of a common homogenous denominator. This struggle means that he is torn between two incomparable categories of importance, and the choice has nothing to do with a comparison of two objects in the context of one homogenous type of importance, a choice made merely on the basis of their degree of this importance, which alone would be the true preference.

But even in those cases of immoral action in which a real preference is found, the wrong preference as such is nothing but a symptom and could thus never function as the real root of the immorality.

For instance, a preference is at stake when someone chooses to send his child to a school where the intellectual education is brilliant but the moral atmosphere is dangerous, because he believes intellectual development to be more important than moral integrity. Let us suppose he hesitated at first. He compared both values, the intellectual and the moral, and preferred wrongly the lower one. He thus disrespected the morally relevant value because of a wrong preference. But we have to ask: how does this wrong preference come about? Is it an intellectual error? We have seen above that errors concerning morally relevant values are always rooted in a misdirection of our will or, as we may put it, that every moral blindness is more than a mere intellectual failure. Obviously, if an intellectual failure alone could cause a wrong preference, the resulting action would no longer be an immoral one. Purely intellectual failures, as deplorable as they may be, are never the object of moral blame. But in fact the wrong preference with respect to a morally relevant value is never the result of a purely intellectual failure. If we approach a good with a pure attitude of value-response, the value of that good is given to us as it really stands in the hierarchy of values. The rank of a value is essentially implied in the data of the value. As soon as a good is underestimated or overestimated in its value, as far as morally relevant values are concerned, there are other elements in play besides the interest in the value for its own sake. Pride or concupiscence are in some way cooperating, and their contribution is responsible for the over- or underestimating of the value of the good. Because the approach is not a completely pure one, because pride or concupiscence play a role in our interest, the good is viewed not only from the point of view of its value but also from the point of view of its significance for pride or concupiscence.

Thus a good, say, the intellectual development of a child, which besides its authentic value also flatters the pride of the parents, their ambitions, hopes, or even the mere interest in an eventual bearer of this good, appeals simultaneously to their pride, whereas moral integrity does not likewise appeal to it. Thus, the child's intellectual development belongs to the category of the merely subjectively satisfying, which obviously must be clearly distinguished from its authentic value, and this is what turns the scale in favor of the child's intellectual development. It is, in reality, preferred not as having the higher value but because it appeals, independently of its value, to the pride of the parents. It does not matter whether this occurs in the form of an intellectual overestimation of this good, whereby the man fools himself into considering it as having a higher value, or whether he prefers it without such an intellectual overestimation, simply yielding to the temptation to satisfy his pride. What matters is to see that a wrong preference is always caused by the intervention of tendencies that differ completely from the pure interest in the value for its own sake and the sincere desire to conform to the objectively higher value.

Thus we may say by way of summary: the immoral action in which we disrespect morally relevant value can never be explained as the result of a wrong choice of a good possessing a lower value over a good possessing a higher one. Firstly, there are many immoral actions that are motivated by no value at all. Secondly, there are other immoral actions where a struggle between two categories of importance precedes the choice, whereby the disparity of the two categories or the absence of a common denominator excludes a real preference. Finally, there exist immoral actions where a preference of a good having a lower value with respect to a higher good is really found, but the reason for this possibility is that pride and concupiscence undermine the pure interest in the value for its own sake, and the wrong preference is thus merely a consequence of the fact that the lower good appeals to our pride and concupiscence independently of its authentic value.

The Immorality of Actions Not Due to the Interference of Passions with Practical Reasoning

There are many who say that the disrespect for a good possessing a morally relevant value is conditioned by the presence of some passion that prevents our reason from leading our will. This theory implies undoubtedly a truth. It is the very nature of passions, in the strict sense of the word, to darken reason and especially to dethrone the free center of the person. We have dealt with this tendency of the passions in the analysis of the freedom of the will.[8]

But it must be said: firstly, the immoral action is not always the result of a passion in the true sense of the term. Already Aristotle distinguishes actions that are accomplished under anger or fear as special cases where moral choice is no longer found. There is no deliberation in these actions. However, he admits that there exist morally wrong actions preceded by a deliberation. There is indeed no doubt that many immoral actions are not accomplished in a state of passionate disorder—in a state where the agent has, so to speak, lost the full power of his reason and his freedom. One of the main questions in judging the action of a murderer by a tribunal is whether he acted under the impulse of a passion or whether his action was premeditated. The premeditated murder is considered much worse than the one perpetrated under the influence of a passion.

Thus, the turmoil created by a passion cannot be considered the exclusive cause of immoral action because there obviously exist many immoral actions that are not perpetrated under the influence of a passion. Secondly, even in the cases in which a passion really is in play, the passion as such explains only the turmoil in the soul that disables our reason and our freedom. But it does not yet explain why something motivates our interest to such an extent that we consent to disrespect the morally relevant value. Or, as we may put it, only the formal element of passion is considered here, its violent character that darkens our reason and tends to dethrone our freedom. But the even more important element in a passion, namely, the fact that it is motivated by something merely subjectively satisfying and not by a value, is not taken into consideration.

There also exist cases in which we lose our head and are no longer able to master the situation, and in which our free center is no longer able in its full power to intervene, but which nevertheless do not con-

---

8. [This reference likely relates to an extensive typescript titled "Freedom," more specifically to its section on "The Role of Our Freedom in the Spheres of Passions." This extended section (pp. 167–215) includes a detailed analysis of passions in their relationship to freedom of the will. Intriguingly, Hildebrand distinguishes in this text passions and affective responses. Cf. Ana 544, VI, 14, 8. Editor.]

stitute immoral actions. Fear, for instance, gives rise to panic. In this agitation we do some unreasonable things, but they are not necessarily morally wrong. Take the man who, in his fear that he will be drowned, holds on to his fellow man who wants to help him, thereby preventing his helper from swimming: he certainly acts against reason, but he does not accomplish a morally bad action. Even if he causes the death of his fellow man, we shall not blame him from a moral point of view. It is thus not the formal character of "losing our head" that is mainly responsible for the immorality of an action, even in cases where the action is accomplished in such a state of being "out of our mind." For what is morally illegitimate is either an interest in something merely subjectively satisfying that makes us indifferent to the morally relevant value at stake, or an interest in something subjectively satisfying as such.

Thus, it does not suffice to say: passion is the root of morally wrong action. Firstly, not every immoral action is done under the influence of a passion in the strict sense of the word. Secondly, it is not primarily the formal character of the passion as such but the fact that the passion is always an interest in something that is merely subjectively satisfying. It is impossible to understand the root of the immorality of an action or, as we may put it, the root of the disrespect for a morally relevant value, as long as we do not start from the clear distinction between the kinds of importance that can motivate our will—as long as we do not discover the essential difference between value and the merely subjectively satisfying. While the formal character of the passion may explain the unreasonable character of an action, its immorality, which is more than its pure contradiction to immanent reason, cannot be explained by it.

I.iii. *The Roots of Immorality: Pride and Concupiscence*

After refuting the different theories about the roots of immorality in the sphere of action, we turn now to a detailed analysis of our problem. In order to understand the specific elements that determine immorality in the sphere of action, we have first to examine the roots of immorality in general.

One's position toward morally relevant values—in the last analysis toward God himself—decides whether a human attitude is morally good or bad. St. Augustine has formulated this fundamental truth, saying: moral goodness or badness depends upon whether someone's life is centered in God or in himself, whether he lives according to God or to the flesh, whereby flesh need not be understood in the strict sense but as *pars pro toto*, embracing pride as well as concupiscence. We would say: just as the ultimate root of moral goodness derives from our interest in the morally relevant values for their own sake and our conforming to their call, so moral badness results from our disrespect of the morally relevant values. In every genuine response to a morally relevant value, a response to the important-in-itself is implied and implicitly a response to God. In every act of disrespect for a morally relevant value, a disrespecting of the important-in-itself is implied and implicitly a disrespect for God. But whence comes the disrespect for the morally relevant values in man? How is it possible that someone consents with his will to a deed that disrespects a morally relevant value, or to a deed that realizes a morally relevant evil? There must be some motive for this attitude, something that has the power to motivate our will. The negative value as such could never motivate our will, nor the positive value as such motivate our disrespect, our negation. We have seen in the chapter about the freedom of will that there must always be a *bonum*, in the widest analogous sense of the term, on the object side in order to motivate our will.[9]

Thus it is never the negative value as such that motivates the will, nor the positive value as such that motivates our disrespect or will to act against it.

And indeed, we see that it is always something subjectively satisfying that motivates our will whenever it consents to disrespect a good possessing an authentic value. Any response that contradicts the important-in-itself is motivated by something subjectively satisfying. But an interest in the subjectively satisfying is not as such something morally negative. If someone plays bridge because it gives him pleasure,

---

9. [It seems that Hildebrand is referring here to ch. 21 of his *Ethics*, "The Two Perfections of the Will," and more specifically to pp. 327–28 (289–90). Editor.]

fully aware that there is no objective value in it, that he is in no way morally called to do so, he does no moral wrong. Rather, his playing bridge is morally neutral, belonging to the vast sphere of the morally allowed. However, as soon as something subjectively satisfying is connected with disrespect for a good possessing a morally relevant value, or with the realization of a morally relevant negative value, his action becomes morally bad.

If we are to understand how it is possible for someone to pursue the subjectively satisfying in such a way as to disrespect a good possessing a morally relevant value, we have to realize that in man live two mighty tendencies that are incompatible with value-response: *pride* and *concupiscence*.

As soon as someone's interest in the subjectively satisfying begins to become preponderant in the attitude of the person, the immanent readiness to yield to the importance of the morally relevant values is lost. In this situation, it is no longer the legitimate center, to which the subjectively satisfying appeals. Pride and concupiscence have intervened and even in some way replaced this center. Or as we may say, as soon as someone's interest in the merely subjectively satisfying detaches itself from the immanent *religio* to the reign of values, as soon as the value-response attitude no longer has the predominant role in the person, pride and concupiscence have penetrated the person's interest in the merely subjectively satisfying and replaced the legitimate center of susceptibility to the agreeable. Similarly, the merely subjectively satisfying on the object side assumes another character: it too is in some way perverted or poisoned, as we shall see later.

What matters for the moment is to understand that the center to which the morally neutral subjectively satisfying or subjectively important appeals remains intact and legitimate only as long as the person is superactually primarily directed toward the reign of values. It belongs to the very nature of this center to be restricted to a subordinate sphere and to coexist with the value-response attitude as its master. This must not be understood only in the sense that the dethroning of this direction toward the reign of values is illegitimate, which would be merely a repetition of that which has been stated already. It means that as soon as the primacy of the value-response attitude no longer subsists, the center to which merely subjectively satisfying goods appeal—for instance good food, a warm bath, a bridge party—is immediately replaced by concupiscence or pride. The unity of the human soul and its God-given order is such that the qualitative character of this center, though it is not directly linked to the value-response attitude, is completely changed as soon as interest in the subjectively satisfying is no longer tamed by the value-response attitude, as soon as it is no longer in the frame of a subservient role, so that it only actualizes itself with an immanent *placet* or *nihil obstat* given by the value-response attitude. The dethroning of the value-response attitude in its primary role is inevitably linked to the actualization of pride and concupiscence. Or as we may put it, pride and concupiscence are always the cause of this dethroning. What causes the apostasy from the reign of values in our soul, the turning away from the attitude of *religio* towards it, is not just a matter of the harmless and innocuous interest in the merely subjectively satisfying becoming too strong. Rather, instead of the legitimate center to which the satisfying appeals, pride and concupiscence intervene and become the center to which the subjectively satisfying goods appeal; interest in them now assumes a completely new and different character.

Certainly, the merely subjectively satisfying potentially entails the possibility of this perversion for man's fallen nature. It is proper to this category of importance to imply the danger of appealing to concupiscence or pride. But the difference between the legitimate center, to which it appeals when the person is primarily directed to the reign of values, when it lives under the influence of their call, and the center of pride and concupiscence must be clearly seen.

The morally legitimate interest in the merely subjectively satisfying, on the one hand, and the interest in it that derives from concupiscence or pride, on the other hand, differ not only by degree but also in their very nature. The disorder, which consists in a formal independence of the interest in the merely subjectively satisfying and entails immanently the dethroning of the value-response attitude, is never only of a formal nature but always includes immediately a complete qualitative change, that is to say, the replacement of this legitimate center by pride or concupiscence. After we have examined concupiscence and pride as the roots of immorality the character of the legitimate center for the subjectively satisfying will become even clearer. For the moment, it suffices to state that it is not this center that is responsible for our disrespect of the values and that when we say that interest in the merely subjectively satisfying is the cause of our indifference or hostility toward the reign of relevant values, we always refer to pride and concupiscence, that is to say, to an interest in the subjectively satisfying that derives from these centers and that thus has a completely different character from the legitimate one.

II

Concupiscence

II.i. *Nature of Concupiscence*[1]

IN ORDER TO UNDERSTAND the nature of concupiscence, we shall first study the man in whom concupiscence plays the predominant role, that is, the man who has become a complete slave to concupiscence. There exist certain types of men whose approach to the world and to life is dominated exclusively by the interest in drawing pleasure out of every situation. The way in which they superactually look at being, and in which they approach every concrete situation, is dominated by the question of how much pleasure they can get out of it. They are indifferent to the important-in-itself. The question as to whether or not something has a morally relevant value does not pose itself for them. They approach even those goods that have a morally relevant value exclusively from the viewpoint of whether or not they may bring them satisfaction directly

---

1. [Some of the wording and most of the content of the following section of the manuscript are identical to the beginning of the chapter on concupiscence in *Ethics*, 455–56 (431–33). The present volume follows the text version in *Ethics*. Editor.]

or indirectly. They are blind to morally relevant values in general, and their indifference has blunted them for every concrete, morally relevant value. The notions of moral good and evil are for them empty concepts—which they know play a role for other persons—and they treat them as we would treat superstitions. Being completely absorbed by the merely subjectively satisfying, they are deaf to the majestic call of morally relevant values.

In the very depth of their soul, they have delivered themselves to concupiscence. This must not be understood in the sense of a decision that issues from a full use of their freedom but, rather, in the sense of a failure to make use of their freedom. This decision is a gliding into concupiscence, a yielding to it, but they had the freedom to avoid this surrender. These persons have become slaves of concupiscence.

Concupiscence is, as we saw before, incompatible with the value-response attitude and the center that we called the reverent, humble, and loving center from which all the value-responses derive.[2] It is also incompatible with the capacity to understand the morally relevant values as well as with sensitivity to their call. The persistent craving for the subjectively satisfying, the blunt outlook toward the world that conceives it as a mere means for one's satisfaction, the brutish cramping of one's soul, the complete egocentrism: all these are ultimately opposed to reverent interest in the important-in-itself, to readiness to submit to the call of the morally relevant value, and to the value-response attitude. This antithetical incompatibility does not involve a consciously hostile attitude toward God and the realm of moral values on the part of the man dominated by concupiscence. His typical attitude toward God and values is one of indifference.

A man given over to concupiscence turns away from the reign of moral values, puts them aside and ignores them. He is indifferent toward them, not in the sense of a mere objective absence of the value-response attitude, but in the sense of a positive indifference toward them. Even if concupiscence has completely blunted his conscience and blinded his capacity for grasping morally relevant values, this outspoken indifference

---

2. [Cf. *Ethics*, 436 (412). Editor.]

toward the important-in-itself is immanent to the concupiscent man, in the depth of his soul. The concupiscent attitude as such necessarily implies this indifference toward the important-in-itself, toward the call of morally relevant values and the fundamental question of moral good and evil. It is inseparably linked to the gesture of doing away with the morally relevant sphere and its majestic obligation.

Not only is man objectively under the obligation of the morally relevant values, not only is he metaphysically ordered to God, but the presence of this call and the obligation to conform to the moral law is such that it simply cannot be overlooked and that an immanent position toward the world of values must in one way or another be taken. Thus, even in the person who is morally blind, in the person who seems to be ignorant of the existence of moral good and evil, there is to be found an immanent gesture of pushing this world aside. His concupiscent craving for the "emancipated" subjectively satisfying entails an immanent direction of his will to ignore the world of morality. Yet if the concupiscent man is primarily indifferent toward the world of values and ultimately toward God, every ignoring of, every positive indifference toward, the reign of values, every apostasy from their lordship necessarily leads to rebellion against the values and the voice of God implicit in them.

Since their call and obligation are by their very nature so relevant, so implacable, the apostasy can never remain a pure indifference but necessarily leads to a gesture against this obligation and against the rule of morally relevant values. Thus in order to clear the way for an unlimited craving for the subjectively satisfying, the casting aside of the obstacle of the moral obligation surpasses the specific indifference that is proper to concupiscence and necessarily leads to a somewhat rebellious or hostile attitude. In this hostility, the reign of values has the character of an obstacle to the unlimited expansion of concupiscence. It differs from the primary rebellion against the world of values that is proper to pride. For it is not a hostility against them as such, but a secondary hostility created by their character as an obstacle to the unlimited acquirement of the subjectively satisfying.

Man cannot become a real brute; he cannot give himself exclusively to the agreeable, as an animal does. In trying to live like an animal, he necessarily falls below the animal level.

Concupiscence can never exclusively dominate man; it must always be supported by an element of pride. But this in no way erases the difference between pride and concupiscence. Those two centers are essentially different. This becomes unmistakably evident in the fact that pride can dominate a person without the cooperation of concupiscence. Satan's rebellion against God does not imply concupiscence.

Concupiscence is characterized by the turning to the merely subjectively satisfying as the one exclusive measure of our life—implying an outspoken indifference toward the reign of morally relevant values and any value or importance-in-itself.[3]

But this first part of this characteristic applies equally to pride. In order to understand the specific nature of concupiscence, we have thus first to examine the nature of the subjectively satisfying that appeals not to pride but to concupiscence. We must further examine the specific fields in man to which this kind of merely subjectively satisfying appeals, which react in the specifically concupiscent way. Equally, we will have to consider the urges that derive from concupiscence. This different analysis will help us understand the *nature* of this center in man that is the root of a great part of the immoral attitudes of man. Before we enter into a minute analysis of the object of concupiscence and of its different manifestations, we have to distinguish three main forms in which concupiscence can deploy itself.

II.ii. *Three Main Concupiscent Types*

The first is the passionate type in whom the craving for the agreeable assumes a violent form and whose temperament has an impetuous character, as, for instance, in the case of the father of the Karamazov brothers in Dostoevsky's novel, or the father of Eugénie Grandet in Balzac's nov-

---

3. [This sentence and the next paragraph are taken from the manuscript Ana 544, VI, 14, 1. Beginning with the description of the three concupiscent types, the present volume follows again the respective text-version from *Ethics*, 461–64 (437–40). Editor.]

el. In such men, concupiscence deploys itself in a passionate form, in an unquenchable thirst for the subjectively satisfying. Moreover, this type is characterized by a specific hardness.

There is, secondly, the vegetative, phlegmatic type in whom concupiscence has the character of a lazy and heavy enslavement to the agreeable. Men in this category do not manifest any passionate impetus, any unquenchable thirst that holds them in a state of perpetual tension. Comfort plays a greater role in their life than the intensely agreeable. Theirs is a bovine heaviness characterized by the predominance of the desire not to be disturbed in the satisfaction of their animal urges. They are too lazy for any passionate craving for the agreeable. But they are nevertheless exclusively absorbed by the subjectively satisfying, mostly concerned with bodily agreeable things, but they also enjoy in a "Fafnerlike" manner the possession of wealth.[4] Their carnal, blunt approach toward the world makes them completely indifferent to the reign of morally relevant values and incapable of being charitable. They share hardness with the first type, but their hardness has more the character of a blunt and pachyderm-like insensitivity.

Thirdly, there is the soft type of person who neither passionately craves the subjectively satisfying, nor is imprisoned by his laziness and dumb inclination toward the agreeable, but who is hypersensitive, yet only insofar as his own person is concerned. He is especially interested in avoiding any "rough winds"; he wants to live in a world where only gentle breezes fan him. Whereas the two former types do not care what attitude other persons have toward them, as long as they present no obstacles to their desires, the latter likes to be petted, to be surrounded by a soft atmosphere, to be caressed and cherished. He is sensitive not to the priceless gift of charity or love directed toward him, but only to a soft and friendly atmosphere or a gentle touch. He does not crave passionately for bodily pleasures, but he reacts in an exaggerated, self-pitying manner to any bodily displeasure or pain. Whereas the two former types are not inclined to weep easily, this type is tearful and easily falls into

---

4. [Fafner, one of the giants in Wagner's *Rheingold,* seems to Hildebrand to embody this second type of concupiscence. Editor.].

a crying mood. But for all that, he is unable to shed noble tears as the result of a true value-response.

This last type differs so much from the two former ones that it seems that the three could have no root in common, and that the latter cannot be considered as another form of the concupiscent man. But a deeper analysis reveals that, notwithstanding the differences, the latter type is also dominated by concupiscence. Not only is he as egocentric as the other two, but he shares with them an exclusive preoccupation with the agreeable. Furthermore, the subjectively satisfying does not appeal to his pride; it is not self-glorification that is his great theme but the agreeable in the narrow sense of the term.[5] Again, he too is indifferent toward values. He is the man who pities himself, who feels himself to be harshly treated on every occasion, who is incapable of abandonment to the important-in-itself and of any interest in it for its own sake. He always thinks of himself and of his own feelings, and relishes every emotion, instead of focusing on the object that motivates this emotion. His tears are rooted only in his pampered softness and brought on exclusively by the slightest harsh or rough touch; sometimes he even enjoys them for their own sake.

There are certainly many different variations in this third type of man. He may respond more readily to the sensational and enjoy being thrilled and put into an inner state of tension for its own sake. Or perhaps he is of a more sentimental mood, eager to savor a specific kind of emotion, for whom the object merely serves as a means for arousing this emotion. Again, this soft type of concupiscence may appear in an aesthete, for whom everything is merely an occasion for aesthetic enjoyment. Upon seeing a fire that destroys the home and threatens the lives of human beings, such an aesthete remains indifferent to their misfortune and is completely absorbed in the beauty of the spectacle. He is the man who says: "Throw this beggar down the steps; the aspect of his misery breaks my heart."[6]

---

5. This does not mean that pride may not also play a great role in this type of man, but it will manifest itself in other ways.

6. In order to avoid any misunderstanding, we must note not only that this aesthete is unable to abandon himself to goods possessing morally relevant values, but also that his attitude is perverted

In all forms of the soft, concupiscent type, indifference toward morally relevant values assumes a character other than that of the two former types, but it is nevertheless an analogous indifference. Whereas the two hard types are so indifferent toward the important-in-itself that it is obvious that they ignore the goods endowed with values, the soft type is seemingly directed toward many goods having an authentic value. Yet he is not really affected by their value, nor does he respond to them in a true value-response; rather, he uses them as means for his subjective satisfaction. He is, for instance, interested in hearing lectures on metaphysics given by a famous philosopher, not because he really thirsts for truth but because he relishes the atmosphere created by the occasion of meeting a famous and brilliant man, and he cherishes the thrill of an intellectual event; or he goes to church because he takes pleasure in a certain religious emotion.

Persons in this category are, in general, more refined than the two former types and are less materialistic. They will not so easily commit crimes as the former types, but they are just as indifferent to the important-in-itself. They completely misunderstand values and are as egocentric as the two former types. Despite their softness they are equally incapable of charity.

II.iii. *The Subjectively Satisfying as Appealing to Concupiscence*[7]

The Bodily Agreeable

This analysis may suffice to reveal the vast frame of concupiscence and to warn us against sticking too much to one special type of concupiscence in our analysis of concupiscence as such. It shows us that concupiscence can assume apparently opposite forms and will help us to disentangle the essential marks of this center from the special features of one or the other species of concupiscence.

---

toward aesthetic values. He does not grasp them in their importance-in-themselves; rather, he enjoys beauty in a refined, self-centered way and degrades it in approaching it as if it were something merely subjectively satisfying.

7. [The present volume continues with the typescript Ana 544, VI, 14, 4. Editor.]

We shall now begin with an analysis of the type of subjectively satisfying that appeals to concupiscence or of the goods that can appeal to concupiscence, and of those that are exclusively satisfying for concupiscence and that would, without this perversion, have no attractive power for us.

We have thus to begin with those goods that are as such satisfying for the legitimate center but can become an object for concupiscence. Within the vast realm of the bodily agreeable, there are three main types that must be distinguished. Firstly, the outspokenly agreeable, pleasure in the strict sense, as good food and drink, sexual pleasures, a warm bath, a comfortable bed or couch, and so on.

Secondly, the satisfaction of urges and the pleasure connected with it, such as sleep when someone is tired, drinking when he is thirsty, eating when hungry, smoking for the smoker, swimming in cool water when the weather is very warm, and so on.

Thirdly, the comfortable in all its different dimensions, to drive in a car instead of going on foot, to be free from efforts to provide the necessary things for daily life, all the conveniences provided for us through the progress of technology, or in former times provided for us by others, such as servants or slaves, in sum, all the things that spare us the hardship of fatigue and bodily efforts.

These three types of the bodily agreeable appeal, more or less according to different temperamental dispositions, to man as such, that is to say, they do not presuppose concupiscence in order to be experienced as agreeable. But they can easily become an object of concupiscence. The concupiscent man is directed toward these three types of the agreeable, but obviously his approach differs completely from the approach of the man in whom concupiscence is not predominant. We saw before in what this difference consists.

Firstly, the agreeable or the subjectively satisfying has become the measure of his life. It is "emancipated" from its legitimate frame, denuded from the yoke of the value-response attitude. Secondly, the interest in these three forms of the bodily agreeable has assumed a new character even in its quality, or a passionate craving for it, or a lazy, blunt being absorbed by it, or a soft dependence upon it. Finally, the intoxication by these forms of the agreeable implies an outspoken indifference toward the important-in-itself and especially toward the reign of morally relevant values.

For the passionate type, the first type of bodily pleasures as well as the second one—the satisfaction of urges—obviously prevail. Whereas for the heavy, lazy type, the comfortable plays a predominant role.

For the soft type, all three types of the bodily agreeable may play a great role according to his temperamental disposition, but with another nuance. As they generally do not have particularly powerful instincts, the avoidance of everything disagreeable is more in the foreground, the comfortable has less the note of a satisfaction of a blunt laziness than the satisfaction of refined needs, of the petting of their hypersensitivity. Equally, an interest in the agreeableness of food and drink has more a character of refined relishing than a passionate craving for it or than a satisfaction of elementary urges. And above all, this whole sphere is not the primary theme of their concupiscence.

The Saint[8]

In order to elaborate the manifestations of concupiscence in this realm, we have to distinguish between the following attitudes with respect to the sphere of the bodily agreeable.

---

8. [In order to flesh out the type of change occurring in the person when the legitimate center in her sensitive to the merely subjectively satisfying is replaced by concupiscence, Hildebrand sketches two idealized typologies of positive moral characters: the saint and the morally upright person. These two idealized types are the positive counterparts of the three aforementioned concupiscent types. Unlike these three morally negative types, the two positive ones are clearly hierarchically ordered: while the saint is the most perfect moral type, the morally upright is not as perfect, although his moral character is decent. In his description Hildebrand skillfully describes how, in both these types, the value-response attitude governs the habitual desire for the merely subjectively satisfying, but in each of these types in a different way. His sketch of the saint makes it understandable why Hildebrand, like Scheler before him, takes Christian saints to be the models of moral perfection. It also explains the claim advanced in the last chapter of his *Ethics*, namely, that Christian morality is the fulfilment of natural morality. The description of the morally perfect attitude of the saint and of the decent attitude in the morally upright person in this section is complemented in the section II.v. by the description of the attitudes of these two moral types to bodily displeasures, particularly to intense pain. Editor.]

Firstly, the attitude of the saint, besides being something incomparably new with respect to natural morality, and necessarily presupposing the revelation of Christ, is also the fulfilment of natural morality. It is here that we find the absolute antithesis to concupiscence and pride. Secondly, the attitude of a noble, moral personality, in whom the value-responding attitude definitely has the predominance over pride and concupiscence, for example, Socrates. Thirdly, the morally unobjectionable attitude. Fourthly, the morally imperfect attitude that is stained with a moral disvalue but does not yet constitute a sin. Fifthly, the definitely morally evil attitude that constitutes a sin.

It is in case four that we shall discover the traces of concupiscence in which the transition of the legitimate center to which the agreeable appeals to concupiscence manifests itself. In the last case (case 5), we are confronted with concupiscence in its full development.

In looking first at the attitude of the saint, we serve a double purpose. First, we want to elucidate the nature of concupiscence in opposing it to its radical antithesis, the victorious domination of the reverent, loving, humble center. Second, we want to elaborate the specific character of Christian morality in contradistinction to the merely natural morality; we want to throw into relief the completely new Christian ideal of moral perfection that is embodied in the saint and is the most specific topic of Christian ethics.

In the case of the most perfect human being, that is to say, a saint, bodily pleasures are not sought for their own sake. He will not make them an object of his striving. On the contrary, he will in general avoid them, fearing that he will yield to concupiscence. He will, moreover, try to substitute them with something neutral or even with their opposite in order to separate himself from any inordinate attachment, in order to make himself free for Christ and His charity. The ascetic self-mortification concerning this sphere is to be found more or less in the life of every saint, as well concerning the quantity and quality of food, the curtailing of sleep, choosing the uncomfortable, fasting, and so on.

That does not mean, however, that saints are not sensitive to these pleasures. If they are bestowed upon them accidentally, they will appreciate them as gifts of God, seeing them completely as objective goods for the person, approaching them in this moderate distance, which enables them to experience them more in their friendly character for the person, that is to say, as results of God's love, than as something merely subjectively satisfying. The category of the subjectively satisfying is here not only tamed and restricted to a subservient role, but it has completely disappeared as a motive for the will. In the cases in which something bodily agreeable is bestowed upon them, though not having sought it, it speaks to them not as something subjectively satisfying as such; rather, the subjectively satisfying is absorbed into the category of an objective good for the person, ennobled and elevated to the status of an instrument of God's superabundant bounty.[9]

This attitude is the pure antithesis to concupiscence, and the perfect one from the moral point of view.

The Morally Upright Person

Another morally legitimate, though much less perfect, attitude we find in the man whose will is primarily determined by the morally relevant values, and the important-in-itself, but in whose life the subjectively satisfying plays, nevertheless, a limited role. Bodily pleasures motivate his will in a subservient role, under the rule of his value-response attitude, whereby they may play a greater or lesser role according to his temperamental disposition. He may not only enjoy good food and wine as such, but he may even to a certain extent decide with his will to procure this pleasure for himself.

The same applies to the other types of the bodily agreeable. If he is pious, he will consider these goods as gifts of God and enjoy them with gratitude toward God. Nevertheless, the subjectively satisfying remains a real motive for his will, and in enjoying the agreeable as such, the category of the objective good for the person has not absorbed the subjectively satisfying as it has in the saint. If he is not pious, he will not make

---

9. [For this meaning of the objective good for the person, see *Ethics*, 414–415 (394–395). Editor.]

this connection with God. However, he will not be without restraint toward the subjectively satisfying, but will always approach it under the rule of the value-response attitude, so to speak, having received the *nihil obstat* of this predominant sphere.

True Moderation

Someone could object: the characteristic of the morally legitimate attitude toward bodily pleasures is moderation. It is the result of self-control, whereby our will does not simply yield to the subjectively satisfying but remains the master and enables us to avoid any excess, and to enjoy these pleasures with a certain reserve (restraint), that is, with moderation. It must be said: self-control only covers one element of the morally right attitude toward bodily pleasures. It is the fact that the person has not fallen prey to the attraction of bodily pleasures and that her free will is able to yield to or to refuse the invitation of the agreeable. It is certainly a very important formal element that concerns the sovereign position of our free will, the making use of our freedom as opposed to the enslavement of the person by her instincts, the letting oneself be ruled by the inclinations of one's desire.

But this formal capacity to submit our desires and instincts to our will does not yet guarantee the morally decisive point. For a concupiscent man, too, may possess this formal self-control; he may be able to control his desires and instincts and to abstain from satisfying them in order to attain a good that satisfies his concupiscence more. The more refined and consciously he craves the satisfaction of his concupiscence the more he will possess this technical self-control, which means that his will has assumed a full master-position toward his desires and instincts, but he will use it only in order to satisfy his concupiscence in a more efficient way. It is the prescription of hedonism, the famous norm of Aristippus of Cyrene, who despises the man who has fallen prey to his accidental instincts and desires, and prescribes that everyone should crave the subjectively satisfying in a reasonable way, that is in deliberating, before we choose a pleasure, whether it is the most intense, the longer lasting, the one that engenders no pains and is the most certain in being obtainable.

Obviously, this technical self-control is not the morally decisive factor, and it is thus not the decisive mark of the approach of the morally good man to the bodily agreeable. What matters is that his will is directed toward the reign of the morally relevant values, and that he approaches bodily pleasures under their rule. Self-control assumes, then, a completely different character. It no longer means only a formal capacity of dominating our passions, our desires, and instincts with our will, but it implies that we remain in the attitude of *religio* toward the reign of morally relevant values, in the last analysis toward God. It implies that we conserve the *habitare secum* [dwelling with oneself], that we remain in this salutary distance from the turmoil of our passions and instincts because we remain anchored in the morally important-in-itself.

But this implies that our free will is turned toward the reign of the morally relevant values, that it is a value-response, that it is not only ontologically but morally free in the Augustinian sense. This freedom concerns not only the relation between our will and the instincts and passions, but above all the relation of our will to the category of importance that motivates it. It implies that we have made the right use of our freedom, conforming to the morally relevant value as the norm of our conduct. It implies not only that our will is the master with respect to passions and instincts, but that it is simultaneously the servant with respect to the moral commandment. And the strength that this self-control of the value-response attitude deploys differs completely from the strength of technical self-control. It draws its power from obedience toward the moral obligation, from the majesty and intrinsic preciousness of morally relevant values, in the highest case, from the love of God.

As such the self-control is thus not the decisive element in the approach of the morally good man toward bodily pleasures. It is the rule of the superactual value-response attitude that restricts the subjectively satisfying *ab ovo* (*a priori*) to the sphere of the "allowed" and to a subservient role.

Similarly, moderation does not yet cover the decisive feature of the morally legitimate approach to the bodily agreeable. First, moderation refers to a use of the goods that are bodily satisfying, the use that abstains from excesses. Certainly, abstaining from any excess is of great moral importance. Immoderate enjoyment of pleasant food or wine, as well as of sleep, and so on, is morally bad. But this covers only one aspect of the morally legitimate approach, in contradistinction to the concupiscent one. The morally legitimate approach differs from the concupiscent one also when every excess is avoided. Firstly, excess may sometimes be avoided by the concupiscent for reasons of health. Someone who knows that the abuse of certain pleasant dishes will cause in him considerable pains, and thus refrains from any excess, certainly acts in a reasonable manner, but he may nevertheless be a concupiscent man. He simply fears pain more than he desires the pleasure because the former surpasses the latter in intensity.

Secondly, the morally legitimate approach to bodily pleasures, besides the abstaining from excess, that is to say, besides using them with moderation, is characterized by an inner distance, a remaining in the fundamental attitude of *religio* to the world of morally relevant values, an approach that avoids losing ourselves in them. This is more than to abstain from an excessive use of them; it concerns not the quantity but the quality of our enjoying them. The most specifically moral reason for abstaining from excess is precisely this inner gesture of our approach to this sphere and not any reason of health or any other extrinsic motives. But this fact does not imply that avoiding excess is a guarantee for this inner attitude. Only in a reversed sense can we say that this inner attitude guarantees the abstaining from any excess.

But someone may object: this is precisely true temperance or moderation. It means not only abstaining from any excess but this inner restraint and distance toward the bodily agreeable as such, of which avoidance of any excess is but a consequence. The concupiscent may for another reason avoid excess accidentally, but he has never this inner distance and freedom toward the bodily agreeable.

It must be said: even if we take moderation in this deeper sense, as an inner distance, an inner reserve, an avoiding of letting ourselves fall into the subjectively satisfying, being intoxicated by it, it does not suffice to characterize the nature of the morally legitimate approach.

The Stoic, who abstains from an immoderate enjoying of bodily pleasures, because he wishes to conserve the consciousness of never abdicating a master-position toward anything, obviously differs from the morally legitimate approach that is our topic. His moderation, his reserve, smells of pride, and his self-control is of a mere technical order. His attitude, though not soiled by concupiscence, is poisoned with the even worse poison of pride and not only differs from the morally legitimate approach toward the bodily pleasures but is even opposed to it.

The morally decisive point is that the superactual value-response attitude, the consciousness of the incompatibility of an unlimited falling into the merely subjectively satisfying of bodily pleasures with the value-response attitude, is what forms "moderation," the distance and reserve in enjoying bodily pleasures. This "moderation" flows organically out of the attitude of *religio* toward the reign of the morally relevant values. It is the attitude of reverence toward the "world above," the consciousness of our role as servants to this world, this being bound to it, which excludes an immoderate jumping into the subjectively satisfying.

Thus we see that the decisive mark of the morally legitimate approach is not moderation and self-control as such, but the fact that the subjectively satisfying aspect of the bodily pleasures remains in a frame that is *ab ovo* ruled and circumscribed by the morally relevant values, that the approach to it is pervaded by the superactual value-response attitude. This means, firstly, that any choice of a bodily pleasure which conflicts with morally relevant value is implicitly excluded; secondly, that the position toward it, even if there is a conflict with a morally relevant good at stake, remains always a moderate position because of the incompatibility of an immoderate enjoying of the subjectively satisfying with our attitude of *religio* toward the morally relevant values.

The Unique Character of Sexual Pleasure

As already mentioned in other works[10], sexual pleasure forms a case that differs in every respect from the above-mentioned bodily pleasures. This

---

10. [Cf. Hildebrand's *In Defense of Purity*, Ch. 1. Editor]

sphere is endowed with a unique mystery. The morally legitimate approach does not require "moderation" here, but it involves above all the strict exclusion of any isolation of sexual pleasure. The very meaning of this pleasure, as a subservient element of the conjugal act that is destined to be a reverent union of mutual love in marriage, requires above all that it never be sought without the specific sanction of God, that is to say, outside of marriage. It requires, moreover, that it never be sought for its own sake, that it never be detached from its organic insertion in the marital love-union, that it never be deprived of its function as an instrument of this spiritual union. Thus here it is no longer the question of approaching the bodily agreeable while maintaining the attitude of *religio* toward the world above and conserving a moderate inner reserve; rather, any thematicity whatsoever of this pleasure, making it as such an object of our will or desire and isolating it from its God-given function as an instrument and medium of the spiritual union of conjugal love, is morally bad.

It is easy to see that the morally legitimate approach requires much more than in the case of other bodily pleasures, and that an isolated striving for it as such is not only a much graver form of concupiscence, but always simultaneously a desecration of a good endowed with a high morally relevant value.

If we mention here sexual pleasure among bodily pleasures, it must be stressed that the attractiveness of the sexual sphere and the urge directed toward it definitively transcends the sphere of bodily pleasures. Besides sexual pleasure in the sense of *libido*, that is, a *bodily* experience, there exists obviously the psychical pleasure engendered by the attractiveness of this entire sphere. It matters for both the bodily sexual pleasure and the psychical charm of this sphere that they form a unique case of their own, incomparable with any other bodily or psychical subjectively satisfying datum. The isolation of either entails concupiscence necessarily, and the morally right attitude toward both requires the fulfilment of the same conditions. Thus, we do not need to deal with them separately in our context, notwithstanding their deep difference as such.

The extraordinary position of the sexual sphere from the moral point of view will become apparent if we analyze the role of our free will with respect to the sexual instinct, embracing by this term the direction both toward the bodily experience and toward the allure of sex.

It is even a specific moral task to dominate those instincts and to control them to such an extent that their fulfillment will be approved by our will only when the morally legitimate presuppositions are given. It must be stressed that the sexual instinct has a quite exceptional position in this respect. As it is by its very nature something destined to be the expression of a spiritual act, namely spousal love, and to be formed and elevated by it, it calls not only for certain conditions under which the will concedes its autonomous fulfillment, but it is formed in an extraordinary way by spousal love and the free act of exchanging vows; in these ways it loses the character of a mere instinct. It has thus a place quite different from that of any other instinct in being by its very nature not a mere vital instinct, but something destined to be part of a complicated higher spiritual experience, to be inserted in it as a serving element. Its normal fulfillment is not a mere satisfaction of an instinct but necessarily much more than that: a personal self-donation to another person of a unique character.

In the case of its God-given legitimate fulfillment, it is simultaneously the expression of spousal love and the full consummation of the solemn, irrevocable self-donation that the exchange of vows constitutes. A mere satisfaction of this instinct, isolated from its function as an expression of spousal love and as a consummation of the marital commitment, is necessarily an outspoken abuse.

It is not a simple vital instinct with its immanent law, the fulfillment of which can be conceded by our will as soon as certain conditions are given. Rather, our will has to abstain from its fulfillment as long as this fulfilment is not the consummation of a marital commitment. The will has not only the task to control it in such a way that its satisfaction will be conceded only under certain circumstances, leaving the instinct then to its autonomous, immanent law, but also the task to transform it completely, making it an integral part of a highly spiritual act. It is by its very nature a part of a whole.

Our freedom thus has here an incomparably greater role than it does with respect to other instincts. Firstly, the satisfaction of this instinct has not only to be controlled by our will from "without," so that it will be conceded only under certain circumstances. Rather, it has to be spiritualized from within, coordinated by our freedom, allowing for the satisfaction only when it is no longer an isolated vital instinct, but something forming a part of a whole, subordinated to spousal love and the marital commitment, following no longer only its immanent laws, but the immanent law of love and of the lovers' commitment to each other, formed from within by them. Love as such is not in the realm of our freedom, it is a gift that has to be bestowed on us, but the sanction of the gift is in an outspoken way a fruit of our freedom. Nevertheless, it is up to our freedom to allow for a fulfillment of this instinct only when it has been spiritualized in becoming a part of spousal love, something engendered and pervaded by it, experienced as the consummation or actualization of the lovers' commitment to each other, and not a mere parallel stream, coordinated from "without" with our spousal love and marital commitment.

Moreover, not only do we have the task of abstaining from a satisfaction of this instinct as long as it is not yet a part of a whole, but we also have to make efforts to place this instinct into its God-given place, to submit it to love, to avoid anything that appeals to its isolated actualization as such, even apart from the question of its satisfaction. We have again and again to realize with our intellect the grandeur and depth of the mystery of this self-donation in marriage, to create by that, apart from all ascetic efforts, the submission of this instinct to spousal love and to the marital commitment, to attain this organic connection from within that is given to certain persons as a gratuitous gift. I am referring to those persons in whom the sexual instinct never arises as an independent, isolated tendency seeking its satisfaction, but where it arises only as an expression of spousal love.

The role of our freedom is thus here an incomparably greater one. Whenever this organic connection is not given by itself, we have to aim to attain it by a complicated process. Our task is not only an abstaining from a satisfaction of this instinct, an abstaining which lies in the realm of our direct command, as any other action; our task is also the spiritualization of this instinct, the integration into a whole that is obviously not in the realm of our direct command but belongs to the vast realm of our indirect influence, which we shall examine later in the analysis of the role of our freedom with respect to the spiritual sphere of the person.[11] It implies the efforts to attain a potential submission of this instinct to spousal love and the marital commitment, and secondly the actual formation of it by love and by the marital commitment in the case of marriage. These hints concerning this instinct may suffice at present.[12]

After having examined the morally legitimate approach to bodily pleasures, it must still be mentioned that an interest in bodily pleasures does not always need to imply an actualized conscious reference to the reign of the morally relevant values in order to remain morally allowed. If someone sees beautiful fruits in a shop and their attractive appearance prompts him to buy them, this action will certainly not necessarily have a morally negative character.

Let us presuppose that there is no special reason that forbids him to buy these fruits, for instance, that the expense is not excessive, that it fits in the frame of his normal living expenditures. The interest in the subjectively satisfying is here not necessarily preceded by a confrontation with the morally relevant values. It suffices that, superactually, this attitude of *religio* is maintained and the subjectively satisfying presents itself *ab ovo* as something "allowed" or, as we said before, as something within the limits of the subservient role that is proper to the subjectively satisfying in the God-given order. The same man would not buy it as soon as any morally relevant value would call him to use this money for another purpose that is important-in-itself. What matters is thus the presence of the superactual value-response attitude that would immediately determine our will to abstain from the subjectively satisfying, whenever a good having a morally relevant value is at stake that calls for it.

11. [Cf. *Ethics*, Ch. 24. Editor.]
12. [The next two paragraphs are retrieved from the original manuscript, that is, Ana 544, VI, 14, 1. Editor.]

II.iv. Bodily Pain[13]

Before we turn to the analysis of the concupiscent attitude toward bodily pleasures, we have still to consider the morally legitimate approach to bodily displeasures.

As St. Augustine has already rightly stated, the situation concerning bodily displeasures differs from that of bodily pleasures. Interest in avoiding outspoken bodily pains for their own sake is obviously not morally on the same level as the interest in bodily pleasures. It is morally legitimate to try to avoid intense bodily pain, and this attitude has as such not the same immanent danger of falling prey to concupiscence, as the interest in enjoying bodily pleasures. A shrinking back from bodily pain does not have the same self-centered character as craving for bodily pleasures. In order to be morally legitimate, it need not be restricted to a certain frame that is determined by the morally relevant values, it need not be tamed and limited to a subservient role.

An extraordinary moral obligation must be at stake in order to render the free acceptance of bodily pain obligatory or the shrinking back from them morally illegitimate, as, for instance, in the case of martyrdom or of being tortured rather than betraying other persons, or of doing something morally wrong. Certainly, it is a heroic moral action of a specific moral value if someone accepts intense bodily pain in order to realize some good having morally relevant value, as, for instance, preventing another person from suffering, but as we saw in the chapters on the "Degrees of Moral Obligation," it is not morally obligatory.[14] The same applies to the elementary goods that are indispensable for our life, such as health, daily bread, and so on. Regarding their moral significance, they are not a real negative counterpart to bodily pleasures.

Let us first examine the intense bodily pain that has a unique posi-

---

13. [We return here to the typescript Ana 544, VI, 14, 4. Editor.]

14. [This chapter is not found in *Ethics*. The text referred to is preserved as the typescript "Degrees of Obligation" (17 pp., Ana 544, VI, 14, 7). The central question discussed in it is whether the call of the morally relevant values always involves a moral obligation of such a character that when someone fails to obey this call, he is becoming morally bad/guilty, or whether this is not the case. Editor.]

tion among bodily displeasures. They have no real counterpart among bodily pleasures, besides sexual pleasure. The bodily pleasure of drinking when thirsty or when relishing a good wine can obviously not be considered as an antithesis to pain, but merely to the displeasure of a violent thirst or of drinking something that tastes bad.

From the psychological point of view, the experience of pain is something quite different from these kinds of displeasures. Firstly, the negative character is much more aggressive and goes in a direction different from the other displeasures; secondly, the formal character of pain, as an outspokenly half objective, half subjective state, differs clearly from urges, on the one hand, and the displeasure that flows out of a bad taste, which presents itself obviously as something bestowed on me by the quality of an object, whereas pains present themselves as something in us, deriving in no way from the quality of an object but merely sometimes as caused by an object.

The only real counterpart to outspoken bodily pain, on the positive side, is sexual pleasure, from the qualitative point of view as well as from the formal or structural one. One could also add that from the point of view of intensity, sexual pleasure can be considered as the only real counterpart of outspoken bodily pains.

No Moral Obligation to Accept Intense Bodily Pain

We have thus, before we examine the morally legitimate approach to bodily displeasures that are the counterpart to bodily pleasures, to analyze the morally legitimate approach to intense bodily pain, because their psychologically exceptional position conditions a completely different role from the moral point of view, independently from the general difference that applies from the moral point of view to bodily displeasures with respect to bodily pleasures.

Obviously, the fact that sexual pleasures alone can be considered as a real counterpart to bodily pain in no way implies that our moral position to the one is in any way analogous to the other. As we saw before, the God-given function of sexual pleasures that by their very nature are elements of the conjugal union is a secondary one, namely, to be an instrument of this union. Every isolation of it and every making it into the main theme is morally bad. Nothing similar is to be found with respect to bodily pain. The interest in avoiding bodily pain, the fear of it, is obviously completely morally legitimate.

Some persons are less sensitive and endure bodily pain more easily; others are more sensitive and react much more strongly. This is obviously no moral question but a mere matter of different psychophysiological structures. Notwithstanding this fact, it would be a grave error to believe that the attitude toward bodily pain is of no moral significance.

The horror of bodily pain as such is not something derived from concupiscence but is rooted in man's nature, and derives from a morally legitimate center. The interest in avoiding them and in alleviating or even getting rid of them, if this lies in the realm of our influence, is equally morally legitimate.

Notwithstanding this fact, one's attitude toward bodily pain varies according to the moral standard of the person in a very characteristic way.

We shall again start by examining first the attitude of the saint toward bodily pain. Not only will he endure inevitable bodily pain with patience, that is to say, without losing his basic attitude of *religio* toward God through bodily pain, but he will do so without irritation toward his fellow man, without interrupting his loving, charitable attitude toward him. He will not be absorbed by them to such an extent that his superactual charity no longer actualizes itself so that he becomes shut up in himself and cut off from his surroundings. He will not only accept bodily pain, in a spirit of submitting to God's will, without any rebellion. He will even accept them with a readiness to embrace the cross as expiation for his own sins and the sins of his fellow man, he will unite himself with the sufferings of Christ and offer them to God. He will thus be concerned not so much with alleviating or diminishing them, but with enduring them in the right way. The natural horror for bodily pain is victoriously absorbed by the love of God and neighbor.

This attitude is obviously a heroic one and constitutes the absolute antithesis to concupiscence and pride. Further, he will not only not strive to avoid bodily pain, but even inflict it upon himself in order to mortify his nature and to expiate his own sins and the sins of others.

He will thus choose bodily pain freely, precisely because his nature abhors it. This again is a heroic attitude, far surpassing his moral obligation; it is even to a certain extent the response to a specific vocation and invitation of God that does not exist for every Christian. The holy Church prays *a peste, fame et bello libera nos Domine*.[15] And it could even be a danger flowing out of lack of sobriety and humility if a person seeks pain without having received special graces.

Finally, the saints will never shrink back from accepting, by free choice, bodily pain, whenever a good having an authentic morally relevant value calls for it. They will not only prefer to endure bodily pain rather than to commit a sin, but they will, for instance, choose to suffer themselves rather than to let another person suffer. That is to say: they will not only prefer to endure bodily pain rather than actively to do something wrong, as for instance, deny their faith (in the case of martyrdom) or to betray or injure in any way a fellow man. Moreover, they will never neglect to follow the call of morally relevant values on the grounds that conforming to their call would result in the suffering of bodily pain. They will raise their voice in protesting against injustice and immorality *opportune importune* ["in season and out of season"], even if they are aware that in doing so they have to accept bodily pain. The threat of bodily pain will never be an obstacle for them to fulfill that which a morally relevant good calls for, which the love of God inspires them to do.

This attitude reveals an extraordinary independence from fear of bodily pain, a victorious predominance of the value-response attitude and of charity, not only over concupiscence but even over a morally legitimate horror of bodily pain. This latter is heroic.

What is the morally legitimate position toward bodily pain that we find in the man in whom the value-response attitude dominates, and

---

15. [The precise formulation is *Ut mundum a peste, fame et bello servare digneris* ("that it may please thee to keep the world safe from disease, hunger, and war"). This invocation appears in section 4, *Supplicatio pro Variis Necessitatibus* (Prayer for Various Needs) in the Litany of the Saints as we find it in the *Graduale Romanum*. Editor.]

who does not yield to concupiscence, but who is nevertheless far from being a saint? It is clear: he will avoid bodily pain and not freely choose it as long as a morally relevant good is not at stake that calls for accepting it freely.

But as soon as such a conflict arises, for instance, when he is threatened with bodily pain if he does not submit to disrespecting morally relevant values, he will accept enduring bodily pain rather than disrespect the morally relevant values. But here we must distinguish the case in which an acceptance of bodily pain is morally obligatory and that in which it is not.

If someone is confronted with the alternative either to endure torture or to do an act in which he disrespects a morally relevant value, he is obliged to accept the torture. For instance, if one tries to force him to kill an innocent person or to torture her, or to betray somebody in such a way that he is put into danger, or to do something impure, he is morally obliged not to yield to this pressure, even if he has to endure the most terrible bodily pain. But when the alternative is between omitting a morally good action and enduring bodily pain, the obligation to accept the pain is no longer as obvious. It depends upon many circumstances whether or not it is obligatory to accept bodily pain.

Firstly, it matters whether our intervention would really prevent the injustice in question or whether it would take place in any case. If we risk being tortured by helping an innocent person to escape or by preventing our fellow man from being injured, our acceptance of this risk is obviously more obligatory than if our intervention has no possibility of preventing the evil and amounts to only a protest against the evil at stake.

Secondly, the nature of the morally relevant value at stake, that is to say, its rank and the character of the bodily pain that threatens us, has a decisive influence on the question of whether it is obligatory or not. Obviously, it makes a great difference whether the life of our fellow man, his freedom, his health, or grave bodily pain are threatened or whether only a violation of his property is at stake. We are not obliged to intervene if we see a robber enter a house, if we can do so only by risking grave bodily pain. By contrast, we are obliged to take this risk if another person's life or freedom are threatened. And, on the other hand, it makes a great difference whether we have to accept grave bodily pain or only minor pain. In the latter case, obviously, the obligation to accept it obtains even if a morally relevant good is at stake that does not rank very high.

Thirdly, we must distinguish whether there is only a risk of enduring bodily pain at stake, or whether it is an absolute certainty. It makes a great difference from the moral point of view whether the mere risk of bodily pain makes us shrink back from an intervention for which the morally relevant good calls, or whether there is the inevitable certainty of enduring bodily pain. The fear of risking bodily pain reveals a self-centered attitude, the fact that the morally relevant good is not able to attract our attention to itself, that the interest in the important-in-itself does not lead us to risk eventual bodily pain, discloses an egotism that has its roots in concupiscence.

Fourthly, it makes a great difference whether we are by our profession or function in a special way called to intervene, or whether this is not the case. For a lawyer or a doctor, it may be obligatory to protest against certain injustices when a client or patient is unjustly treated, even if he risks bodily pain and even if his intervention is not able to prevent the injustice. This applies still more to a priest or bishop who has *ex officio* the obligation to raise his voice against injustice and moral evil, whether he can prevent the injustice or not, and independently of the question whether he has to accept bodily pain in doing so.

Finally, it makes a difference whether the alternative presents itself as a clear *aut-aut*, where he has to choose between the intervention or bodily pain, as in the case of danger from a tyrant, or whether he is called by a morally relevant good to intervene, and the bodily pain is only accidentally connected with the means that he has to employ in order to attain his goal, for instance, the pain that someone risks in saving the life of his fellow man who is in a burning house; whereby we suppose for the moment that he risks not his life in doing so but only bodily pain. Obviously, in the latter case the avoidance of bodily pain is a much less morally legitimate motive for abstaining from an intervention than in the former case the acceptance of bodily pain does not presents itself in the same outspoken way, and the very fact that we take it into consideration already reveals a greater amount of self-centeredness.

Summarizing, we may say: being deterred from intervening by the risk of bodily pain when a morally relevant good calls us, is morally bad under certain circumstances but not in every case. It depends on different circumstances whether the interest in avoiding bodily pain that leads us to omit a morally desirable intervention is a fruit of concupiscence, or whether it remains still in the frame of the morally legitimate. We shall examine the cases in which concupiscence is at stake in the omission of an intervention demanded by a morally relevant good, as soon as we turn to the analysis of the concupiscent type. First, there remains the examination of the morally legitimate attitude toward bodily pain that occurs inevitably without having been accepted by a free choice, as for instance through an illness.

The way in which such pain is endured is very significant for the moral standard of a person. One's interest in alleviating or even getting rid of pain is completely morally legitimate and implies no element of concupiscence. But as long as it is present it must be endured, firstly, without any rebellion. The revolt against it, in the worst case in cursing, is a fruit of concupiscence and even of a certain element of pride. Moreover, the pain must never disturb the superactual *religio* toward the reign of the morally relevant values. One must not let oneself go. He must not lose his rootedness in the world of morally relevant values and abandon himself to his bodily discomforts. He must endure them in patience, in a humble acceptance that has a specifically noble character.

Finally, he must also be patient in the sense of not losing his temper toward the persons who surround him, abstaining from irritation, anger, and even from being unable to direct himself with charity toward them, from being so absorbed by pain that he becomes closed, shut up in himself, and indifferent toward everything else.

By contrast, the Stoic attitude that endures bodily pains with courage as a pure result of a technical self-control, that does not shrink back from them but accepts them with an imperturbable mood, has no moral value. It may evoke our admiration as a fakir does, but it lacks any moral value because it is a fruit not of the value-response attitude but, on the contrary, a result of an idol of virility that is rooted in pride. It is thus not only morally worthless but even morally negative. It derives from a desire not to admit our human frailty, our situation as a creature, from an attempt to place ourselves above everything, to enjoy the consciousness of our master-position of self-esteem. For this proud virility, it is a horror to show any weakness, to admit that one's *ataraxia* is limited, to fear that someone could think of one as coward.[16]

The Concupiscent Attitude When Undergoing Intense Bodily Pains as Expressed in Cursing

The analysis of the attitude toward bodily pain in the person in which the value-response attitude has overcome pride and concupiscence has prepared the way for determining how concupiscence intervenes in the attitude to bodily pain. As far as the two "hard" types of concupiscent persons are concerned, the passionate and the lazy one, their attitude toward bodily pain, when it occurs without leaving us a choice, is a rebellious one. Their self-centered direction toward the bodily agreeable, deprived of any *religio* toward the reign of morally relevant values, in the last analysis, toward God, makes them react with hostility against bodily pains. It shows itself in a rebellious, impotent struggle that expresses itself in a typical way through cursing. To curse is the most outspoken antithesis to the fundamental attitude of *religio*. It is the gesture in which one does away with all respect, all reverence, in which we throw away, so to speak, all that is "above" because we come across something that is negative from the point of view of the subjectively satisfying. It may be that an obstacle hinders us from attaining our subjectively satisfying goal, that something does not go as we wish it; it may be that we have to sustain something that is bodily painful.

Certainly cursing implies also an element of pride, but the main root is concupiscence; it is not the master-position sought for its own sake,

---

16. [Hildebrand alludes here to the Stoic interpretation of eudaimonia as the highest end of one's life consisting in an unperturbed, peaceful state of mind. Editor.]

but the rebellion against God occurs because something hurts our concupiscence, because we are hindered in the unlimited unfolding of our desires or instincts. It is the anger of coming across something disagreeable that one cannot overcome by one's own force, and the reaction is a revolt against the world above upon which we depend. Concupiscence is the root of this cursing, but it is also supported by pride. The difference between this secondary rebellion, being more a brutal letting ourselves go, throwing away the bounds of any *religio* because of our concupiscence, and the thematic rebellion of the proud against God is obvious.

The first feature of the concupiscent attitude towards inevitable bodily pain, as far as the two hard types are concerned, is thus this brutal revolt against it, this antithesis to the *religio* which finds its typical expression in cursing.

The second is a letting oneself go in general, showing irritation against the persons who surround us, showing no appreciation of their kindness in helping us, no gratitude, taking for granted that we are the center of everything, laying claim to any and every service. It is not a relishing of feeling ourselves important but a brutal undisputed arrogance, a changing mood in asking for this and that, and a furious, impatient reaction to the fulfilling of wishes that contradict each other. The absence of any *religio* toward the reign of morally relevant values expresses itself in this letting ourselves go, in our impatience, as well as in being completely shut up in ourselves.

It must be said that the man in whom concupiscence is predominant possesses no *religio*, no charity, is shut up in himself and dominated by his egotism, even without needing special objects that appeal to his concupiscence.

The Yielding to Fear of Bodily Pain and Concupiscence

But bodily pain may also lead certain persons, in whom there normally lives a superactual value-response attitude, to yield to concupiscence. It is a harder test for someone in whom there is a predominance of the value-response attitude to endure bodily pain in the right way, than to keep away from the concupiscence awakened by bodily pleasures. A higher degree of the domination of the value-response attitude is required here in order not to yield to concupiscence. It is therefore often the case that persons in whom the value-response attitude dominates fundamentally, lose their temper and yield to some extent to concupiscence when they have to endure grave bodily pain.

The hard concupiscent types will obviously not shrink from doing wrong if they are threatened by bodily pain if they do not do wrong. It does not even form any problem for them as the disrespecting of morally relevant values does not mean anything for them. Their general indifference toward the important-in-itself makes them also disposed to disrespect every morally relevant good, if they risk bodily pain in not doing so. Thus they will, without any inner conflict, disrespect any morally relevant value under the menace of bodily pain. The avoidance of anything subjectively disagreeable suffices as a motive for them to accept something morally negative, as the morally relevant values are something neutral for them. We must take this into account, as the hard types of concupiscence are not necessarily especially sensitive to or fearful of bodily pain. In order to attain something subjectively satisfying they may be disposed to accept bodily pain.

These types of concupiscence have often a certain courage, and absorbed by their desire to attain something agreeable they do not think of possible bodily pain. It is not a horror of bodily pain that makes them concupiscent. This is, as we say, a morally legitimate feature of our nature; it is not even because they fear bodily pain more than others do that they accept without struggle a disrespect for the morally relevant good. They do so because of their indifference toward the important-in-itself. The specific character of concupiscence consists not in a greater fear of bodily pain but in the indifference toward the morally relevant value. In the unfolding of concupiscence a horror of bodily pain does not play a role analogous to a craving for bodily pleasures.

Also, these hard types of concupiscence will omit any morally obligatory intervention rather than endure bodily pains. But it must be said that they would, even without the risk of bodily pain, not intervene because they are indifferent toward the call of the morally relevant values. Thus, an interest in avoiding bodily pain does not play a decisive role in their omission of a morally obligatory intervention. It is their general indifference toward the important-in-itself that plays this role.

It is, rather, the man in whom the value-response attitude coexists with concupiscence who will, in yielding to the fear of bodily pain, reveal in his attitude the relative power that concupiscence still has over him. The connection of the fear of bodily pain and concupiscence becomes visible when someone, under the threat of bodily pain, disrespects reluctantly a morally relevant good or omits reluctantly a morally obligatory intervention, for instance, the man who reluctantly kills innocent persons under the threat of a Nazi or a Bolshevik concentration camp, or who does not dare to help a fellow man because of the same threat. In these cases, it is really the horror of bodily pain that motivates the disrespect of the moral obligation.

Someone may object: the root of these moral failures is not concupiscence, but a lack of courage, a weakness of the will; it is the absence of a kind of self-control that makes him yield to his fear of bodily pain. This weakness has no relation to concupiscence.

It must be said: the weakness in question is in reality a symptom that a person's interest in the morally relevant value is not yet so great that it is able to overcome the horror of bodily pain. It is not a pure formal strength of the will, such as energetic persons possess, or the courage that can be proper also to a morally bad man. It is not the technical self-control but the degree of our abandonment toward the morally relevant values, in the last analysis, the degree of our love of God.

Here we come across the general problem: which elements are responsible for the different degrees of the ardor of our value-response, or the degrees of our love of God? Is it that concupiscence or pride to a certain extent still obstruct the full and unhindered unfolding of our response to values and of our love of God, or is it some other element besides them?

It is the same problem that we find when comparing someone who is ready to accept great sacrifices in order to conform to the call of a morally relevant value, with someone who is not ready to do so, though he would certainly conform to this call if he would not need to make a sacrifice or need to make only a minor one. The problem is twofold. Firstly: is the difference between the heroic attitude of a saint who surpasses his moral obligation, and the person who restricts himself to the fulfillment of his obligation, to be found in a complete overcoming of pride and concupiscence? Or has the man who conforms to the strict moral obligation already fully mastered his pride and concupiscence, so that it is something merely in the setting of the morally positive that determines this difference?[17] Or as we may put it, is it rather the interference of something morally negative that is responsible for the lack of a superabundant heroism that surpasses moral obligation?

Secondly: consider the difference between the man who accepts a sacrifice because a morally relevant value obliges him to do so and the man who, though he wishes to conform to the moral obligation, has not the strength to do so because of a fear of accepting the sacrifice. Is this difference determined by pride and concupiscence or by another imperfection?

The first problem does not concern us here as we shall deal with it in the chapter about the difference between Christian morality and natural morality.[18] The second, on the contrary, refers to our present topic because bodily pain is a typical example of sacrifice and of something that we desire to avoid independently of concupiscence.

We have thus to examine the root of yielding to the fear of bodily pain and so disrespecting the moral obligation. Obviously, bodily pain, though repulsive to our nature in a morally legitimate way, is not something negatively important-in-itself but only an objective evil for the person. The concupiscent man may look at it merely as something subjectively disagreeable. In any case, it presents itself to us not as something important-in-itself, and still less as something having a morally relevant negative value. We are not morally obliged to avoid bodily pain or to try to get rid of it when it occurs. In order to avoid any misunderstanding,

---

17. [That is, the difference between the saint and the morally upright person. Editor.]
18. [Hildebrand refers here probably to ch. 36 of his *Ethics*, "Christian Morality." Editor.]

it must be said that as soon as other persons are concerned, their bodily pain is always and necessarily given to us as objective evil for them. Our interest in their being free of pain is a necessary consequence of love, which is essentially a value-response. Thus, the suffering of bodily pain assumes a character of something that is negatively important-in-itself, which has not only a negative value but also a morally relevant one. It is morally obligatory not to inflict bodily pain on another person if it is not necessary for higher reasons, as in the case of a surgeon performing a surgery on a patient, and it is morally obligatory to mitigate the bodily pain of our fellow man if we are able to do so.

This is one of the many cases where from the moral point of view some good or evil changes its character completely according to the question whether we ourselves are concerned or our fellow man. The general difference in those two cases concerns obviously only the sphere of the objective goods for the person and never the values as such: interest in a moral value never assumes a different aspect depending on whether we ourselves are concerned or another person. Our interest in being just, pure, or charitable ourselves, in sum, our interest in our moral perfection, is as good and obligatory as our interest in the perfection of another person. Also the objective value that the knowledge of truth possesses is to be desired for us as for others, or interest that a building may be beautiful is as pure whether we ourselves are the architects or another person.

The same applies to the highest objective good that forms the point where the objective goods for the person join the important-in-itself: our eternal welfare. Here again, it is as obligatory to strive for own eternal welfare as it is to strive for that of our fellow man.

But for all the other objective goods for the person that are not simultaneously important-in-themselves, the great difference lies in whether we ourselves are concerned or other persons.

It is the problem of egotism, on the one hand, and charity, on the other. Not as if the interest in attaining an objective good for ourselves would be egotistic. Far from that. It is even, as far as the higher objective goods are concerned, morally good to be interested in them and, moreover, morally obligatory to preserve and protect great gifts that God's bounty bestows on us. The question of egotism arises only when we try to attain something for ourselves while simultaneously depriving a fellow man of the possibility of attaining it.

The Attitude of the Soft Concupiscent Type towards Bodily Pain

We have now to examine the attitude of the soft concupiscent type to bodily pain. He has, firstly, the tendency to exaggerate every bodily pain, not because of a greater sensitivity but because of his egocentric softness, because he considers every rough wind as an intolerable injury inflicted upon him. Compassion with himself is a basic form of his egocentrism, and he thinks that everything that he has to endure is vastly greater than everything that others have to endure. He is so imprisoned in his self-centeredness that the suffering of others is merely disagreeable for him. He shrinks away from it because it gets on his nerves, or because he is reminded of the existence of something that could also happen to him, but in no way because he has a real compassion for his fellow man. He will be at ease as soon as he does not have to witness them; the fact that the other person suffers ceases to bother him as soon as he does not have to witness it. This substitution of true compassion flowing out of charity by a hypersensitive reaction, and being concerned only with the horrifying aspect of suffering, is very typical for the soft type of concupiscence. Whereas the hard types are likewise indifferent to the sufferings of their fellow man and to the aspect of bodily pain, the representatives of the soft type may fool us by reacting strongly to these things.

But in reality, they are as self-centered as the hard types, and just as indifferent toward their fellow man. Their sensitivity makes them shrink back from all that has the aspect of something subjectively disagreeable, but not because it is an evil for their fellow man. The category of the subjectively satisfying is also the only decisive factor for them. The difference is only that their softness and sensitivity make them experience this aspect as disagreeable. Whereas the tough, hardboiled, concupiscent type remains indifferent to "aspects" and finds no harm in them, the representative of the soft type fears bodily pain even more than he craves bodily pleasures. His sensitivity makes him fear bodily pain much more than the hard type does. He will especially consider small bodily pain as intolerable, which the hard types would not bother with very much. His concupiscence shows itself in taking every pain as a very serious injury inflicted on him, as something incomparably worse than the grave bodily pain of another person, and it will lead him to compassion with himself.

He will not so much revolt against pain, he will not curse, but his letting himself go will assume the character of making a great fuss over his pain, and having a desire for compassion, a desire to be nursed and petted. He will also be shut up in himself, inclined to criticize surrounding people, to find that they do not adequately realize what he has to undergo, that they do not take care of him in the right way. He will always be offended by their lack of interest and will display this kind of egocentrism, which may also express itself in irritation. In any case, he will never appreciate the attention given to him by other persons. He will never shrink from annoying his fellow man by always asking for more attention.

The important point is to see that his attitude is completely egocentric: he is concerned only with the subjectively satisfying, indifferent toward the moral values. He will feel no gratitude, for instance, for the kindness of other persons. He lets himself go. He also has no attitude of *religio* toward the world above; but he has fallen prey to the subjectively satisfying or, rather, to the subjectively dissatisfying.

It is not the lack of self-control, not the lack of virility, that makes this way of enduring bodily pains morally bad. Rather, it is the self-centered indifference toward the important-in-itself, the being absorbed by the subjectively satisfying that frustrates every true charity in him and closes him up in himself. In sum, what makes this way of enduring bodily pain to be morally bad is this kind of concupiscence.

In what concerns the free choice of bodily pain, when a morally relevant value calls for it, it is clear that the soft types will never accept it. Their indifference toward a moral obligation is perhaps not as great as that of the hard types. These soft concupiscent types are generally not criminals, thieves, or murderers. Their effeminate sensitivity and their cowardice prevent them from such brutal crimes. We say "in general" because there exist even criminals of this soft type, but these are rather an exception. They will thus, in general, not kill other persons in complete indifference but not so much because the morally relevant value means something to them but because they shrink back from every shedding of blood as a shock to their sensitivity. But there is no doubt that they will do anything under the threat of bodily pain. Their fear of bodily pain suffices to overcome an obstacle that is of a moral order. In reality, their choice is between the disagreeable experience of bodily pain, and the disagreeable shock to their nerves that a brutal act against their fellow man would include. It is a choice in the frame of the category of the subjectively satisfying. And obviously, the subjective evil of bodily pain tips the scale for them more than the evil of a disagreeable aspect.

Again, in this case, we must say that the fear of bodily pain is not the decisive factor in disrespecting a moral obligation or in omitting something morally obligatory. There exists, as in the other concupiscent types, an indifference toward the morally relevant values that is not a cause of the fear of bodily pain. They are in general indifferent toward it. It is not as in the case of the weak man who has a fundamental direction toward morally relevant values but yields reluctantly to his fear of bodily pain. Nevertheless, the fear of bodily pain plays a different role than in the hard types.

The difference is not so much a moral one, but a merely psychological one. That is to say, their concupiscence presents itself in a specific way, namely in their fear of bodily pain, whereas in the hard types, the fear of bodily pain is not the typical way of unfolding their concupiscence.

It must be added that their shrinking away from certain crimes, which as we saw is merely motivated by their disagreeable horrifying aspect, is found only in evildoing that implies such a bloody aspect. Killing or torturing other persons may be repugnant to them, and they may yield thus only to the fear of bodily pain that will result from opposing it; but to betray somebody, to do any injustice to someone, to do something impure, and so on, will not be repugnant to them from the point of view of the merely subjectively disagreeable.

Summarizing, we may say: to abhor bodily pain is not, like craving bodily pleasures, a typical expression of concupiscence. Whereas the interest in bodily pleasures becomes illegitimate as soon as it is no longer tamed and ruled by the superactual value-response attitude, the interest in avoiding bodily pain is as such, even without this *placet* of the value-response attitude, not morally illegitimate and not rooted in concupiscence. The typical expression of the difference between the concupiscent and the morally good attitude is visible only in the way in which inevitable pain is endured. The same holds for the case where morally relevant values call for an acceptance of bodily pain.

II.v. *Bodily Displeasures*

Bodily Displeasures Caused by Unsatisfied Urges

We now have to examine the other bodily displeasures that are in a stronger sense, at least psychologically, a negative analogy to bodily pleasures. Firstly, the unsatisfied urges imply a bodily displeasure. But the degree of analogy to the pleasures connected with the satisfaction of bodily urges varies very much.

There exist, firstly, certain imperative urges, the fulfillment of which is necessary for our bodily existence, such as a bowel movement or urinating. The displeasure of not being able to satisfy them is obviously much more intense than the pleasure connected with their satisfaction.

Secondly, there exist other urges that are also imperative but of another character, such as hunger and thirst. Here the discrepancy between the displeasure when they are not satisfied and the pleasure in their satisfaction is not so striking as in the former case, but still it seems that the displeasure surpasses the pleasure. The same applies to the desire for sleep when one is exhausted.

Thirdly, there are less imperative urges, as, for instance, the desire to plunge into cool water when it is very hot or to be fanned by fresh air. In this case, it seems that the displeasure of the unsatisfied urge or of the suffering of heat equals the pleasure of the satisfaction of the urge.

Fourthly, there is the sexual urge, where obviously the pleasure of satisfying surpasses the displeasure of the unsatisfied sexual urge. Obviously, the whole question depends upon the degree to which the satisfaction of an urge bestows upon us a positive pleasure besides the satisfaction of the urge as such. For, as we saw before in the chapter about happiness, the positive bodily pleasure and the appeasement of an urge or satisfaction as such must definitely be distinguished.[19]

In what concerns the first and second type of imperative elementary urges, the displeasure connected with them has an analogy to bodily pain, and from a moral point of view it has the character of an elementary evil.

The first type is even of such an automatic character that to yield to it is inevitable, and the reaction against this displeasure as well as the interest in satisfying it is no object of concupiscence.

Only the attitude of yielding to them without making use of our freedom, the animal-like giving way to them without taking notice of the situation, without regard for decency and shame, can be a typical symptom of concupiscence. It is again the lack of distance from one's own bodily sphere, an animal-like imprisonment in our bodily instincts, that characterizes this type of concupiscence. It applies only to the two hard types of concupiscent man, and here even more to the second lazy type, whereas the soft type of concupiscence will not express itself in this way.

In what concerns the second type of elementary urges, the concupiscent attitude again will express itself in an uncontrolled craving for the satisfaction of these urges, in getting wild and impatient, in pushing every obstacle aside, in a self-centered ignoring of every regard for other persons. It is again the lack of any distance of the spirit to the bodily sphere, being imprisoned by bodily instincts, failing to take a free stance with our spiritual ego toward it.

---

19. [There is no chapter on happiness in *Ethics*. The author refers here probably to some material preserved in the *Nachlass*. Editor.]

Again, this applies above all to the two hard types of concupiscence. The concupiscence of the soft type will express itself in a whimpering compassion for one's own person, in exaggerated complaints, in being cut off from one's surroundings in a self-centered preoccupation with this displeasure, unable to engage in any other activity, unable to show interest in the suffering of others. Here equally the inner distance to one's own body is lacking, the self-centered imprisonment in our own body is also present, but it presents itself not in the brutal hard but in the soft whimpering manner.

The morally legitimate attitude, on the contrary, will express itself here in the distance of the spirit to one's own body. Of course in the legitimate attitude we react against this displeasure, but this reaction does not absorb us to the point of losing all regard for our surroundings, all awakedness for the call of values. The presence of this bodily displeasure throws into relief precisely the preciousness and nobility of the spiritual character of man.

In what concerns the third type of displeasures resulting from unsatisfied urges, concupiscence expresses itself in a similar manner. The two hard types, sometimes less sensitive to heat and cold, will not react specifically against them. But when they are sensitive to this displeasure, they will again reveal the lack of distance and this animallike craving for a relief or a satisfaction of their urge, ignoring all contrary circumstances. The soft type, on the contrary, will react in a whimpering way, trying to make himself the center of compassion, and having compassion for himself above all.

The fourth type of displeasure, the one that derives from an unsatisfied sexual urge, reveals the same features in the concupiscent man as the craving for sexual pleasure. It does not need, therefore, any special analysis. The especially odious passionate craving for the satisfaction of this urge, in the first hard type, brutally pushing away every obstacle, indifferent toward the call of the reign of morally relevant values, shows us, similar to the animal-like desire of the lazy type, and the whimpering sensuality of the soft type, the aspect of pure concupiscence in its worst form.

Bodily Displeasures Caused by Eating Unpalatable Food or Smelling Unpleasant Smells

Another type of bodily displeasures are associated with unpleasant tasting food and drink and unpleasant smells. Obviously, we abstract from hunger and thirst and concentrate exclusively on the displeasure of unpleasant taste as such. This displeasure appears to form a more proper negative antithesis to the pleasure of good tasting food and drink.

What is the attitude of the concupiscent man toward them? Here again we must say that the horror of eating something with a repugnant taste, bad fat, for instance, castor oil, or a rotten egg, is completely legitimate. The non-concupiscent type will prefer to abstain from eating anything if he is confronted with the alternative of swallowing something with a horrible taste before he may eat something that tastes good. If he has to choose between the successive consumption of something that tastes bad and then a refined food, or to eat neither, he will certainly choose the latter. Whereby it is presumed that he is not hungry. But he will courageously swallow something having an unpleasant taste as soon as a value calls for it, for instance, the preservation of his health. He will further patiently eat something which tastes unpleasant if he has nothing else to satisfy his hunger. He will also have here the necessary distance to his body and its reactions.

The soft concupiscent type, on the contrary, will especially give in to his repugnance of anything that tastes unpleasant. He will make great fuss about taking a bad tasting medicine, even if his health requires it imperatively. Again, the compassion with himself and the soft whimpering imprisonment in his bodily sphere, his weak yielding to his instincts will be on full display. And what is characteristic of him is that his horror of unpleasant tasting food and drink is much stronger than his craving for the refined pleasures of the table.

The hard types, on the contrary, will care less about this type of the disagreeable. The passionate will desire more the good tasting food than he will shrink back from the unpleasant tasting. The lazy type will be rather insensitive with respect to taste, more concerned with the satisfaction of his greediness. The soft type will not only not accept the unpleasant tasting food but also refuse the bland, neutral tasting food that gives no opportunity for a refined pleasure. He will be especially presumptuous in this sphere.

Unpleasant smells will not form an object of special horror for the lazy concupiscent type. The passionate concupiscent type will also have no special reaction to them. The soft type, on the contrary, will abhor them and will again in his attitude of an aesthete reveal an exaggerated avoiding of anything disagreeable in this field. He will, for instance, shrink back from helping someone who is sick, because of an unpleasant smell, he will take the avoiding of the disagreeable and unaesthetic as much more important than the call of charity or any moral value. The features of concupiscence clearly stand out in his attitude.

After having examined the role of concupiscence in the sphere of bodily experiences, we now turn to the subjectively satisfying in the psychical sphere.

II.vi. *The Subjectively Satisfying in the Psychic Sphere*

Games

Firstly, this sphere comprises all kinds of games, such as cards, football, and so on. The subjectively satisfying here consists in the thrill of a certain tension of the game as well as in the eventual satisfaction of winning. We abstract from the gain of money that may occasionally be connected with winning. The thrill of the game as such appeals to a morally legitimate center. Certain persons may be indifferent to it, others may enjoy it; it has obviously no value that calls for a response. Everybody has the clear consciousness that it is up to his temperamental disposition or to his momentary mood as to whether he will partake in a game or not. Eventually charity or some other reasons referring to a morally relevant value may motivate our partaking, for instance, when other persons who are eager to play a game could not fulfill their desire because of our abstaining from it. But this case would obviously include a motive that is beyond the subjectively satisfying nature of the game.

In themselves games are typical goods that, having no value as such, do not require a response on our part. It is up to our mood to play a game or to abstain from it, as long as no special moral circumstances are at stake that require us to abstain from the game or to partake in it. Games are, further, an especially innocent type of the subjectively satisfying, appealing to a natural desire for relaxation. The man in whom concupiscence dominates is generally not especially attracted by this form of the agreeable. It is too innocent, too childlike, to form a typical satisfaction for concupiscence.

Nevertheless, it would be wrong to deny any possible connection with concupiscence. People who lose much time with games, in whose life this kind of amusement plays too great a role, are obviously yielding to concupiscence, though to a more innocuous form of it.

A certain laziness, not the heavy negative one but the infantile dislike for work and its hardship, on the one hand, and a thirst for this kind of amusement, on the other hand, are at the basis of this disproportionate role of games. They are both fruits of concupiscence. As soon as a value at stake calls for a more serious occupation and someone wastes his time in playing cards or tennis, he yields to concupiscence. But it is obviously a more innocent type of concupiscence that is therefore more likely found in such people who are not fundamentally dominated by concupiscence but where an unconscious, infantile direction toward the agreeable survives, notwithstanding a fundamental value-response attitude (but which still lacks a fully conscious character).

Another type is the man in whom the interest in certain games has assumed the character of an outspoken passion. In this case the connection with concupiscence is still more obvious. The "untamed" role of this kind of subjectively satisfying, the formal disorder that the passion as such implies, the fact that something which is not important-in-itself but merely subjectively satisfying assumes such a power over the person, that it threatens to enslave her, to do away with her freedom and her fundamental stance of *religio* toward the world above—all of this is a typical mark of concupiscence.

We abstract hereby from the passion for gambling, as the chance of winning money plays here an important role as well as the appeal to a sensationalism, both surpassing the pleasure of games as such, and also being rooted in concupiscence in their very quality in a much more obvious manner.[20]

Superficial Forms of Socializing

A second type of amusement are parties, all kinds of superficial social gatherings, dancing, and so on. The pleasure in question is appealing to certain natural and legitimate desires. Again, we must say that this kind of pleasure is not the typical object of an outspoken and dominating concupiscence. They are not the type of agreeable things that kindle the flame of concupiscence in its typical and most serious forms. Nevertheless, it would be wrong to overlook the fact that they may also form the object of concupiscence, even if in a more superficial form.

The behavior of a man who craves those pleasures, running from one party to another, who wastes his time, his energy, and his money in such entertainments, is certainly morally wrong, and concupiscence is at the root of his moral failure.

The tendency to fly into the periphery, to thirst for a superficial jolliness, is a fruit of concupiscence. We must distinguish here different types: firstly, the man who is desirous of parties, dancing, and so on, where he can let himself go, which give him the opportunity to revel in wild jolliness, where the presence of comrades seeking the same pleasures creates an atmosphere of superficial jolly independence. We abstract from the incidental appeal to sexuality that may occur in these entertainments because this appeal obviously surpasses the frame of the pleasure here in question, and is as such immoral in a much deeper sense.

In this type of person, interest in parties and the like is a fruit of the desire for letting ourselves go, which is a typical fruit of concupiscence. To throw ourselves into a dissolving jolliness, into a wild laughter and uncontrolled chattering, into a stratum of our nature where we relish the

20. [This will be explained in section II.viii. Editor.]

absence of *religio*, where we feel, so to speak, in a kind of state in which responsibility is suspended: these are all signs of concupiscence.

Secondly, the elegant man who does not desire to let himself go, is craving not those informal, wild parties but the salon with a conventional, superficial atmosphere, where politeness and good manners reign.

He is much more refined than the former, and that which appeals to him is the superficial atmosphere that accepts him and supports him, giving him the opportunity to dwell in the periphery of his self without having the desire to let himself go, the opportunity to take delight in light and unsubstantial conversation, to find a place in society. The tendency to leave the fundamental stance of *religio* toward the world above by dwelling in the periphery, is here not open and conscious as in the former case, but is covered by the illusion of being on his best behavior. The *religio* is substituted with the conventional forms of politeness, elegance, and a peripheral self-control.

And this substitution has precisely its roots in concupiscence and pride. In concupiscence insofar as he craves the empty exaltation of these parties, the illusion of a world without suffering and serious problems, the soft atmosphere of politeness and compliments. In pride insofar as he wants to yield to his concupiscence without having the humiliating consciousness of letting himself go. He wants to conserve his consciousness of self-control, of being a gentleman, because of the support of convention, because this society presents itself as something serious, and finally because he delights in the brilliant social image of himself.

Thirdly, the man who throws himself into these peripheral amusements in order to escape sorrows and troubles, who uses them as a narcotic in order to distract himself rather than as the source of pleasure. What is the root of this wrong way to overcome troubles and sorrows, of this flight from himself? It is the unwillingness to face reality and to endure sorrows and troubles, to embrace the cross; it is the general tendency of fallen human nature to shrink from an inner effort to overcome hardship, sorrows, difficulties; instead of overcoming them from the depth one does away with them by trying to ignore them, to close our eyes to them, and to flee to the periphery of our being. This tendency is also rooted in concupiscence.

The untamed desire to get rid of something unpleasant, disagreeable, painful, depressing, regardless of the call to give the adequate response to the distressing object or event in question, the self-centered gesture of escape by considering a merely subjective withdrawal as a legitimate solution—all of this is incompatible with the value-response attitude, the direction toward the inner meaning of the object, its *logos*, and results from concupiscence, for which not only the subjectively satisfying is the norm of life, but for which also our subjective state alone counts and not the object, its meaning, its positive or negative value.

To prefer an illusion to reality is already a result of concupiscence. A respect for reality, a desire to face it, to remain in conformity with reality and truth is an important formal element of *religio* and the fundamental value-response attitude. But the attitude in which one tries to do away with something depressing by ignoring it, by lulling oneself into the illusion of its non-existence, by attempting to forget it through plunging into superficial distractions and pleasures, lacks the respect due to reality and reveals a formal subjectivism that is a fruit of concupiscence.

Also the tendency to fly into the periphery of our being, to escape the cross in stepping down to a lower level, to live in a lower stratum of our life, to yield to the easier way, to avoid the inner effort and *élan*, is a typical fruit of concupiscence. The deep metaphysical laziness that incites us to choose the easier way, to fear any actualization of our depth, is rooted in concupiscence, as is every laziness. And the readiness to give up the deeper stratum, to fly into the periphery, which means as such an ignoring of the general *sursum corda* of the reign of the values, an indifference toward their call, is equally rooted in concupiscence.

Obviously, this form of concupiscence is not restricted to this special case of using entertainment as a narcotic for troubles, sorrows, and pains, but it extends itself to all the domains of life in which man escapes the adequate response to the object and glides into the periphery, in which he gives himself over voluntarily to illusions instead of being determined by reality and truth, in which he flees from himself and in the last analysis from God. We shall thus come across this dimension of concupiscence again and again.

Light Literature, Movies, Pop Music, and So On

A third type of the subjectively satisfying in the psychical sphere are the different kinds of light literature, movies, plays, operettas, and light music. We abstract here from everything that has an artistic value and belongs thus to the realm of the important-in-itself.

Those goods that are amusing in the narrower sense of the word are again not necessarily relative to a morally illegitimate center in the person. But it depends, obviously, on the very nature of these goods that exist exclusively for the purpose of amusing us. Many of them appeal to a deep sentimentality, to an evil sensation, to sexual excitement, and so on. If this is the case, they are repugnant for the unperverted man as soon as he feels this appeal. This must be said because sometimes this appeal is not even experienced by certain innocent types.

It is obvious that these appeals are directed to concupiscence and that those who delight in them do so because of their concupiscence. But if we abstract from those cases and examine light literature, music, novels, that, though lacking any artistic value, are just amusing without appealing to illegitimate centers, the problem arises whether and when they become an object of concupiscence.

Again, it is the type who nourishes himself too much with this light mental food, who has a disordered inclination to dwell in this light, superficial tension, perhaps as the opportunity to escape boredom or in order to relish the thrill of something exciting.

The fact that someone wastes time with such amusements, that he employs time that should be dedicated either to work or to contact with goods having an authentic value, with the *frui* of beauty or truth, is a symptom of a disorder that has its roots in concupiscence.[21] The

---

21. [The term *frui*, to enjoy, comes from St. Augustine, who contrasts it with *uti*, to use. In his *Ethics*, Hildebrand describes *frui* as "enjoying high goods endowed with values which bestow a true and noble happiness on us." See *Ethics*, 72 (69). Editor.]

following elements must be distinguished that are all rooted in concupiscence. Firstly, the "untamed" yielding to the merely subjectively satisfying, the lack of the fundamental stance of *religio*, which restricts us *ab ovo* to the frame of the merely amusing. Since we objectively live under the reign of and in the presence of the world of value, we feel void and empty if we dwell too much in the sphere of mere amusement.

Secondly, the very fact that one seeks to overcome boredom by means of these amusements instead of turning to a *frui* of goods having an authentic value, the very fact that one considers amusement as the only alternative to work and does not see the alternative to work that lies in the *frui* of the great goods of life that have an authentic value, the fact that, when work is done, we see only the periphery instead of depth and recollection, reveals a concupiscent attitude, a being dominated by the subjectively satisfying. The perversion that substitutes the mere "exciting" for the thrill of real values, the peripheral distraction for the blissful being affected by real values, is typical for concupiscence.

Thirdly, this craving for amusements of this kind reveals an attitude in which periphery is preferred to depth, in which we avoid the inner *élan* of abandoning ourselves to a good with an authentic value, and in which the uplifting call of value is avoided, and we delight in something that is deprived of any call, in which we can let ourselves go in the enjoyment of it—all of this is very typical for concupiscence.

Fourthly, every flight into an unsubstantial illusionary peripheral world is a symptom of concupiscence. Here we come across a general tendency of a certain concupiscence that is not restricted to these entertainments but occurs in many other spheres. The tendency to dream, to detach ourselves from reality, to retire into a world of agreeable images where our desires can unfold without being limited by reality, which is proper to certain persons, is a very typical fruit of concupiscence.

It is something similar in its root to the escape from troubles and sorrows by means of distractions and illusions. But it is not identical with it. The tendency to "dream" is not necessarily the consequence of an effort to escape from troubles and sorrows. It is found even when the person in question has no particular trouble. It is often the mere attempt to build up an illusionary world in which our desires can unfold undisturbed and in which our drive for happiness encounters no obstacles. The person of this type may in her dreams seek not only the subjectively satisfying but even goods that have an authentic value. She may transfer herself in her dreams to a beautiful country, imagine herself united with beloved persons, enjoy in her fantasy being loved and understood, and so on.

Nonetheless, this dreaming is a result of concupiscence. This is because of the detachment from reality, from its unique seriousness that alone can give us true happiness. It is because of the subjectivism that consists in trying to satisfy our thirst for happiness with illusions, by creating for ourselves a world other than the real world, a world in which we choose *ad libitum* instead of letting reality bestow happiness on us. We saw before that a respect for reality is an essential element of *religio*. This respect is here absent and with it the seriousness and validity of a truly human life. We are undoubtedly dealing with a fruit of concupiscence when we are drawn to this effeminate subjectivism in which it is no longer the presence of a real good, its very existence, that affects us and calls for a response, but our wishes that determine the object. And in our special case of throwing ourselves into superficial entertainment by craving mere excitement in order to "fill" our life, we encounter this general attitude of the "dreamer" insofar as one tries to overcome boredom not by turning to the world above and to the real goods having an authentic value, but to the mere excitement of imaginary things.

In order to avoid any misunderstanding, it must be said that this kind of literature, music, movies has, by its very nature, a tendency to escape from reality in a manner that is completely alien to every authentic work of art. The theme of the work of art to unfold a specific beauty is not something imaginary, or a world of illusions; it is certainly a world of its own, and though it presupposes sometimes an artistic illusion (as in novels), the values at stake are real and speak to us of a higher world that is eminently real. The real work of art does not draw us into an illusionary world that, like the dream-world, is destined to be a substitute for reality, but it presents itself *ab ovo* as something quite different, as something that strengthens our receptivity to values and to the deeper meaning of reality, thereby throwing a new sublime light on life.

Concupiscence in the Satisfaction of One's Psychical Urges and in the Releasing of One's Mental Energies

A new type of the subjectively satisfying in the psychical realm are the different natural urges which it is pleasant to satisfy. We have to distinguish two main types. Firstly, certain urges that, similar to bodily urges, tend to attain an object that is able to appease them. Such is, for instance, the longing for communion with other persons, or the desire to speak, to express that which we feel. Secondly, the different psychical energies that tend to diffuse themselves. Such are the urge to unfold a talent, perhaps a practical talent to organize, an ability for sport or cooking, perhaps an intellectual talent, such as the capacity for philosophical or scientific research, or perhaps an artistic talent.

The difference between the two types is that the first kind, like thirst or hunger, results from a natural need for certain objects that appease or satisfy this urge, whereas the second type results from a superabundant plenitude that tends to diffuse itself. The object has here the function of offering an opportunity to display this capacity.

To the first type belong the need for communion with other persons, the need for being understood and spiritually supported, the thirst for seeing new countries and people. To the second type belong, besides all the different talents and abilities, the desire to display motherly instincts in nursing and taking care of other persons, the desire to teach and inform other persons, the desire to speak to many persons. The satisfaction in the first type results from the aptitude of the object to appease it; in the second case it results from the activity as such.

But in both types, we cannot simply subsume the satisfaction under the category of "the subjectively satisfying." As Aristotle has already shown in his *Nicomachean Ethics*, Book 10, the nature of the pleasure varies according to the urges and activities in question.[22] The difference between those kinds of pleasures is obviously determined by the nature of the objects that are able to satisfy the urges, and by the nature of the activities in which the mental energies display themselves. And the decisive point regarding the nature of the object and of the activities is whether they possess an authentic value or whether they are merely subjectively satisfying.

The delight in displaying a spiritual activity, as for instance for a musician to compose, or for a philosopher to actualize his capacities in the search for truth, or of the actor to act, presupposes the value that is proper to these activities, and is in its quality and depth obviously beyond the merely agreeable. Similarly, the appeasement of the urge for communion with other persons or for being understood is directed toward a good that has an authentic value.

By contrast, the satisfaction that the activity of speaking as such bestows on loquacious persons is emphatically something merely agreeable. This is shown by the nature of this activity as something that has no value. But precisely in the case of the urges and energies the satisfaction of which is not merely subjectively satisfying, we have to face the fact that this satisfaction has essentially to play a secondary role in order to remain morally legitimate. This statement seems paradoxical at first sight, but a brief glance at the fact will reveal its correctness.

Every spiritual energy that tends to diffuse and display itself in certain activities, whenever this activity is noble and possesses a value in itself, such as knowledge, creating a work of art, or reproducing it, is concerned with objects that have an authentic value, a value which calls above all for an interest in itself.

Knowledge is directed toward being and truth and should primarily be motivated by the desire for truth, by the love for truth, in sum, by the value-response to truth and not by the mere desire to dwell in this activity. The theme has to be truth, for its own sake, the respect for truth, the value that consists in the fact that truth is grasped. And the main

---

22. [Aristotle, *Nicomachean Ethics*, bk. 10, chaps. 4–5. Editor.]

delight has to be the contact with truth, the superabundant gift that the value of truth bestows on us when we seek it for its own sake. As soon as the primary theme would be our intellectual activity as such and the main delight would be the displaying and working of our mental energies, a complete perversion would take place that is incompatible with the true value-response attitude. Instead of being the servants of truth, we would use it as a mere means for relishing the display of our mental energies, that is to say, an egocentric attitude would have replaced the value-response attitude.

And by that the entire value and preciousness of the activity of knowledge would be frustrated, because its value and intrinsic nobility is essentially rooted in its inner gesture of submitting to truth, of being directed to it for its own sake. An intellectual activity of searching for truth in which the main theme would be the displaying of this activity for its own sake, would assume the character of an intellectual sport and lose its entire dignity and value. The satisfaction resulting from this "sport" would have the pure character of something merely subjectively satisfying and would never be the blissful delight that results as a superabundant gift from the contact with truth, nor even the noble enjoyment that the activity as such implies as long as it preserves its inner dignity by respecting its subservient role.

The same applies to all these activities that have an authentic value. The artist who is not primarily concerned with creating something beautiful for its own sake, who does not feel himself as a servant of the world of aesthetic values, whose main intention is not to glorify God and to exalt his fellow man by his work, whose delight is not primarily the contact with the world of beauty in his creative process and being deigned worthy to "give birth" in this beauty, but who seeks above all to delight in the creative process as such, in his own activity, or even in the well-functioning of his activity, would also make of his creative process a kind of "sport" and frustrate its inner nobility and value.[23] It will not be

---

23. [It seems that Hildebrand alludes here to the famous passage in Plato's *Symposium* where Diotima speaks about *tokos en kalō* (206b7–8, e5). This Greek expression is normally rendered in English as "giving birth in beauty." Editor.]

discussed here whether the works of art created in this perverted attitude are necessarily bad from the artistic point of view, that is to say, whether the perversion of the intention frustrates the capacity of creating something really beautiful. It seems improbable that the great deep works of art could ever result from such an attitude. But this is obviously not the point here.

What matters is to see that this attitude deprives the artistic activity of the person of its inner nobility and value, independently of whether the work at stake is frustrated by this perversion in its artistic value, that is to say, whether the instrumental power of this creative activity is destroyed by this perversion. As a human act it loses its dignity, and it is incompatible with a true value-response attitude. The artist becomes, instead of a minister of beauty, a refined spiritual sportsman, and by that, egocentric. And the satisfaction that this "sport" procures for him obviously differs completely from the blissful delight that is bestowed upon him when in the attitude of a minister of beauty he strives for the authentic beauty of his works for its own sake. This satisfaction is of the merely subjectively satisfying order. The destructive character of this perversion where the object assumes the mere role of a means for our activity, where the activity in its immanent unfolding is sought for its own sake, becomes obviously still much more serious when the object of this activity is a morally relevant good.

To nurse a sick person primarily in order to display motherly instincts or to relish our skill, instead of being motivated by our interest in the sick person, in mitigating her sufferings, in serving her, is repugnant and frustrates the moral value of this action. An action in which we fail to respond to the morally relevant good because we aim merely at displaying of our talents is completely incompatible with the value-response attitude. It is obvious that any sport-like approach is still much more incongruous as soon as a morally relevant value is at stake. The satisfaction flowing out of the activity or the working as such has to remain a definite secondary theme as far as activities are concerned that deal with an object having an authentic value, and this is precisely the case in those activities that are noble as such and themselves have a value. As soon as the activity is chosen for its own sake, as soon as the delight in which the displaying of our energies and talents would be the motive, a perversion takes place that frustrates the value of this attitude and substitutes something merely subjectively satisfying for the true blissful delight that the values of the object and the activity itself can bestow on us. More than that, even if our motive would originally be the value of the object, as soon as we are absorbed during our activity by the satisfaction of displaying our talents or energies, and this satisfaction overtakes our interest in the value for its own sake and in the delight resulting as a gift from the value, then our attitude is perverted and loses its genuine value. The satisfaction of displaying our talents thus remains legitimate and preserves its higher quality only as long as it is a secondary theme, definitely subordinated to the main theme, the value-response, having a merely accompanying character, a modest subservient role.

The susceptibility and the desire to display these talents and energies is thus something morally legitimate and even noble as long as they remain in this subservient, secondary role that is the essential *conditio sine qua non* for their genuine character. But as soon as this perversion takes place whereby they become the main theme, concupiscence or pride has been substituted for the value-response attitude.

Here are typical fruits of concupiscence: the indifference toward the call of the value at stake, the egocentric imprisonment that reveals itself when noble activities destined to serve an objective value are degraded to mere spiritual sports, the desire of relishing the subjectively satisfying, a mere unfolding of an energy for its own sake when a value calls for us to abandon ourselves to it. As soon as this perversion goes in the direction of relishing the consciousness of how perfectly we accomplish it and how satisfied we are with ourselves, it is pride that intervenes.

The egocentrism that lies in making the satisfaction of noble spiritual energies into the main theme, depriving them of being formed and pervaded by a value-response attitude, is as such rooted in concupiscence. Yet pride displays itself in relishing elements that, though connected with the displaying of these energies, are no longer the mere satisfaction in their unfolding as such. Pride goes, so to speak, a step further in turning away from the value-response attitude or in reflecting on ourselves. It directs our interest toward the perfections that we actualize in our activities and that are as such beyond the normal field of our experience, for instance, our intelligence, our genius, our moral values. Or it directs our interest toward being admired by others, toward making an impression on them (not for the sake of the goods which we serve, but for our own sake).

The perversion resulting from pride will have to occupy us later on. It is, on the one hand, a general continuous danger threatening us in the accomplishment of anything that has a value, and, on the other hand, it is easier to overcome, being less unconscious and having very often the character of an unmasked temptation.

The perversion deriving from concupiscence by which the satisfaction and pleasure of the working and the unfolding of a spiritual capacity as such becomes the main theme of our activity and eventually even the motive is more "masked" in its morally negative character than the one conditioned by pride. It presents itself to us even as something innocuous and legitimate because it is something good as long as it is a merely accompanying subservient element, and is only perverted by becoming the main theme. By contrast, the appeal to pride reveals itself more obviously as perversion.

II.vii. *Money*

An important object in the sphere of the subjectively satisfying is money, not insofar as it is an indispensable basis of our daily life but as riches, insofar as it provides comfort and gives us the possibility of appropriating many goods to ourselves.

The first distinction that has to be made here is between a purely instrumental function of money, as a means to procure for ourselves certain goods, and the attraction that money possesses for man in itself, being wealthy, the position that wealth implies, the independence, might, security, the *Lebensgefühl* that riches provide. Money or wealth possesses undoubtedly an attractive power as such, in its potentiality to procure for us various goods, before any direct concern with certain concrete goods to which someone may aspire. Interest in money, the desire to possess it, the aspiration for wealth is as such a normal human tendency. Wealth belongs to the sphere of the legitimate subjectively satisfying. To prefer to be rich rather than to be poor is not necessarily a fruit of concupiscence. We shall briefly analyze the different approaches to this sphere, starting again with the one that is morally most perfect, that is to say, with the approach of the saint.

The saint is not interested in wealth. Money as such has no attractive power for him; he will neither strive to become wealthy nor consider it a great fortune if wealth should be bestowed on him without his intervention. This applies, obviously, only to his own personal wealth. Should he be married, the duty to take care of his family, and especially if his profession is business, may impose on him a certain interest in making money. But even in these cases he will keep an inner distance toward money and wealth and remain free of the spell that this sphere casts on man. He will always be aware of the immanent danger that the attachment to money and wealth implies for inner freedom. He will tend to poverty and never concede the interest in money as such any role in his life. When circumstances impose on him a certain prosperity, he will consider himself a mere administrator, always concerned to make use of his wealth for doing works of charity or for goods possessing genuine value in themselves. Whatever may be his position, he will remain poor in spirit, that is to say, he will possess an indifference to wealth as such, and the whole sphere of money will mean something to him only as a mere means for accomplishing something that has an authentic value. The value-response attitude has absorbed in him any interest in the subjectively satisfying character of money. Wealth as such no longer has any attractive power. Even more, his approach to wealth will be penetrated by the consciousness of the immanent danger of this sphere, and his aspiration will go in the direction of partaking in the poverty of our Lord, flowing out of his heroic charity. He will prefer, as far as his direction of will is concerned, poverty to wealth.

If we abstract from the saint and consider the morally obligatory attitude, it must be said: the interest in money and wealth, being affected by its attractive power as something subjectively satisfying, is as such nothing morally bad as long as one remains in the attitude of *religio* and as long as this interest remains tamed by the value-response attitude.

This implies, firstly, that the moral man experiences responsibility concerning the use of his money. Secondly, that this interest is never isolated, never separated from his basic value-response attitude. He must never abandon himself to the immanent law of this sphere; he must never yield to this interest in a way that is deprived of the rule of the morally relevant sphere. It is not just that, in any case in which some morally relevant value is in conflict with the gain of money, the readiness to abstain from such a gain lives in him, or as we may put it, it is not just that he is *ab ovo* disposed to give up any possibility of making money that would imply a lack of charity or *a fortiori* an injustice. Rather, interest in earning money as such must never play a predominant role in his life; it must not form a constitutive element of the normal outlook of his life. The moral man will not seek happiness in wealth and riches, but besides an interest in securing the possibility of a life in conformity with his social position, the acquisition of wealth as such will not preoccupy him. He will always be aware of the immanent danger of wealth and especially of the attitude of aspiring to wealth.

But the problem arises: is it not completely legitimate that he rejoices in receiving an inheritance, or in any way receiving wealth without having strived for it? Obviously, there is always a fundamental difference from the moral point of view between striving for a legitimate subjectively satisfying good and a susceptibility to it when it is bestowed on us without any intervention on our part. There is certainly no moral objection against rejoicing about such a gift for which we have not been striving. But this joy must *ab ovo* be penetrated by a consciousness of the responsibility connected with all wealth, the consciousness of the obligations of charity, of our duty to use it for goods having an authentic value, for the common good, and so on. It must not be the mere joy about wealth as such, but about the possibility of doing good procured by this wealth.

However, our main interest is, in this context, to investigate the role that this sphere plays for concupiscence. Obviously, money and wealth are a classical object inciting concupiscence. As soon as the desire for wealth is no longer kept in a subservient role, tamed by the value-response attitude and inserted in the frame of an authentic *religio*, this tendency assumes a completely new quality and is soiled by concupiscence.

The first, hard type of concupiscent man is normally aspiring to money and wealth in a specific way. It is one of the main objects of his concupiscent interest. He will strive for it at any cost and ignore in this pursuit all morally relevant values that might form an obstacle for his aim. Obviously, there are many degrees concerning his disrespect for morally relevant obstacles, from the hard and uncharitable attitude of a ruthless capitalist to the thief and gangster who will not even shrink back from killing someone in order to satisfy his craving for money. But as different as the attitude of this type of concupiscent man may be concerning the degree of his disrespect for morally relevant values, his attitude always has an outspoken concupiscent character.

We are not yet concerned with the immorality of this attitude that is the result of the concrete disrespect for morally relevant values, which form an obstacle for acquiring money, but exclusively with the immorality of the concupiscent attitude as such that is also found when no disrespect for morally relevant goods is connected to it.

The way in which this type of man is interested in money, his greedy, passionate desire for it, is a typical actualization of concupiscence and necessarily implies in the measure to which it dominates his soul a corresponding indifference toward the realm of morally relevant values. If we look at this greedy, passionate craving for money, the specific quality of concupiscence reveals itself in a most drastic and typical way.

The second, lazy type of a concupiscent man is not so much characterized by the craving for money as by the possessive way in which he holds on to the money he possesses. He is too lazy for the restless, passionate tension that the craving for money implies. I am not yet thinking of the avaricious type here. He forms a quite special phenomenon that we shall analyze later on. I am thinking of the lazy, Fafnerlike, satisfied man sitting on his riches, characterized by a readiness to defend them against anybody who would touch them.

The third type, the whimpering, soft type of concupiscence is generally less directed toward the possession of money as such than toward the comfort that wealth provides, toward being spoiled and being able to avoid any hardship. He will not crave money; nor will he aspire to wealth in a passionate way.

Nor will he hold on in a greedy, heavy way to what he possesses. But he will have a tendency to live continuously in fear of losing his comfort, of being exposed to hardships. His concupiscence will express itself in an exaggerated dependence upon comfort and an easy life, in complaining about any loss in this direction, in being preoccupied by the aspiration to acquire wealth insofar as it assures him of an easy life in which no effort and hardship will touch him. This type is not necessarily stingy. But he will generally be very particular concerning his own property, unwilling to let others share the things that belong to him because of his self-centered, petty mentality. What matters for us is to see the specific role that money, wealth, and riches play for the different concupiscent types and the specific appeal to concupiscence that this sphere implies.

Again, we have to state that the decisive difference between the concupiscent interest in this sphere and the legitimate, innocent interest in money, riches, and wealth is not the mere quantity, the size of the role which it plays. It is not the mere difference between a moderate and passionate interest, but a definite qualitative difference.

A completely different center in the person is actualized as soon as the subjectively satisfying power of this sphere is no longer "tamed" by the value-response attitude, as soon as it unfolds outside of the setting of the fundamental attitude of *religio* toward the realm of morally relevant values, and in the last analysis, of God. Whether it is a reasonable, moderate striving for money or a passionate craving for it does not make the decisive difference from a moral point of view. We must not be fooled by the fact that passionate craving has *a fortiori* the character of a concupiscent attitude because any passion in the strict sense of the term implies turning away from the fundamental attitude of *religio*.

This is not merely a consequence of the intensity of the passion but of the very nature of the passion, its tendency to dethrone our reason and our free spiritual center, and thus also our value-response attitude. But this separation from *religio* does not necessarily presuppose passion. It is not a mutual relation. Passion implies always this separation from *religio* if it dominates a man; but passion is not the only form of this separation. A moderate man may also be concupiscent; he too may crave the subjectively satisfying in his way of relinquishing *religio* and the value-response attitude.

In what concerns the specifically avaricious man, it must be said that it represents a concupiscent type *sui generis*. Insofar as avariciousness is opposed to genuine generosity, it will be found in different forms in every type of radical concupiscence. The lack of charity, the absence of any genuine interest in the needs and happiness of our fellow man, is deeply linked to concupiscence as such. But this does not yet constitute the typical stinginess. There also exists a prodigal type of the concupiscent man. He spends money without any restraint in order to procure for himself subjectively satisfying goods, but he refuses to give anything to his fellow man, because his own pleasure alone counts for him.

And even when he should rejoice in bestowing money on other persons, it is not real charity that moves him. He enjoys, firstly, the gesture of spending money, and secondly, he may enjoy the superior position that bestowing gifts on others implies, and thirdly, he may like the atmosphere of jolliness in his surroundings, not for the sake of his fellow man but in order to be undisturbed by the disagreeable aspect of misery. In what concerns the second motive, relishing the superior position, an element of pride intervenes besides concupiscence. In any case, it is obvious that his prodigality is separated from genuine generosity by an abyss. It is a fruit of his concupiscence as well as the avaricious attitude.

But in order to understand the specific character of concupiscence present in the avaricious person, we must stress, besides the lack of genuine generosity that he shares with every concupiscent type, the particular kind of enslavement that makes him prefer the potential element of money to real goods that he can enjoy by his money. It is a specific form of a paradoxical perversion where the means are more appreciated than the end that objectively endows the means with its importance.[24]

He is more attracted by the consciousness of preserving the potential of enjoying goods than by the real enjoyment of them. Thus he will not only lack generosity and be unwilling to give anything to his fellow man, but he will also shrink from spending money for subjectively satisfying goods for himself—given that this implies a diminishing of his money.

This perversion is not only found among men who are dominated by concupiscence and indifferent toward the world of morally relevant values, but also sometimes in persons who have an outspoken respect for morally relevant values, who will even spend money for goods endowed with an authentic value rather than for the merely subjectively satisfying. The specific mark of their stinginess will be the regret with which they spend money for any kind of good, their peculiar attachment to money as such that makes it a great effort for them to spend money, their concern to attain their end with the least possible expenditure. Money seems to them something so precious, sometimes even so dignified, that they shrink from spending it. Sometimes money and preserving their riches assumes the character of an idol, and is treated as if it were an authentic value. People under the spell of this idol feel disturbed in their conscience when spending money, and they will spend as little as possible, always attempting to avoid any expenditure that is not strictly indispensable or imposed on them by some strict moral obligation.

The point that is of a specific interest for us is that avariciousness represents a type of concupiscence *sui generis* insofar as its object is, in a new sense, money and the preserving of one's own property. It is to be found not only in the morally indifferent man, who is dominated in general by concupiscence, but also in man who remains in *religio*, who possess basically a value-response attitude. But it is nevertheless always a fruit of concupiscence.

We have thus to distinguish two different kinds of concupiscence

---

24. [Famously, it was already Aristotle who alludes to the paradox in the fact that what by its nature is a mere means, namely wealth, is by many considered to be their eudaimonia, and hence the final end of their life. Cf. Aristotle, *Nicomachean Ethics*, bk. 1, Ch. 3. Editor.]

in the typically avaricious man. Firstly, the general concupiscence that is opposed to charity and shuts the avaricious person up against the needs of his fellow man, which makes him an egoist, imprisoned in his self-centered interests. It is this concupiscence that makes him specifically hardhearted, which is the same in the luxurious, prodigal type, as found in the rich man in the Gospel who gives nothing to Lazarus, does not hesitate to spend money for his own pleasures, but refuses to give anything to his fellow man.[25] Secondly, there is a more specific tendency of concupiscence that is specifically directed toward money as such, toward the possession and preservation of the possessed money, the peculiar preference of something potential over real goods.[26]

The first element of avariciousness, that is to say, the hardheartedness and indifference toward the morally relevant values, which the avaricious shares with every man who is a slave of his concupiscence, which excludes every value-response attitude, and especially charity, is obviously, from the moral point of view, much more negative than the specific paradoxical attachment to money as such. The morally negative value of avariciousness is above all due to general concupiscence, which is equally to be found in the covetous man, who is not specifically avaricious, but equally hardhearted and shut up in his own selfish interests, and even in the luxurious, prodigal egoist. But it would be wrong to overlook the fact that the specific perversion of the avaricious person also has a morally negative value of its own. It may seem at first glance that the attachment to money as such, when we abstract from the general immorality of concupiscence, is more a ridiculous and repulsive temperamental disposition, but not something specifically immoral. The fact that someone prefers the possession of money rather than the enjoyment of the subjectively satisfying goods seems to be something morally neutral as long as no morally relevant value is at stake. Someone could, for instance, ask: is it something morally bad when someone does not grant himself any plea-

---

25. [Luke 16:19–31. Editor.]

26. This latter type of concupiscence reveals itself, so to speak, in its specific character, without connection to general concupiscence, in those cases in which it appears as a mere obstacle, in persons whose general attitude is directed toward the important-in-itself.

sure because of his stinginess? In this case, in which the love of neighbor is not at stake, in which no moral obligation compels him to spend money, is the attitude of stinginess morally negative?

It must be said: even this stinginess is morally negative, though not comparable to the immorality of the lack of charity and egoistic hard-heartedness. Firstly, this attachment to money is as such a fruit of concupiscence and as such immoral, just as much as concupiscence directed toward any other subjectively satisfying object, regardless of the disrespect for any morally relevant value to which it may lead. But this would not yet concern the specific perversion of stinginess, that is to say, the preference of the potential over the real subjectively satisfying good. We have to ask: is stinginess as such endowed with an element of immorality that the prodigal does not possess? Why should it be morally worse to hold on to money as such than to spend it unreservedly in order to plunge ourselves into the satisfaction of our concupiscence? It must be said: stinginess represents as such a higher degree of self-centeredness; preferring the possession of money to the enjoyment of a subjectively satisfying good, for instance, a luxurious meal, implies a still colder and harder attitude; the idolization of money and the possession of it as such contains a moral poison *sui generis*. Not only that it deprives us in a continuous way of inner freedom, that it imprisons us in a more fixed way, but it implies also the danger of an idolatrous respect for money, which in many cases makes the stinginess appear to the avaricious as a virtuous attitude. The luxuriously prodigal is at least more sincere, more unmasked in his concupiscence, whereas the avaricious is in some way still less human, still more self-centered.

II.viii. *The Sphere of Pure Concupiscence: Sadism and Curiosity*

After having analyzed the concupiscent attitude insofar as it is directed toward the kind of subjectively satisfying that, as such, can also form the object of an innocent legitimate interest, we have to examine the objects that already presuppose concupiscence in order to became subjectively satisfying.

Only in the sphere of pure concupiscence, in which an object would remain neutral, possessing no attractive power, or even being repulsive to our legitimate center, can the object assume the character of something that is subjectively satisfying because of its appeal to concupiscence.

A typical case of this kind of subjectively satisfying object is sadism. Relishing the sufferings of other persons can be satisfying only with respect to the concupiscent center. It presupposes concupiscence in order to be satisfying and even to be a specific perversion. The nature of concupiscence reveals itself here in a naked way. For to the legitimate center to which the normal subjectively satisfying appeals, such as bodily pleasures, the satisfaction of natural urges, wealth, and so on, the bodily sufferings of other persons, and especially inflicting of pains on others, are in no way attractive or agreeable. It already involves concupiscence in its attractiveness. It is thus already morally evil as such, independently of the disrespect for the morally relevant values connected with it. The mere desire is already immoral because of the intrinsic quality of concupiscence that is due not only to its separation from the setting of *religio* and of the value-response attitude. It can, by its very nature, never exist in this setting, as the interest in the normally subjectively satisfying can. It is by its very nature necessarily concupiscent.

The same applies to some other urges that, though less venomous than sadism, are *ab ovo* necessarily an offspring of concupiscence. Such is idle curiosity, that is to say, the desire to know all kinds of things that in no way concern us.

Sometimes one has called curiosity the noble thirst for knowledge, for an intellectual penetration of the world. Obviously, we do not use the term curiosity in this sense, in which it indicates a classical spiritual desire of man. Regardless of how one may use this term, the two things must be clearly distinguished. The desire for knowledge that is directed toward truth, of which St. Augustine asks, *Quid enim fortius desiderat anima quam veritatem?* has nothing to do with the attitude of the curious man, who is always eager to know every detail, especially when it concerns the private life of his fellow human beings.[27]

---

27. [St. Augustine, *Tractates on the Gospel of John*, 26, 5. Editor.]

Curiosity in this specific sense has a petty, sensational character, it finds satisfaction in dwelling on things that do not pertain to us and the knowledge of which has no value whatsoever for us. The curious man loses his time in aspiring in an indiscrete way to know the private affairs of his fellow man, an attitude that not only differs radically from the true interest in the knowledge of truth, but also generally is incompatible with this noble interest.

The curious man is in a specific way self-centered, ridiculous, and childish; pettiness and something even mean-spirited is proper to him; he is concerned with *pettegolezzi*, which excludes a genuine thirst for truth.[28] The specific objects of curiosity are always personal affairs. The curious man is not eager to be informed about scientific or philosophical truths. He craves knowledge of concrete facts that are at least related to some persons. But above all his eagerness for knowing concerns intimate affairs of other persons and details concerning their private lives, the more so if they are secret and still unknown to other persons. To be informed about the secret affairs of his fellow man and, if possible, to be the first to know them is what he relishes the most. He will be still more satisfied if he succeeds in knowing such things that his fellow man wants to hide. The *chronique scandaleuse* attracts him above all.

The more something is kept secret, the more his curiosity will be incited. And generally, the curious man is equally loquacious, eager to spread the secrets he has succeeded in discovering. The same indiscretion that incites him to discover all the private and secret affairs of his fellow man pushes him to tell them to other people. Sensationalism is at the basis of curiosity, or as we may put it, curiosity is a special form of sensationalism. Its being rooted in concupiscence, as is every sensationalism, is obvious. It is morally much less harmful than other forms of concupiscence, though it is *ab ovo* concupiscent, as its object has no attractive power to the legitimate center of the subjectively satisfying. It does not engender the hard-heartedness and ruthless egoism that is proper to some of the aforementioned forms of concupiscence and will

---

28. [*Pettegolezzi*—an Italian word for a gossip containing inappropriate or indiscrete information about other persons. Editor.]

not lead to the disrespect of elementary morally relevant values. But it is firstly, in its intrinsic quality, mean-spirited and petty, and secondly, it implies a disrespect for our fellow man, arrogating to oneself the right to know things that the person in question wants not to be known; it implies a disrespect for the private life of a person that is proper to every indiscretion of this kind. Moreover, it is immoral in the deep indifference toward the fate and affairs of these fellow men, in approaching them merely or at least primarily as something that appeals to one's concupiscent sensationalism.

The curious man makes of things that should engender sympathy a mere object of his curiosity. But above all, his attitude implies a lack of reverence. The moral man respects the private sphere of his fellow man, and especially of his secrets. This kind of indiscretion, a putting our nose into the affairs of other persons that in no way concern us, is an outspoken lack of reverence. Moreover, the attitude of spreading those secrets implies an outspoken lack of consciousness of responsibility. The curious man is not concerned with the damage and suffering that his delivering of these secrets may imply for his fellow man. This again implies a lack of charity. We see thus that curiosity, though less virulent than other forms of concupiscence, is immoral and incompatible with a true value-response attitude, with the reverence and charity that are proper to the moral man.

All other forms of sensationalism look similar. They are rooted in concupiscence and are as such morally negative. They are in themselves soiled with a self-centeredness that is opposed to the value-response attitude and implies a lack of reverence and charity. It always looks at the world from the point of view of the satisfaction of concupiscence and is thus *ab ovo* not responsive to the real meaning of the object and *a fortiori* to its value or disvalue. Sensationalism is as such unobjective and implies an abuse of the object.

A new and worse type of concupiscence is at stake when the object that is experienced as satisfying is not only neutral for the legitimate center of the subjectively satisfying but possesses even an outspoken disvalue. It is the concupiscence that relishes an evil, as, for instance, sadism. The pains and sufferings of other persons are as such an evil and engender sympathy and compassion in the moral man, determined by his value-response attitude, and they make him suffer. The perversion that experiences them, and especially the inflicting of them, as something satisfying is a new and worse type of concupiscence.

The disrespect for morally relevant values here is not only accidental, as in the case in which the values form only an obstacle to the satisfaction of our concupiscence. The thief craves money and is disposed to disrespect the property of other persons in order to satisfy his desire. The connection of the disvalue, that is, the violation of the property and the right of a fellow man, with his concupiscent desire to enrich himself is only accidental, or as we may put it, the disrespect of this value is not the formal object of his desire.

He does not delight in stealing as such but in the money that he acquires in an easy way. Certainly, his concupiscent attitude in itself implies his superactual indifference toward the morally relevant values. But the subjectively satisfying object that appeals to his concupiscence is not the disvalue as such. By contrast, in the case of sadism, the inflicting of pains and sufferings on one's fellow man, this being a flagrant disvalue, is as such the formal object that the sadist relishes. Certainly, it is not satisfying for him because of its formal character as a disvalue, but only because of its material content. It is not like the case of the satanic type whose pride and rebellion against the reign of values and ultimately against God makes wrongdoing and the realization of a disvalue as such into something satisfying.

Still, it is obvious that the role of the disvalue here is completely different from the role in the case of the thief or the gangster. At least materially, the evil itself is the source of the sadist's satisfaction. The much more intimate connection of the disvalue on the object side with his concupiscent satisfaction endows this type of concupiscence with a specific, venomous, morally negative character. Certainly, the sexual perversion that is implied deals with the sufferings and pains of other persons not to the extent that they are an evil but insofar as they incite a specific sexual pleasure. But the very fact that the inflicting of pain and suffering can become as such a source of sexual pleasure constitutes a new type of concupiscence in which the object appealing to concupiscence is not only not something that appeals also to our legitimate center, that is to say, something that is neutral for the legitimate center of the subjectively satisfying, but is even an outspoken evil.

Something similar is given in the case of revenge. The satisfaction that revenge implies is also drawn out of an outspoken evil. The pain and suffering that we inflict on the person who has wronged us, independently of the question whether he has really injured us so as to be responsible for this *injuria*, or whether he, without any fault, injured us, or whether he has even done something objectively good for us which we experience as evil only because of our perversion, are experienced as the source of great satisfaction. But the vengeful attitude is obviously a fruit not only of concupiscence but primarily of pride.[29] Hence, notwithstanding its formal affinity to sadism because of the fact that something possessing an outspoken disvalue attracts us as subjectively satisfying, revenge does not belong to the analysis of the cases in which concupiscence is, at least primarily, at stake.

II.ix. *Concupiscence in the Realm of the Objective Goods for the Person*

We have now to examine the role of concupiscence in the realm of the objective goods for the person. We started by distinguishing the concupiscent attitude from the legitimate interest in the subjectively satisfying and acquired a notion of the nature of concupiscence insofar as it constitutes one main form of the "untamed," isolated direction toward the subjectively satisfying.

We then examined the cases in which concupiscence is directed toward an object that exclusively appeals to our concupiscence, which pre-

---

29. [For a detailed treatment of the nature of revenge, see below, section IV.iv. Editor.]

supposes concupiscence in order to become attractive. We now have to examine whether or not concupiscence interferes with our relation to objective goods for the person.[30]

As far as the objective goods for the person that are merely legitimately subjectively satisfying are concerned, we do not need to examine the role of concupiscence because we have dealt with it when we analyzed the sphere of the legitimately subjectively satisfying. As far as one's own person is concerned, those goods do not present themselves qua objective goods for the person, except in the case of those persons in whom the value-response attitude has absorbed the interest in the subjectively satisfying, as it is with the saints, and here the intervention of concupiscence is *a fortiori* excluded. In all other cases, those goods attract us qua subjectively satisfying and not insofar as they are objective goods for the person.

We can thus omit this type of objective goods for the person in our present research. The problem of the role of concupiscence in the sphere of the objective goods for the person is limited thus to the other types of the objective good for the person. Let us firstly examine the realm of useful goods. Are they objects that may incite concupiscence?

It must be said: notwithstanding the gray and rather sober character of these goods, they may incite concupiscence. Certainly, they will never be the proper object of concupiscence. Besides the fact that their monetary worth may appeal to concupiscence just like anything that is valuable from the monetary point of view, they also have an importance for the concupiscent man insofar as they are means for something agreeable or subjectively satisfying. The concupiscent man may crave useful things insofar as they facilitate the possession and enjoyment of the subjectively satisfying.

---

30. [By "objective goods for the person" Hildebrand is referring to one of the three foundational categories of importance in his ethics, the other two being "value importance" and "the importance of the merely subjectively satisfying." Within the objective goods for the person he distinguishes several kinds (see his *Ethics*, Ch. 29) one of which he calls the legitimately subjectively satisfying, another of which he calls the elementary goods, including minimum of basics such as food and drink and shelter. In the present text he discusses the ways in which concupiscence can distort our pursuit of these elementary goods. Editor.]

The concupiscent man will try to appropriate different useful goods to himself and will crave their possession in a ruthless way. But it is not this type of good that will in itself incite concupiscence. As far as they are valuable due to their market price, he will crave them as he does anything which increases his wealth. Or his interest will be incited by certain subjectively satisfying goods for which these useful goods are mere means.

But there also exists a type of less obvious concupiscence that is concerned with those goods as such. A certain type of housewife, for instance, may reveal in her interest for useful goods a disordered attitude that is penetrated by a certain type of concupiscence. The useful attracts them even more than the specifically agreeable that bestows pleasure on them. Their practical humdrum outlook directs them in a specific way toward this type of good and sometimes their interest in them assumes the character of a concupiscent craving for them. They reveal, for instance, an egoistic attitude, full of eagerness to possess them characterized by an unwillingness to let other people share them. They are not only eager to possess them, but they are always on the *qui vive* that nobody else should use them. They are unwilling to lend them to others and are irritated toward anybody who would ask them to do so. The petty attachment to these household articles without any proportion to their objective meaning, shuts them up in themselves and creates a rivalry against anyone who would, without imposing on them any real sacrifice, want to share these goods temporarily with them. This tendency reveals undoubtedly an element of concupiscence. Even if we abstract from the general irritability concerning any intrusion into the sphere of our rights and property that is at least as much rooted in pride as in concupiscence and that we shall analyze later on, the useful goods become, in these special cases, an object of concupiscence. The narrowing effect that engenders an outspoken egoistic attitude excluding charity and generosity as well as a potential irritability toward all fellow man who are eventual rivals in this sphere reveals undoubtedly the presence of concupiscence. The peculiar mark of this concupiscence is that the same persons may be less interested in the specifically pleasurable and agreeable goods than in the useful ones. These persons may lead a life full of hardship and possess even the readiness to make many sacrifices with respect to the sphere of the agreeable.

The reasonable, sober character of the useful appeals more to them than the merely pleasurable. Their interest turns around the useful. It assumes in their eyes a specific dignity and even the character of something possessing an authentic value. Whereas the merely pleasurable seems to them unnecessary and childish, they approach everything that is useful with awe and respect. It seems to them even more serious than objective goods possessing an authentic value, such as friendship or the enjoyment of beauty in nature and art.

A similar attitude is typical for the *banausos*, or philistine. We find it in many businessmen, in certain capitalists. The category of the "useful" is for them the decisive one and dominates their outlook. Everything enjoyable seems to them superfluous, unserious, whether it is merely subjectively satisfying or endowed with an authentic value and thus able to bestow authentic happiness on us.

The attitude of the *banausos*, in which the useful goods assume a disproportionate rank in the hierarchy of the objective goods for the person, is not only characterized by a dull lack of sensibility to many authentic values, but implies also always an element of concupiscence. This concupiscence is more veiled and masked than the untamed craving for the subjectively satisfying. It has not the same greedy, passionate character, but as soon as it makes those types egoistic, hard, or petty, as soon as it excludes charity and generosity, it is obviously rooted in concupiscence.

This form of concupiscence is often related to being absorbed by the immanent law of certain activities and a certain rhythm of life. The housewife striving to assure a well-functioning household, or the businessman striving for success in his business, may, if the value-response attitude is not strong enough, be absorbed by the danger to which human nature is generally exposed, namely, by the immanent logic of their activity.[31]

This immanent logic of an activity tends, as soon as it captivates us in

---

31. [The theme of the immanent logic of certain activities as a root of moral evil is treated bellow in section VI. Editor.]

a disordered way, to give a disproportionate weight to the end of this activity, and even to the subordinated ends that are objectively only means. We lose the distance to the object and isolate it, without confronting it with the reign of values. It is something analogous to relinquishing *religio* in the case in which our interest in the subjectively satisfying is no longer under the reign of the value-response attitude. Analogous obviously in a purely formal sense because the quality of the two kinds of relinquishing *religio* differs completely. Something of this absorption by the immanent logic of an activity is always at stake when we fall prey to the weight that something assumes merely because we have made it into an end for our will, independently of its importance as such. The mere automatic dynamism of our will, of the very fact that we have proposed something to ourselves, tends to give to our purpose a weight in addition to the importance that it possesses as such.

II.x. *Property*[32]

One of the main areas in which concupiscence manifests itself is property, the desire to possess something, to own it, the satisfaction deriving from possession as such. We are not concerned here with the satisfaction, joy, and pleasure that various goods, when we possess them, may bestow on us. A house or an estate that we own may be a source of joy as well as a car or a horse. We have to distinguish the joy that derives from the beauty and atmosphere of the house and garden or the pleasure and satisfaction deriving from the comfort of the house, from the joy of possessing them as property. Likewise, we have to distinguish the joy that making beautiful excursions in a car bestows on us and the pleasure of using this comfortable means of transportation, from the satisfaction of owning a car.

The joy of dwelling in a beautiful house and garden, of living in it, could also be experienced when friends have offered us their beautiful

---

32. [Ana 544, VI, 14, 9. The theme of this short typescript is closely linked to concupiscence. Hence it was included in this edition and placed immediately after the materials analyzing concupiscence. Editor.]

house and garden. The same applies to the car or the horse. But there exists a specific elementary satisfaction that is rooted in owning something as property.

We are here interested in this satisfaction based on possession as such, resulting from being the possessor, and not the satisfaction that is drawn out of a good as such that we happen to possess. The nature and quality of the latter satisfaction obviously varies according to the nature of the good in question.

But the satisfaction of owning something, the satisfaction resulting from the property relation as such, of being able to call something *mine*, to be its master, has a definite quality independently of the nature of the possessed object. It is this good, the good of property as such and the satisfaction deriving from it, that is here our topic, and that can become a specific object of concupiscence, a source of concupiscence.

That property as such is experienced as a good, that the relation of possession to an object is a source of satisfaction, is as such something completely legitimate. To possess something is a natural unfolding of our human personal being, it is an elementary gesture of man connected with his character as "lord of creation." Property is not only something that presupposes essentially a personal being (impersonal beings cannot own anything), but it belongs also to the plenitude of human existence.

Already in children the vehement desire to own something reveals itself. Early on they contend that a toy is theirs, and they quarrel with other children in saying "this is mine." To own something is a normal continuation of man's individual life, a normal self-assurance, a normal expression of his sovereignty toward impersonal beings as well as of his right and independence as an individual from any community, an expression of the private zone of his person.[33]

But legitimate as a sensitivity to the satisfaction given by property is, as well as the desire to own something, here we also find a source of many different types of concupiscence.

---

33. Obviously this relation of owning is possible only in relation to certain objects. Between objects that are destined to be consumed, such as food, the relation of property cannot be established properly. The object must have a lasting character and offer itself for repeated use or enjoyment.

As soon as the interest in possessing as such and the desire of owning something is no longer subservient to the reign of the morally relevant values and no longer "tamed" by *religio*, the interest in property is perverted. The craving for possessing much is a typical form of concupiscence: covetousness. The spasm of egocentrism, the insatiable thirst for possession, independently of the nature of the possessed goods, is above all found with respect to money: to possess much money or valuable objects. We may say that, as soon as someone is more interested in the possession of a good than in its fruition, concupiscence has made its entrance. Something is wrong if someone, without any sense for art, is the owner of a great work of art and is very eager to possess it, though he is not able to enjoy it. And there is something wrong if someone owning a beautiful house and estate never lives in it, does not care for it, but finds a great satisfaction in the mere possession as such.

Yet the full danger of the craving for possession as such manifests itself primarily in egoism, in the gesture to snatch possessions from others, to want everything for oneself. Given any good, the egotist wants to have it for himself, not in order to be able to enjoy it but because of the possessive gesture..."for me."

Egoists suffer when others possess something valuable, not because they are not able to enjoy it but because they are frustrated in their potential possession. Even sometimes they will worry more if another person possesses something instead of them, than if it were "no man's property."

Apart from the meaning of property as an expression of a fundamental feature of the human person, as "lord of creation," and of his right to a private life (*Eigenleben*), the relation of belonging or possession has still another profound meaning and function. This function of possession consists in a specific intimate union with things that we like and that are dear to us. Besides the fruition of an object, the fact that it *belongs* to me, that it is mine, establishes a spiritual relation *sui generis* to the object. That I can call a beautiful book "mine" is a source of joy, not only because I can read it any time I want. This could be also the case if someone lends it to me for an indefinite time. The very fact that it belongs to me implies a unique union with the object. That I can call a house that I love *mine* is a source of joy not only because I can dwell in it and enjoy it, but also because the relation of property constitutes a specific union with the object. The nature of this unique union discloses itself especially when we consider the nature of a gift.

In giving someone a gift, for instance, a jewel, a work of art, or a beautiful book, it belongs essentially to the very nature of this act that the object in question becomes related to the other person, in a new intimate manner, as his property. Certainly, the preciousness and value of the object is presupposed in order to make the gift a token of our love or friendship. But the very essence of "giving," of transferring the property to the other person, refers to the specific union with the good that consists in its belonging now to him. For the act of making a gift, this relation is twice implied. Firstly, the donor must possess what he wants to give. Hence the principle, *nemo dat quod non habet*.[34] The donor must give of his own, if the gift is to have the character of a token of the donor's love. Secondly, it belongs to the very essence of a gift that the good is handed over to the other person as his property, that it becomes related to him in a unique way. The inner intention of the donor, the inner word of the act of donation—"To thee"—is fulfilled by the very relation of property, the object being bestowed on the other by the fact that he owns it now. The character of belonging to or being possessed by as a unique union with the object clearly discloses itself here.

The same manifests itself also in our desire to possess something that we especially like. The desire is directed not only toward the fruition but also to the appropriation, to the insertion into my life, to bringing it near me, making it "mine."

This aspect of property has an analogy to the incomparably higher union that is possible among human persons. If we said before that only persons can possess something, we must now add that only impersonal beings and never persons can be possessed as property. But there is an analogy to possession on an incomparably higher level, in the union

---

34. ["No one gives what one does not possess." Editor.]

established by love. By saying to a person whom we love, "I am thine" or "Thou art mine," this analogy to "property" is expressed. *Ich bin Din; Du bist min.*[35]

And in the ninth symphony of Beethoven, we hear the words: *Ja wer auch nur eine Seele Sein nennt auf dem Erdenrund.*[36] Here the idea of being mine embodies a climax of union and the gift of one's heart to another person. It is the very *causa exemplaris* of all donation. But we must emphasize that it would be more correct to state that the relation of property constitutes a union with impersonal objects that is a faint analogy to the incomparably higher and deeper union established in the mutual love of persons.

The desire to possess something that we like is thus as such completely legitimate and a natural outgrowth of our liking the good. But here again this desire can become a typical outgrowth of concupiscence if it is no longer tamed by the superactual value-response to the morally relevant values.

II.xi. *Laziness*[37]

A typical outgrowth of concupiscence is laziness. We saw in the beginning that there exists a concupiscent type who is above all characterized by his laziness. It is the vegetative, cowlike, heavy man whom we mentioned as being the second among the three main concupiscent types. As long as it is only a temperamental disposition, it has no moral significance. A man with a phlegmatic temperament can become a saint as well as the man with a sanguine or choleric temperament.

The phlegmatic temperament forms no obstacle as such for a full

---

35. [Famous first verse of the arguably oldest example of German medieval lyrics. Anonymous author, around 1150. Here is the whole short poem: Dû bist mîn, ich bin dîn; des solt dû gewis sîn; dû bist beslozzen in mînem herzen; verlorn ist daz slüzzelîn; dû muost immer drinne sîn. Editor.]

36. ["Indeed, who even has just one soul to call his own in this world!" Editor.]

37. [Besides property, also the theme of laziness is closely linked to concupiscence. Hence it was included in this the present volume to conclude Hildebrand's treatment of concupiscence. The theme of laziness is developed in a manuscript (Ana 544, 14, 1) and a typescript (Ana 544, 14, 9). As in all other cases, where there are two versions of the text, the present volume is based on the typescript. Editor.]

value-response attitude, though it will cost the phlegmatic man greater effort in some respects than it will cost the sanguine or choleric. In other respects again, it will cost him less effort, for instance to overcome wrath or anger.

But as soon as the inertia becomes a direction of the will, a resistance against any effort, we discover its concupiscent character. It is the man who relishes the comfort of an undisturbed abandoning to a dumb vegetative rhythm of life and a turning away from everything that compels him to any strain or movement. This man has a blunt obtuse attitude toward life and being, toward the world of values, which is incompatible with the value-response attitude. It is obvious that this attitude is incompatible with any value-response attitude.

But obviously this form of concupiscence is not restricted to this type alone. As in all other forms of concupiscence, it lives at least as a danger in every man. It is also, as concupiscence in general, a part of the perversion of man's fallen nature.

Its specific object is easiness or the avoidance of any effort. The lazy man abhors any tension, any *élan*, any strain, and he relishes above all that which is easy, which corresponds to the law of gravity of his nature. What he seeks is to remain undisturbed, to enjoy the absence of anything that compels him to make an effort.

Strain is certainly something that is as such disagreeable to man. Also, for his legitimate center, strain is something disagreeable, and in paradise life did not imply strain, and what requires in fallen man an effort was granted to him without strain. Notwithstanding the absence of work in sweat, this applies as well to all the effort of overcoming moral obstacles in order to conform to values and to God's will. But as strain and effort are inevitable in our present situation on earth in order to attain what is necessary for our life, in order to conform to the commandment of God and the call of the morally relevant values, for any earthly happiness, and for attaining our eternal end, every avoidance of strain and effort that forms an obstacle to live according to God's will is an outgrowth of concupiscence. It is the same situation that we found with respect to all the merely subjectively satisfying goods. Even when they appeal to a legitimate center in us as such, they become an object of concupiscence as soon as they are no longer under the reign of the morally relevant values and as interest in them is no longer tamed by the fundamental attitude of *religio*. But the tendency of avoiding strain, though strain is as such an evil, is not on the same level as the tendency to avoid bodily pains. This latter tendency is nobler than the interest in the agreeable, whereas the resistance to strain is on the same level as the tendency toward the agreeable.

We shall now inquire into the different main fields where laziness occurs in order to discover its specific nature and the main different forms of laziness. This will show us that some types of laziness are *ab ovo* rooted in concupiscence.

Firstly, we speak of laziness concerning the strain that work implies. Here again we may distinguish between the work of hands and intellectual work. As long as the unwillingness to do the work of hands is rooted in bodily insufficiency, it is obviously not laziness. A refusal to accept a strain that surpasses our bodily capacity is completely legitimate and manifests no kind of laziness.

It is the refusal to accept physical labor as such and the normal strain that it always implies, the tendency toward idleness, that characterizes laziness. The lazy man tries to avoid every work as much as possible, he relishes the state of idleness and tries to cover the necessities of life in an easy way, without working. He will rather live in disorder and dirt than accept the strain that putting our house in order implies. He will try to place the burden of work on the shoulders of others. He will try to choose in every situation that which implies no bodily strain, even when he has to neglect duties in order to do so. He will even sacrifice a pleasure if attaining this pleasure implies any bodily strain. In the worst case, he may steal or accept some indecent way of earning money that is indispensable for his life because he shrinks from any bodily strain. It is obvious that this laziness is rooted in concupiscence. As innocent as a tendency to avoid bodily strain may be in children, as true as it is that bodily strain is as such an evil, the refusal to accept this inevitable strain, which belongs to our earthly situation, is a manifest sign of a tendency to shake off the bond of *religio*, which compels us to conform to the God-given reality and to accept everything that is as such unpleasant if it is an inevitable element on the path leading to the fulfillment of something necessary or even something possessing an authentic value. It is something analogous to the case of escaping into dreaming, which we analyzed before. The refusal to accept the God-given reality is always a shaking off of the *religio* and a self-centered yielding to our concupiscence.

The same applies with respect to the strain of intellectual work. Again, we do not mean the shrinking back from strain implied in this work because of a lack of competency. This is obviously not rooted in laziness but is a completely legitimate attitude. It is the refusal of the strain as such, the resistance against the unpleasantness of this strain, though it is indispensable. The fact that neither the value that may be connected with some intellectual work, nor the necessity to accomplish it in order to earn our living, nor the duty that we have assumed in accepting a job that entails intellectual work, make one willing to accept the strain connected with it, clearly manifests concupiscence and the shaking off of the *religio*. But there are many deeper forms of laziness besides the refusal of working, that is, laziness in the narrowest sense of the term.

There is the spiritual laziness that shrinks back from every *élan*, from any *sursum corda*, from the movement upward to which every value invites us, and invites us all the more when the value has a high rank. The lazy man in this sense of the word has the inclination to dwell in the periphery, to seek superficial goods, which do not call him to this *élan* and do not compel him to dwell in the depth of his soul.

He shuns the strain which this depth implies. When an inevitable situation calls for spiritual *élan* and going back to one's depth, he will escape this call and, if necessary, situate himself on a lower level of existence where he avoids this effort. If a cross is imposed on him, for instance the loss of a beloved person, he will avoid the strain of really enduring this cross by taking refuge in peripheral distractions and amusements, in living on a level where this cross burdens him no longer. This lazy man is also unable really to love because he shuns the immanent *sursum corda* of every true love. He will also have the tendency to let himself go, to accomplish this gesture of relaxing, taking it easy, which is especially opposed to the immanent *élan* of the *habitare secum* and of every authentic value-response.

It is the burden of the fundamental stance of *religio* as such that he shuns. He refuses the *élan* to which he is invited by the call of the morally relevant values, the yoke of God, the effort of moral awakedness, of recollection. He differs from the other types of concupiscence in that he is, firstly, not completely blind to values and does not ignore their call. This is not so much because the call of values hinders him in the undisturbed craving for the subjectively satisfying, but because he shuns the *élan*, the effort that these values call for. Although he shares with every form of concupiscence the turning away from the fundamental attitude of *religio*, he does so for a different reason: though he is aware of the obligation and of the call issuing from the values, he tries to escape from it because of the effort which this conforming costs him.

Now this deeper spiritual laziness differs also from the above-mentioned laziness in the narrower sense of the term to such an extent that many people who are very assiduous and hard working are characterized by a deep spiritual laziness. It is even a typical perversion of modern times to see in work the only serious part of life and to live in the false alternative: either work, the serious part of life, or relaxation and amusement, the light part of life. The *unum necessarium* [the one thing needful] has no place in this alternative, nor does the noble *frui* of goods possessing a high value.[38] The contemplative element of life has been eliminated. This attitude is a typical outgrowth of spiritual laziness because work as such, apart from work that is dedicated to the realization of a good possessing a high value, for instance, the work of an artist, of a philosopher, and especially of a priest, does not call for the spiritual *élan* and the recollection that the spiritually lazy man shuns. Many assiduous and efficient businessmen, employees, farmers, or workers are typically lazy in this spiritual sense. Work may even become a flight from the spiritual *élan* and the *sursum corda* that value-responses and especially

---

38. ["one thing ... necessary" (Luke 10:42). Editor.]

contemplative prayer imply. Work as such implies not a dwelling in one's depth, not a *habitare secum* nor a spiritual awakedness. The active attitude in work as such is even opposed to a full recollection to which only the contemplative attitude can lead us. It is a specific and difficult task to preserve recollection during work, an end that can be attained only if contemplation plays an important role in life.

We have further to distinguish different degrees of this spiritual laziness, or different strata in our soul in which this laziness displays itself. Firstly, the laziness concerning the spiritual *élan* and *sursum corda* that religious awakedness implies, living in the light of supernatural reality, emerging to Christ from our earthly absorptions, accomplishing the *sursum corda* in the sense of the Holy Mass. Secondly, the laziness with respect to the inner *élan* that every full value-response implies, as well as the *frui* of a high good possessing an authentic value. This type of lazy person shrinks from the spiritual *élan* and the dwelling in one's depth that an adequate and genuine *frui* of these goods implies. Thirdly, the laziness with respect to the spiritual effort that obedience toward the call of the morally relevant values implies, laziness that displays itself in the sphere of morally obligatory actions.

These three types of spiritual laziness that refer to different spheres are also qualitatively distinct because the kind of *élan* that each of these spheres require is a different one. There are many people who are not lazy concerning the effort of obedience to the moral law, but who are nevertheless lazy with respect to the spiritual *élan* in the first and second sphere.

As already mentioned, the third type of spiritual laziness displays itself in relation toward moral obligations. This type of lazy man will not refuse to submit to strict moral obligations, but he will firstly restrict his obedience to act in conformity to moral obligations without accomplishing the inner *élan* that the confrontation with an authentic morally relevant value requires. He will look at them as something necessary, self-evident, without understanding this situation as something fundamentally different from conforming to the immanent logic of his professional work. He will conform to them because one has to do so.

Instead of grasping the sublime appeal of the obligation to awaken and emerge from our absorption through our concern for the inevitable necessities of our life and the immanent logic of our professional work, instead of the *élan* that every true value-response implies, he conceives the moral obligation as mere duty whereby even the notion of duty has lost its solemnity and grandeur and is restricted to the mere character of something that one has to do, a matter of mere loyalty.

Secondly, he will tend to restrict the scope of moral obligations. Instead of an unlimited readiness to follow the call of God wherever it may be addressed to him, and instead of the desire to remain in a state of spiritual awakedness so that he may not neglect to hear the call of God, this spiritually lazy man will limit the scope of moral obligations to the most obvious ones, that is to say, the ones he can grasp without this awakedness. The spiritually lazy man may be conscientious in conforming to moral obligations insofar as his spiritual laziness does not conceal them from him, but the manner of his response as well as the limitation of the scope of his moral obligations clearly reveal the obstacle that this spiritual laziness forms for his moral life.

We can clearly see how deeply spiritual laziness differs from the two aforementioned types of inertia and laziness in the most common sense. The most assiduous man, efficient in his work, endowed with a great potential for activity and agility, whom we would contrast with the inert and lazy man, the man who could not live without work, who relishes business, who is reliable, punctual, self-controlled, may still be typically lazy in the sense of spiritual laziness. He may shun the spiritual *élan* in the *sursum corda* as much as the lazy one in the former sense, sometimes even to a higher degree. But as different as it may be from the two forms of ordinary laziness, it shares with them the character of concupiscence. Certainly, there exists also a form of resistance against the call of values and the *sursum corda* they imply, which is rooted in pride and not in concupiscence. But it differs widely from spiritual laziness by having the character of a hostile rebellion against it and directing itself more against the element of submission and abandonment as such that the *sursum corda* implies than against the element of spiritual effort in it. We shall clearly see this later on when we discuss the second main root of moral evil, that is to say, pride.

Spiritual laziness, on the contrary, is definitively rooted in concupiscence. It is the resistance against a spiritual effort, an unwillingness to leave the level of our normal existence with its immanent logic, the specific comfort that even all horizontal...[39]

In the last analysis, there lies in spiritual laziness a resistance against losing our own soul, a refusal to conform to the words of our Lord: "He who loses his soul shall find it."[40] This death to self shows itself in the gesture of keeping our soul from dwelling in the comfortable possession of ourselves, remaining on the firm ground of our natural existence. It is especially the unwillingness to accept the effort that implies any movement which contains an element of this loss of ourselves. It is the concupiscent holding on to the subjectively satisfying that lies in the preservation of this "pseudo" self-possession, in the avoidance of the strain of self-donation. We distinguished before two degrees of spiritual *élan* and spiritual laziness. With respect to the former there is the specifically religious *élan* and the *élan* that every true value-response attitude and every authentic *frui* of a high value implies. We can now clearly see that every religious *élan*, that is, every act that is a direct response to Christ and *per ipsum* and *in ipso* to God the Father, requires this loss of ourselves to a much greater extent and in a formally new way. This manifests itself, for instance, in a typical way in the effort of mental prayer in which we should become completely void, die in a certain way to ourselves and open ourselves to the irradiation of Christ, losing ourselves in Him.

Compared with this religious spiritual effort, with this *sursum corda*, the spiritual *élan* implied in every true value-response that is directed to a created good or to the noble *frui* that is required in any confrontation with the world of values, by far does not contain the same gesture of losing ourselves to the point of death to ourselves.

Even the man who does not shun the spiritual *élan* that the full value-response to earthly goods and the *frui* of values such as beauty in

---

39. [The next page of the typescript is missing. Editor.]
40. [Luke 17:33. Editor.]

art and nature, truth, and especially moral values implies may still try to escape the religious *élan* because it requires much more. Spiritual laziness in general lives to some extent in every man, and it is but the saint who has victoriously uprooted this form of concupiscence. We all know the resistance in our nature to emerge from absorption in our daily activities to the ultimate valid reality of God and to recollect ourselves. We all know the tendency of dwelling in the periphery and of relenting in our spiritual vigilance. We are aware of the tendency of our fallen nature to draw us downward and to resist the spiritual *élan* that the world of values and God require of us. We experience the tendency to avoid this lifting up, this "conspiring" with the rhythm of values and especially in the religious sphere, even when with our will we conform to their call in accomplishing the respective acts in a routine way. We participate, for instance, in liturgical prayers in a routine manner, notwithstanding the ever repeated appeal in the text of these prayers to accomplish this spiritual *élan*, to emerge from the automatism of our everyday life. Even concerning mental prayer, the danger exists that it is accomplished like any other work whereby we remain in the tension toward the next future moment and do not pierce through to a real presence and a recollection in our depth.

And even concerning the full *frui* of sublime music or the presence of a beloved person, we often discover this tendency in us to refuse the spiritual *élan* that a full confrontation with the world of values requires. We discover that our spiritual laziness hinders us from exposing our soul to the deep happiness that these values can bestow on us. We are not ready to enter into the depth of our soul as these goods require.

Summarizing, we may say: apart from the different forms of concupiscence that we examined above, concupiscence manifests itself also in the main forms of laziness. As surprising as it may seem at first sight that laziness, which has always the character of persisting in a certain state, should be a form of concupiscence, with which we always associate a gesture of vehement tension toward pleasure and the subjectively satisfying, our analysis has shown that laziness issues from the same root as all the other forms of concupiscence. Notwithstanding all the differences, we find in laziness the same fundamental gesture of self-centered absorption by the agreeable. We find the same incompatibility with the value-response, the same intrinsic indifference toward values, the same satiated self-affirmation. We can clearly see the role that laziness, and especially spiritual laziness, plays among the roots of moral evil.[41]

There exists also a specific form of spiritual laziness that manifests itself in the field of knowledge. We do not realize that a laziness of the second type shows itself in a superficial and inaccurate accomplishment of scientific or philosophical work.

We mean the unwillingness to "conspire" with the nature of the being that is the topic of our knowledge in philosophical research. Instead of conforming ourselves to the nature of a being, instead of accomplishing the spiritual *élan* that is necessary in order to exist on the level on which alone we are able to grasp the object and, above all, to understand it, we remain on the lower level and thus become unable to grasp and penetrate this being. This intellectual laziness is typical of the materialist. He looks in but one direction, and in the easiest one, the one that requires the minimum of *élan*, and thus does not find psychical and spiritual reality. He behaves as a man who would want to see tones or to hear colors. In his lazy obstinacy, he refuses the spiritual *élan* that conforming to something higher requires.

Also, the knowledge of a being requires a moral attitude besides the concentration of our intellectual capacities, and it requires this more for the knowledge of what ranks higher. It requires precisely the readiness to accomplish the spiritual *élan* that conforming to and conspiring with the nature of a being implies. The greatest intellectual effort, the most intense concentration, the greatest accuracy can never replace this spiritual *élan* that alone will enable us to grasp something higher, and not to

---

41. [The following text is an additional remark that is placed in the typescript after the overall summary of the theme of laziness. It develops further the notion of spiritual laziness. It deals with the manifestations of this laziness in the sphere of knowledge. In the present volume the theme of laziness concludes with this remark, although the typescript continues with another version of the distinction between laziness as inertia and laziness as the tendency to avoid the strain of work. This section is not included in the present volume as it only repeats in a different way and with slightly changed accents the same substantial points made in the description of laziness as inertia and laziness as the tendency to avoid the strain of work. Editor.]

delimit arbitrarily the plenitude of reality. It is not often said that a great part of philosophical error and blindness is a result of spiritual laziness. Certainly, there are still many other moral attitudes that can frustrate our philosophical knowledge, such as pride, lack of reverence, and others. But concupiscence exerts its sinister function also in the domain of philosophical knowledge and even pre-philosophical knowledge. In emerging from this spiritual laziness, we find that the higher the object, the greater the importance of the spiritual *élan*, the more indispensable it becomes, until we reach the sphere of which St. Bonaventure says: these things can be understood only by him who, like Daniel, is a man of desire.

III

Pride[1]

WE SAW ABOVE THAT THE SECOND main root of evil is pride. Its negative role extends even further and deeper than the role played by concupiscence; above all, it is still more negative from a moral point of view. The Gospel, St. Augustine, and the whole of Christian theology and philosophy consider pride to be the deepest and most fundamental root of moral evil: "... because the head and origin of all evil is pride which reigns without flesh in the devil."[2]

Both the proud man and the concupiscent man are completely egocentric, but whereas the latter plunges into subjectively satisfying goods and throws himself away on them, the former is characterized by a reflexive gazing at himself. The relation between the subjective satisfaction

---

1. [The introductory section of the treatment of pride consisting of twenty-three handwritten pages (Ana 544, VI, 14, 1) was transformed into chapter 35 of *Ethics*. There are no substantial differences between the manuscript and this chapter of *Ethics*. Since the text in the *Ethics* is grammatically and stylistically superior, it is used here. The same editorial policy was already applied in the case of a similar overlap in the section on concupiscence. Editor.]

2. St. Augustine, *De Civitate Dei*, XIV, 3, trans. J. Healey.

and the *ego* (self) differs completely in each case. Whereas the concupiscent man exclusively seeks to taste the various pleasures and views the world under the category of the agreeable, the proud man is centered on his self-glory, the consciousness of his own importance and excellence, and his masterly sovereignty.

Concupiscence refers to a *having*; pride to a *being*. Concupiscence is a perversion in the sphere of the possession of a good; pride is a perversion in the attitude toward one's own perfection. In concupiscence man renounces his birthright, as it were, for a mess of pottage; in pride man arrogates to himself a right that is above him; he exalts himself in an illegitimate way. St. Augustine admirably expresses the nature of pride in saying: "This then is the mischief: man, liking himself as if he were his own light, turned away from the true light, which, if he had pleased himself with, he might have been like.... But man desiring more became less, and choosing to be sufficient in himself fell from that all sufficient God."[3]

Pride manifests itself in different main forms that correspond to different strata in the person, and that also embody different degrees of moral wickedness. We shall see that these main forms of pride completely differ in their quality and nature, notwithstanding their common basic character. In order to make clearer the nature of these main different forms, we shall consider them in men who are completely dominated by pride.

III.i. *Satanic Pride*

The first main type is the man of satanic pride. Here pride reaches its climax and reveals itself in its most naked, radical, and typical way. Satanic pride is first of all characterized by its object: metaphysical grandeur and metaphysical lordship. Mere exterior power, the opportunity to be a despot and dominate others exteriorly, the glory of being a hero—none of these can quench the insatiable thirst of this pride. Everything important-in-itself, every value, seems to this pride to entail an injury to

---

3. St. Augustine, *De Civitate Dei*, XIV, 13, trans. J. Healey.

its own glory. Thus the man dominated by this ultimate pride hates all light and the intrinsic beauty and harmony of every authentic value. The fundamental gesture of this pride is an impotent attempt to dethrone all values, to deprive them of their mysterious metaphysical power. The war that the man who is victim of this pride wages is directed against the reign of values as such, and ultimately against God Himself. The higher the rank of a value, the more this man will view it as an unbearable rival, and the more he will hate it. His hatred, therefore, is directed primarily against the moral and religious values. He not only wants to wage war against the reign of these values by bringing about the triumph of moral evil on earth, but he also aspires to a dethronement of moral values themselves and ultimately of God. His attempt is intrinsically futile, an impotent attempt at something essentially impossible. His attitude is metaphysically destructive and nihilistic. His pride and his thirst for metaphysical lordship, combined with the awareness of his own nothingness, engender in him a hatred against being as such. The most general value of being, as such, is for him already detrimental to his desire of himself possessing the plenitude of being.

The innermost word of this satanic pride is the reversal of St. Catherine's prayer: *Che tu sia e io non sia*—"That Thou be all and I, nothing." Its innermost gesture repeats to God: *Che tu non sia ed io sia*— "That I may be, and Thou shalt not be." This satanic pride is embodied in Lucifer and his rebellion against God. In man this pride exists only in an analogous form. It is found in Cain, who hated Abel because of his goodness; it is found in Rakitin of Dostoevsky's *Brothers Karamazov* and in Shakespeare's Iago. The man who has fallen prey to this satanic pride is blind to the real nature of values, to their intrinsic beauty and dignity, but, unlike the concupiscent man, who in his complete bluntness ignores values, he grasps their metaphysical power. Certainly, he misunderstands the nature of this metaphysical power, otherwise he could not attempt to dissociate it from values. He sees the metaphysical "throne" of values, and simultaneously he misses the very nature of this "throne." He does not try to appropriate moral values to himself in order thereby to acquire their metaphysical grandeur as does the Pharisee. He wants to rob them of their metaphysical grandeur and to place himself on their throne, not by possessing them but by dethroning them. Because he sees in them a rival, he wages war against them, and does so in an insidious and infamous way. He tries to replace the true order of values by a fallacious order of pseudo-values; he tries to dethrone them by placing their negative counterpart on their throne. His whole personality is pervaded by a deadly hatred: hatred against all light, all goodness, hatred against God, hatred against other men; the higher their moral rank, the greater this hatred.

This type of man is further characterized by metaphysical haughtiness. He abhors all submission, all obedience. *Non serviam* ("I will not serve") is the second archword of satanic pride.[4] The first feature of this pride is the specific hatred of the infinite goodness and divine light of God; the second is rebellion against God as Absolute Lord. Satanic pride shuns every kind of submission; the man possessed of it refuses to acknowledge any authentic authority; he refuses any submission to a God-given authority, any obedience, any admission of indebtedness to another. He shuns being helped by other persons, and, if forced by circumstances to accept help, instead of being grateful he will hate the one who helped him.

III.ii. *Pride of Self-Glorification*

If we now proceed to a brief analysis of the other main dimensions in which pride deploys itself, we must first observe that we are no longer referring to certain types of men but to dimensions of pride that may in part coexist in the same man, although one dimension will usually prevail and become the most specific trend of his pride. In satanic pride, as the summit of all types of pride, all the other dimensions of pride are, so to speak, surpassed and included *per eminentiam*. But the other main forms of pride, far from excluding each other, may be found in different degrees in one and the same man. They refer to different spheres of life, and their nature is characterized by their specific object. Thus, one and

---

4.[While the term "arch-word" sounds awkward in English, it is a (perhaps too straightforward) translation of the German *Urwort*. Editor.]

the same man may manifest different dimensions of pride according to the situation with which he is confronted.

The second main type of the proud man draws his consciousness of grandeur from values and perfections that he either believes he possesses or that he aspires to possess. He accepts values as the source of grandeur; he does not wage war against them, nor does he attempt to dethrone them, but he desires to adorn himself with them for the sake of his self-glory. He is also blind to the true nature of values and grasps only the metaphysical power that they embody. He is interested in them only as means for his self-glory. But their existence, as such, does not appear to him as something detrimental; he does not hate God. He accepts values as something valid and wants to use them for his self-glory; he even wants, in the worst case, to use God Himself for this purpose.

This type of pride has not the metaphysical aspiration of satanic pride; it lacks the rebellious character and the attempt to dethrone God. It aspires to grandeur in the frame of the existing metaphysical order and hence does not make its possessor a nihilist. But this type of proud man shuns every value insofar as it adorns and exalts persons other than himself; he wants all grandeur and exaltation for his own person. He is incapable of any response to value since he considers values only as means for his own grandeur. The specific objects of this type of pride are one's own values and any excellence proper to one's own activities. The possession of values as a means for self-glory is the specific end of his striving for them; in other words, self-glory through the possession of values is his specific and exclusive aim.

The specific nature of this dimension of pride will be determined greatly by the nature of the values in which the person glorifies himself or that he aspires to possess. There is, patently, a great difference between the pride of the Pharisee who seeks his glory in the possession of moral and religious values and the pride directed to the glory resulting from intellectual values that characterizes the man who glorifies himself in believing himself to be a genius.[5]

---

[5]. The fundamental importance of this factor determining the nature of the different types of pride has been elaborated in detail in chapter 7 of *Transformation in Christ*.

The pride of self-glorification through the possession of values, implying, as a whole, a specific reflexive gesture toward one's own person, manifests itself in two dimensions: first, the glorification in values that one believes himself to possess; second, the craving for the acquisition of new values. We could call them the static and the dynamic dimensions of pride. Both will mostly be found in one and the same person, but it may also be that one of the two prevails, or even that one exists without the other. There is a self-satisfied type of pride in which a person relishes the possession of the wished-for grandeur, and likewise a pride that craves for climbing ever higher. The prevalence of one of these two dimensions, either static or dynamic pride, will first depend upon the image that a man has of his own person, and sometimes even on the capacities and perfections he possesses in reality. Hence we must distinguish the case of a man's satisfaction in certain values of his own person that he believes he possesses, from that of a man thirsting for values that he knows he does not yet possess. Secondly, the prevalence of static or dynamic pride depends upon whether the thirst for grandeur is limited to certain values and can be satisfied by their possession, or whether it is unlimited. This difference in the aspiration to grandeur is independent of the question of whether the person believes himself to possess a value or not. Not the real underlying situation but the nature of the pride itself determines, in this case, whether this pride takes on the rhythm of a restless climbing higher, or whether there is a satisfied repose in the person's own perfection. Here the difference between static and dynamic pride reaches its full significance.

Finally, we have to distinguish three stages in the pride of self-glorification: the first consists in the conviction a man has that he possesses a value, the attribution to himself of some perfection or the feeling that he himself is endowed with it; in the second we find him relishing it, taking delight in his own beauty, intelligence, or goodness; the third consists in the specific self-glorification, the incense that he offers to his own grandeur, the outspoken antithesis to the humble attitude in which every perfection and value is considered as a pure gift from God.

These three stages constitute three degrees of pride, the second surpassing the first and the third surpassing the second. We shall see later on that in some persons pride reaches only the first stage, in others the second, in again others the third. Each further stage presupposes the preceding one, and thus everyone who has the second also has the first, and whoever has the third necessarily has all three stages. But it may be that one has the first and not yet the second, or that in having the second one has not yet reached the third.

Obviously, these three stages of pride refer to the attitude concerning a value that a man believes himself to possess, and not to the attitude resulting from a consciousness of one's own insufficiency and the craving for the acquisition of values that he does not yet possess. They refer, therefore, to the static dimension of pride and not to the dynamic one.

III.iii. *Vanity*

We now come to the third type of pride: vanity. It has much in common with the pride of self-glorification, but it also differs from it in many respects. It, too, refers to values of one's own person and to the excellence of one's activities, as does self-glorification. But vanity is essentially static, and not dynamic. It is not craving for new perfections but relishing the possession of real or imaginary perfections. A second difference is that vanity does not imply a general blindness to values as such, and still less a general approach to them as mere means for one's own grandeur. The vain man may have a certain understanding of values and a readiness to conform to their call. Vanity, notwithstanding all the degrees of vanity, does not imply the poisonous, hard, and tense ethos that the pride of self-glorification always possesses in one way or another. It has the pseudo-harmony of self-satisfaction. The vain man is, above all, characterized by his naïve and ridiculous self-centeredness. Though he may have a certain understanding of values, they never play an important role in his life, since he is absorbed by his own perfection and has the tendency to refer everything to his own person. Moreover, the second stage of pride prevails in vanity, in the relishing of one's own superiority and excellence.

Finally, vanity may restrict itself to a certain sphere of values, for instance, the beauty of one's face, the elegance or grace of one's exterior appearance. Vanity may be satisfied with these perfections and be indifferent to other perfections such as intelligence or moral perfection.

Vanity has some affinity to concupiscence; it is, so to speak, the representative of concupiscence in the realm of pride. It results from a certain combination of pride and concupiscence. The ethos of vanity is soft and not hard, as are all other dimensions of pride. Vanity also displays itself in the enjoyment of admiration received from other persons. Yet it does not so much crave this admiration as take it for granted. The vain man thinks that admiration is due the perfections that he believes himself to possess, and he considers any man who refuses to offer him this admiration to be stupid and inferior.

But it must be said that vanity alone is never able to cut us off completely from the reign of values. Either it is an addition to other dimensions of pride, as in the case of the man who is predominantly motivated by pride, or it is a residuum of pride coexisting with a value-response attitude, perhaps taking the form of a struggle between them.

III.iv. *Pride of Exterior Lordship*

Pride displays itself not only with respect to the grandeur issuing from the possession of values but also with respect to the grandeur connected with might, exterior glory, and influence over other persons. The proud man of this type is not content simply with the admiration of others, which acts as a confirmation of the glory issuing from the possession of perfections, but he seeks and reposes in the grandeur that is connected to exterior glory: an outstanding position, might as such, the exterior domination of other persons, an exterior lordship.

He seeks the consciousness of "exalted being," of superiority, not in the possession of values but in the exterior superiority that a leading position, the possibility of commanding others, or an exterior domination of a group or society conveys to him. The object of this pride is a grandeur that is not derived from the possession of values but that originates in the exterior position that the person holds in relation to other men. Lordship, as such, manifesting itself in a dominating position in the world, is the specific aim of this pride.

This pride is clearly distinguished from satanic pride since, firstly, its aspiration toward lordship does not extend to the metaphysical sphere and hence does not see moral and morally relevant values as enemies and rivals of its own grandeur. Secondly, this pride does not blind its owner in the same way to moral and morally relevant values. This pride does not even recognize the metaphysical power essentially connected to values, especially moral values. It regards them as the naïve concern of lowly and weak-minded people; in its fascination for exterior lordship, it bluntly overlooks them. It may lead to a denial of their objective validity in principle and to a complete indifference *de facto*. The value blindness of this pride is more akin to the value blindness resulting from concupiscence. The call of values is unheeded, being regarded as an unimportant obstacle for attaining exterior lordship. Only things that present themselves as tangible forces in the exterior world, or ideas embodied in a movement, are considered as rivals and thus approached with hostility and the tendency to bring them under domination. No war is waged against God and the morally relevant values, but every moral and religious force that can be evaluated by that category that alone counts for this pride, that is, exterior might, is considered as a rival. The typical rival for this pride is not the saint, the man of genius, the great philosopher, the great musician, the great poet, and so on, but the man who either possesses great influence or a powerful position or whose gifts may lead him to such influence or position.

Though this dimension of pride may vary according to the degree of exterior power to which it aspires, this difference does not affect its moral character, since it is essentially dynamic. Even the man who aspires only to become the chief of some subordinate group has, in his pride, the potential ambition to climb still higher. The frame for possible power that is imposed on him and that he may take for granted is an accidental limit; it does not essentially alter the character of this dimension of pride, which manifests itself typically in ambition.

III.v. *Haughtiness*

We come now to the fourth main dimension of pride, which we may term "haughtiness." We have already mentioned it in relation to satanic pride. It displays itself in the refusal to submit to any other human person. The haughty man does not crave a great position, might, or exterior lordship. But he idolizes his own individual position of mastery or his independence; he shuns the admission of any weakness or any dependence. This haughtiness makes a man incapable of admitting any fault on his part. He will never place himself in the weak position of asking someone to pardon him. He will look at contrition as a despicable weakness. He will make an idol of his dignity, his virility, his honor, and his rights. He lives on the *qui vive* concerning any offense against his honor and his rights. He possesses a hard and irascible ethos; he walks through life with head held high, conscious of his imperturbable strength and independence, shunning any help from other persons. He refuses to be grateful to anyone because this would be an admission of dependence. He wants to be undisturbed in the consciousness of his autonomy and autarchy.

This man does not necessarily refuse to submit to the moral law. He may be disposed to perform his duty and even to submit to the legitimate authorities. But he will never admit a fault even to himself, and certainly never to other persons. Obeying the moral law to a certain extent does not seem to him a weakness or a diminution of his autarchy and virile independence. But the admission of a fault, as well as indebtedness to another person, are regarded by him as incompatible with his honor and virile strength. Haughtiness is centered on the idol of independence and virile strength. The haughty man avoids above all bowing before other people. Anything like compassion or being moved, which implies an element capable of softening his hard and imperturbable virility, is considered by him as a weakness. Shakespeare's Coriolanus is such a haughty man; thus he regards yielding to the prayers of his mother, his being moved by her, as an unpardonable moral defeat.[6]

6.[Coriolanus is the main character in a tragedy of the same name by William Shakespeare. The tragedy is based on the life of the legendary Roman leader Caius Marcius Coriolanus. Editor.]

The contrast between haughtiness and the other dimensions of pride is obvious. In this pride, as such, there is no tendency to dethrone the values, as there is in satanic pride. Furthermore, it conditions no complete value blindness, but it frustrates the full understanding of values. It allows an understanding of the important-in-itself and of the category of duty, especially insofar as it assumes a legal character. But it frustrates the understanding of the intrinsic beauty and goodness of moral values and excludes especially the understanding of every value that presupposes a humble, unpresumptuous mind. Every value that seems to the haughty man incompatible with his virile strength and self-affirmation—for instance, charity, compassion, contrition, and gratitude—is not understood. This pride acts more as a narrowing and falsification of value perception than as a radical frustration of it.

Finally, this pride is not concerned with the acquisition of values in order to exalt its own grandeur or to relish them or glory in them; rather, only one value matters: strength, independence, autarchy. It considers only the possession of this value as indispensable for the desired grandeur. And it does not strive to acquire this strength but instead starts from the consciousness of possessing it and takes it for granted as an indisputable basis. It is concerned only with a refusal of anything that could injure the possessor's independence and virile strength. Pride imprisons its victim in a cramp of self-affirmation, a continually defensive position against any offense to his honor, his rights, his independence. This pride knows only one fundamental evil: weakness. To give up the fortress of the hard, cramped, self-affirmation, to surrender the grandeur that virile strength and autarchy conveys to him: this alone is evil.

Haughtiness has a static character. It is not a craving for more and more independence, a direction toward a higher and higher exaltation. It implies not the gesture of ascension but the refusal to descend from the height that one presumes to possess, the resistance against anything that would imply a humiliation. The man who is obsessed with this pride does not want to be exalted, he is not filled with unrest and tension for a grandeur that he believes himself not yet to have attained. But he defends continually the grandeur that he takes for granted that he possesses and shuns every attitude or situation that he considers incompatible with his grandeur. This is the pride of the Stoic who speaks: *Si fractus illabatur orbis, impavidum ferient ruinae* ("If the world should collapse in ruins about him, struck by its fragments he would remain fearless").[7] To this pride, fear appears as the incarnation of weakness, the very antithesis to its idol of virile strength and dignity.[8]

III.vi. *The Role of Pride in the Different Spheres of Life*[9]

After having distinguished the main dimensions of pride—satanic pride, the pride of self-glorification, vanity, the pride of exterior lordship and haughtiness—[10] we have now to inquire into the role of pride in the different domains of life and the specific objects of pride in detail. We abstract hereby from the satanic form of pride, which, as we saw, offers a radically different approach to every good. We shall first examine the role of pride in the different domains of life with respect to such types as are dominated by pride and in whom the value-response attitude is more or less silenced. This will enable us to grasp the specific nature of pride more clearly. Secondly, we shall examine the role of pride in all those cases in which pride coexists with a value-response attitude and may be present as a mere tendency and potential danger.

We begin by examining the role of pride in the sphere of the different activities of man. As soon as any activity offers any occasion of self-glory, there is a possibility of pride arising. As long as an activity does not offer the possibility of distinguishing between an efficient or perfect achievement and an imperfect and inefficient accomplishment, it is not an object of pride. Eating, sleeping, walking, riding in a bus or in a subway, offer no occasion for pride to arise. But as soon as there is the question of doing something well or not, there is the possibility of pride.

When playing a game, someone may be proud of playing it well and

---

7. Horace, *Odes*, 3.3.7–8.
8. [The end of the passage taken from *Ethics*. Editor.]
9. [Ana 544, VI, 14, 1. Editor.]
10. [Ana 544, VI, 14, 2. Editor.]

especially of playing it better than others. Or his pride may be hurt because he does not play it well and others play it better than he does. In this case the theme is no longer the amusement of the game but his own perfection, feeling of superiority, relishing his own glory, or being irritated and hurt because of his inferiority.

The same applies to any sport. To excel by being more able and efficient, to have greater bodily strength, to be able to run faster, or to have more skill, all this can become an object of pride. It is always a turning away from the objective theme and a focusing on or at least a squinting at one's own ego, at one's own perfection.

The same holds when we consider activities in which the question of perfection is in some way at stake. In any professional activity, in any work, in public speaking, in lecturing, in preaching, in speaking a foreign language, in teaching, in any political activity, in helping some other person, in any moral action, pride may intervene. In every case the proud person will turn away from the objective theme of his activity and will relish his own excellence and perfection, or he will be offended and hurt when he does not succeed.

We see thus that pride may poison every activity in which there is a possibility for one to feel superior, perfect, efficient, or possessing any value. But the nature of pride varies according to the nature of this activity.

The primary object of pride is obviously one's own perfection or, as we may put it, pride is primarily directed toward one's own perfection. Here the specifically self-reflective gesture of pride finds its most authentic expression. Whether it is the beauty of one's face or figure, the elegance of exterior appearance or bodily strength or any ability or intelligence, a special talent or moral qualities, they all can become the object of our pride. It is obvious that in all these cases our interest in possessing those values never has the character of value-response. The value as such does not interest us but rather the self-glorification that results from our being endowed with such a value.

The proud man, apart from the satanic type, is not completely blind to values but he never fully understands them in their true character of important-in-itself, and above all he is not interested in them for their own sake but looks at them exclusively as an adornment of his own person, as a means for his self-exaltation, for feeling himself superior, outstanding, elevated. This self-glory is the source of his satisfaction. Therefore, the fact that other persons are perfect not only means nothing to him but is also a source of dissatisfaction for him. He sees in them rivals for his self-glory, and they hinder him from feeling superior. He is not interested in the glorification of God that his own perfection or the perfection of his fellow man imply. The value has become for him a mere means of self-glorification.

III.vii. *The Character of Pride Depends on the Values That Are the Object of Pride*

But pride assumes a quite different character depending on the personal values that form the object of one's pride. The higher a value ranks, the worse the nature of pride is. The man who is proud of his beautiful mustache or his tall figure is obviously much more innocent than the man whose pride relishes being intelligent. And the self-satisfied correct man who relishes his moral reliability or the Pharisee who relishes his religious standard are still much more morally evil.

It seems, firstly, that the higher a value ranks, the worse it is when someone makes it an object of pride, when he relishes its possession. But in this respect even more important than the mere rank of the value is, secondly, the question whether the value in question presupposes a collaboration of the free will in order to possess it or not. Thus, pride relishing moral values or even piety is so much worse than pride that refers to a talent or exterior beauty, which we receive as a pure gift, without the collaboration of our will.

We encounter here a surprising paradox. On the one hand, a self-glorification, a feeling of superiority and of grandeur because of our fine mustache or the tallness of our stature or the beauty of our face is more stupid and unreasonable than being proud because of great intelligence, erudition, or talent. But morally the latter pride is more serious than the childish and infantile former form of pride. And the paradox increases still when we compare being proud about moral or religious virtues with the pride referring to intellectual and vital values, or even to mere exterior perfections of our body. The less we are responsible for being endowed with a value, the more stupid and ridiculous it is to be proud about it and to draw out of this perfection a consciousness of superiority and glory. But being proud about moral and religious virtues, which presuppose collaboration of our free will, is morally much worse. The more we are *de facto* responsible for being endowed with a value, the worse it is from the moral point of view to be proud of it.

We have now to inquire into the reasons for this paradox and the fact that the moral wickedness of pride increases according to the rank of the value to which the pride refers, and especially according to the role of our freedom in acquiring this value.

It is obvious: the Pharisee is morally worse than the man who is proud because of his exterior beauty, his powerful temperament, or even because of great musical talent that he possesses. Our task is now to understand why. The reasons are the following:

Firstly: to be proud because of tallness of stature or the beauty of the face is especially ridiculous and stupid because the perfection in question is, firstly, too superficial for drawing a general consciousness of superiority and grandeur out of it; secondly, because it is too exterior and not enough our own for constituting a basis for a consciousness of superiority; thirdly, because it is obviously a pure gift, and we are in no way responsible for it.

But the superficiality of the perfection that is here at stake also determines the very quality of the pride. The pride too is superficial and can never possess the dark, poisonous character that corrodes the whole being of the person to its very depth.

Thus we can understand that the very wickedness of pride increases dependent on the rank of the values to which it refers because the nature of the values conditions the quality of pride as well its depth.

Secondly: the exterior perfections and vital values, for instance, a great vitality or vivaciousness of temperament, do not imply a direct reference to goods possessing a value on the object side. They are simple facts, gifts that imply no specific call with respect to objective goods. Great musical talent, on the contrary, or high intelligence imply a call to use them for the creation of objective goods—they unfold their meaning with respect to an object. The man possessing great musical talent does not possess it as a mere adornment of his person but as something that is ordered toward the world of aesthetic values, which implies the call to create musical works of art or to reproduce the masterworks of other artists. To be proud of them thus means to turn away from these values, to relinquish the attitude of abandoning ourselves to the values on the object side by serving the realization of objective goods having an authentic value. To look at these perfections and to draw out of them a consciousness of superiority and self-glory is a more radical abuse of them, an attitude that opposes in a new way the general value-response attitude.

This element of abuse assumes a much greater importance with respect to moral virtues. Here it is no longer a capacity's merely being ordered toward certain goods on the object side possessing a value, but these values come to existence only through a superactual value-response and imply this superactual value-response as their very core. As they are not only capacities but superactual attitudes, the role of the values on the object side is an incomparably greater and essential one. To make them into the object of pride, to look at them and to draw out of them a consciousness of superiority and grandeur means to destroy their very nature by relinquishing the value-response attitude that is their soul. To use them, as it were, for our self-glory means to lose interest in the values on the object side, to counteract the call for humility that issues from those values, to give up the gesture of abandoning ourselves to them.

Thirdly: it is a unique fact that by being proud of such exterior perfections as tallness of stature or the beauty of the face we do not alter or destroy the existence of these perfections. It may be that this pride affects the expression of a face and thus frustrates the beauty of expression. But, firstly, this is not necessarily so, and, secondly, it never frustrates the beauty of form as such, as in the case of the tallness of stature or great bodily strength.

Intelligence or a great artistic gift, on the contrary, are already greatly affected and altered by making them an object of our pride. Firstly, intellectual pride as such implies an element of narrowness and stupidity, which limits the intelligence as such. Secondly, the direction toward self-glory is in its specific lack of objectivity an obstacle for the real penetration of being and the fecundation by it that are both essential elements of an authentic intelligence. The same applies to a great artistic gift. The non-objectivity of pride hinders the genuine inspiration and abandonment to values that are both necessary for the creation of a great work of art. Nevertheless, pride does not dissolve and frustrate those perfections. A powerful intelligence and a great talent are not completely deprived of their substance by a basic proud attitude.

But as soon as we come to moral or religious virtues, we clearly see that pride completely frustrates and dissolves them. The man who relishes his justice, purity, or charity, who uses them as a source of his consciousness of grandeur and superiority, is no longer just, pure, or charitable. Pride is so incompatible and antithetical to the value-response attitude, and especially to the response to morally relevant values, that by looking back on our own moral values and by making them an object of our pride, we immediately destroy the superactual value-response attitude that is the very core of the moral virtue.

To these people the word of the Gospel applies: "They have already received their reward."[11] Moral and religious virtues are not only completely frustrated and destroyed from within by relishing them as a source of our grandeur and "exalted being," but they can never come into existence in a man who is radically dominated by the thirst for exalted being. We are not thinking here of the man dominated by the satanic type of pride, who *a fortiori* can never possess a moral virtue and does not even desire to have it because he strives in his hostility toward the moral values to dethrone them. We are rather thinking of the Pharisee and the morally proud man who accepts the existence of values and wants to possess them, but only because of his self-glory, as a mere adornment

---

11. [Luke 6:24. Editor.]

of his person, as an instrument of his consciousness of grandeur and superiority. In his desire for self-glory, he is unable to accomplish a real response to God and the morally relevant values. In looking at the morally relevant values only as an instrument for acquiring a moral value, which again interests him only as a source of his self-glory, he is unable to accomplish the superactual abandonment to God and to the morally relevant values that is the very core of any moral virtue. Already the fact that he is interested in the morally relevant values only as a means for the acquisition of his own moral perfection frustrates the acquisition of moral virtues that necessarily presuppose and imply a genuine interest in the morally relevant values and a self-abandonment to them without any squinting at his own perfection. But notwithstanding this fact, our own moral perfection can and must also legitimately form an object of our preoccupation, as for instance in all ascetic practices. As long as this interest is itself a value-response, as it is the interest in being good because of the intrinsic importance of moral goodness and above all because of the glorification of God that it implies, it can never be in conflict with genuine interest in the morally relevant values on the object side and will never lead to using morally relevant values as a mere means for the acquisition of a moral value (cf. the chapter on value-response).[12]

The real feature of pride is the absence of any real interest in values, be it the morally relevant values on the object side or the moral value of one's own character. The important-in-itself and the glorification of God through moral value means nothing to proud persons. Their own value interests them exclusively as a means for their self-glory. They accept that their values are something glorious, in contradistinction to the satanic type, but without understanding their real nature. This attitude obviously bars them from the real acquisition of any moral and religious virtue. If they conform to certain commandments of God in this attitude, as the Pharisee does, they substitute a pseudo-justice, a pseudo-purity for the real virtues. And they glorify themselves in something that in reality does not exist.

---

12. [Hildebrand refers here to *Ethics*, Ch. 17. Editor.]

Now we can understand why pride destroys moral virtues or frustrates their acquisition, whereas in the case of other perfections it only alters and diminishes them, and in the case of mere exterior perfections, it does not affect them at all. This also reveals that the higher the value that forms the object of pride and the more its possession implies a collaboration of our freedom, the worse the pride.

Fourthly: even the preliminary stage of pride, that is, the consciousness of possessing some value, or the conviction of possessing it, already assumes a completely different character, the higher a value ranks. The tallness of our stature or even the beauty of our face is more or less obvious. We need not be proud in order to affirm it or to know it. A specific turning back to ourselves is not necessary in order to grasp it. The pride begins here, so to speak, only when we draw a consciousness of superiority and grandeur from it, a consciousness which already intervenes when the possession of such a perfection preoccupies us to a great extent and creates a false "consciousness," a continual "feeling" ourselves to be beautiful.

The conviction and knowledge of our being endowed with a great intelligence or a great artistic gift has a different character. As obvious as it may be for us, the conclusive conviction of possessing it contrasts with the consciousness of being limited in intelligence or artistic talent. Real intelligence, which manifests itself to us in a completely different way from the exterior perfections, that is, manifests itself only in its inner aspect and in the connection to the intellectual penetration of being or the fulfilment of any intellectual task, implies always a consciousness of the limitedness of our achievement compared with the ideal fulfillment of our task, given the mystery of being that we never completely penetrate. The absence of this consciousness of our limitedness when confronted with our task is always a lack of intelligence and condemns us to superficiality. Thus, already the conviction of possessing a great intelligence is incompatible with a true possession of it. The background awareness of the objective task that is indispensable for the experience of our intelligence implies a simultaneous consciousness of the relativity of our intelligence. A blunt description of intelligence as an obvious and conclusive fact is here impossible, in contrast to the exterior perfections. The full conviction of being intelligent implies already the presence of the first stage of pride and a turning back to ourselves. The same applies for artistic talent.

Obviously, we do not exclude by this statement a person who inevitably has a consciousness of his intelligence or of his artistic gift and even of his superiority in this respect to one or another person. But this perfection must always present itself to him in its relativity and with the inner disposition to recognize other persons as superior in this respect, if they really are so. And above all, this knowing about his intelligence is inserted into the consciousness of his insufficiency in the face of the objective task to which he is called by the gift that he received.

A completely new situation is at stake with respect to knowledge about moral and religious virtues. As long as we do not turn back and look at ourselves, no knowledge of the moral values of our person, whether of the moral virtues or of the moral values of our actions and attitudes, is given to us. Moral virtues of our own person manifest themselves only in a consciousness of inner harmony and in the unique bliss that the conformity with the call of the morally relevant values and the will of God conveys to us. The normal direction of our mind is completely focused on the reign of the morally relevant values, and as the Gospel says, "Do not let your left hand know what your right hand is doing."[13] The same applies to every moral value of an action or an act of charity or forgiving. It is the very nature of these attitudes to be completely focused on the morally relevant values on the object side. Besides the inner harmony and peace, our conscience indicates to us that we are in conformity with the will of God. But, unlike the knowledge of the moral values of other persons, the knowledge of the moral values that our attitude objectively bestows on us is not given to us. The difference with respect to the exterior perfections and even to such values as intelligence is obvious.

I cannot avoid seeing the beauty of my own face as I can see the beauty of another person, if I happen to look in a mirror. I cannot avoid experiencing being endowed with a relative intelligence in certain works,

---

13. [Matthew 6:3. Editor.]

although the way in which the intelligence of another person is given to me differs completely. But in the moral sphere, the way in which the moral values of our fellow man are given to us possesses no analogy with respect to the knowledge of the moral values of our own person. In order to grasp them, we would have to accomplish a reflexive gesture toward our own person, to become our own spectator, and this gesture is incompatible with the very nature of our being focused on the morally relevant values. Whereas the consciousness of our moral vices and the moral wickedness of morally negative actions is something to which the confrontation with the morally relevant values call us, whereas the call of the morally relevant values compels us to examine our conscience and to look at our own person in the light of God, no such call is to be found concerning our own moral goodness. It is very characteristic that our conscience speaks to us first of all to warn us of moral faults and to indicate to us when we have failed. There exists also no positive counterpart to the contrition in which we are directly concerned with our own moral faults, our sins, that is to say, there exists no act in which we would rejoice in our moral perfection.

If the way in which our own values are experienced completely differs in the moral and religious sphere, the reasons that prevent us from a conclusive conviction of being intelligent or highly gifted also assume a new character concerning moral or religious virtues. As we saw before, moral and religious values are not only ordered to objective goods having a value, but they also constitute themselves only in a superactual or actual value-response. They presuppose that we are focused on the morally relevant values and God. This fact requires that we measure all our acting and doing against the background of the call of the morally relevant values and of God, and thus necessarily experience that we are only "useless servants."[14] We are aware of the abyss that separates our responses to the call of the values from the ideal conformity to them, and above all from the infinite goodness of God. We realize our insufficiency, the more we grasp and understand the call of the morally relevant values and the higher we objectively rank morally. The saint is more convinced than any

---

14. [Matthew 25:30. Editor.]

other person of his moral insufficiency because he grasps the call of the morally relevant values in a much deeper way, because he realizes much more that which he could and should do. Therefore, even a conviction of a relative moral goodness is here impossible as long as pride does not intervene.

Moreover, the confrontation of our being and doing with the call of the morally relevant values, and above all with our goal of becoming saints, refers to a moral obligation, whereas in the field of intelligence and great artistic gifts the confrontation with the task to which these gifts are ordered does not imply a moral obligation in the strict sense. We are aware of an insufficiency that does not refer to the "one thing necessary."[15] The parable of the talents in the Gospel refers to the moral and religious sphere. This element of obligation brings about in a completely new way that the consciousness of our insufficiency pervades our conscience necessarily and continuously and frustrates any conviction of being good, even in a relative sense. Living under the sword of divine justice endows every conviction of our moral goodness with awe and makes us speak with the Psalmist: "If you, O Lord, mark iniquities, Lord, who can stand?"[16]

Summarizing, we may say: the analysis of the difference according to the nature and rank of the perfections and values at stake in the first stage of pride, that is, the conviction of possessing a value, has added a new reason for the above-mentioned paradox. The higher a value ranks, the less it is in the normal focal point of consciousness (*Blickfeld!*), and in the case of the moral values of our person, they are invisible as long as we do not look at them. If we try to do this we become the spectator of ourselves and assume a gesture that contradicts the very nature of the value-response attitude.

The higher a value ranks, the more it is impossible to have a conclusive conviction of possessing it because we are confronted with an objective task, and in the case of moral values that are based on our freedom, every consideration of ourselves as being morally good involves pride

---

15. [Luke 10:42. Editor.]
16. [Psalm 130:3. Editor.]

because here the understanding of the call of the morally relevant values and of God necessarily engenders in us the consciousness of our moral insufficiency.

A fifth reason for the aforementioned paradox is that the true moral attitude necessarily implies the consciousness that we may go astray every moment, that we have always to be vigilant not to fall. We can never look at our moral state as something settled and conclusive. As soon as we do so, we fall prey to pride because such false security is a specific outgrowth of pride and is strictly incompatible with the true value-response attitude. In considering ourselves morally stable and immune to any moral fall, we have lost the true understanding of our metaphysical situation, we are no longer aware of our frailty, we live in an illusion into which only our pride can lull us. More than that, in believing ourselves to be morally invulnerable and no longer endangered, in not realizing that we can every moment fall, we have already fallen, and even to a greater extent than the sinner who is aware of his moral insecurity.

Concerning exterior perfections, by contrast, we can consider the possession of beauty, bodily strength, the skill of our hands, the richness of our hair, vivacity of our temperament, as something stable. We do not need to have the consciousness that we can lose them at any moment. In considering their possession as something settled, we do not lose them. The same applies *mutatis mutandis* to such values as intelligence or artistic gifts. Here again we encounter a surprising paradox. All the exterior perfections are as such perishable and of a passing character: an illness, an accident, and above all age can deprive us of them. The same applies analogously to intellectual values. Here, as with respect to the exterior perfections, it depends not upon us whether we lose them or not; an exterior force can deprive us of them. As we received them without our collaboration as pure gifts, we also can lose them without any responsibility on our part.

Only the moral and religious values cannot be taken away from us by any exterior force. Neither age, nor illness, nor any accident, nor any influence, no situation whatsoever can deprive us of moral or religious values. As these values can be acquired only with our collaboration and depend in their very existence on our freedom, they also can never be lost without our responsibility. St. Paul says, "Nothing can separate us from the love of Christ."[17] They are the only values that can as such subsist. But on the other hand, they can also be more easily lost than any other values. Precisely because they depend upon our freedom, they are incomparably more endangered than any other value of the human person. The same reason that makes them inaccessible to any exterior force and thus in principle something that can subsist, notwithstanding all the inevitable changes to which our human life is exposed and the frailty of our existence, requires that we live continuously in the salutary fear of falling. Because they depend upon our freedom, we can remain in conformity with the commandments of God only if we go through our life "in fear and trembling," only if we are constantly aware that we may at any moment go astray. This consciousness of insecurity is the indispensable condition for the objective subsisting of moral and religious values. It is the same paradox that manifests itself in the fact that our weakness is our strength or, as we may put it, that only in realizing our own weakness and seeking our strength exclusively in God are we strong. The very fact that the subsisting depends upon our own freedom makes it necessary that we prepare ourselves against any possibility of falling, that we remain constantly morally awakened, and this again implies that we constantly realize our frailty and weakness.

Moreover, the moral and religious virtues, because they are in a completely new and different way our own, have also a deep and mysterious connection to the continuity of our personal being. They are not only able to subsist and cannot be taken from us by any exterior force, but they are also destined to subsist, they partake in the rhythm of man *in statu viae* to prepare him for his eternal end. They have an inner disposition to subsist and increase until we reach the decisive hour of judgment by God. To fall and lose them also has retroactive importance. As a deep contrition and the pardon of God has the power to do away with all former sins, the fall without contrition as such does away with all the former moral and religious values, it takes away their validity. Moral and

---

17. [Romans 8:38. Editor.]

religious values are so deeply related to the person that the person who falls without contrition loses also all the merit of the moral and religious values she possessed before her fall. The mysterious role of presence and of the final attitude of man shines here. To the penitent thief our Lord said, "Amen, today thou will be in paradise."[18] And all the former moral and religious virtues of the apostate until the last hour will not save him. The difference of the moral and religious values, on the one hand, and all the other values of the person in this respect is obvious. The former intelligence or the former great artistic gift do not become invalid because a stroke or age deprive the person of these perfections. And the former beauty is not rendered invalid because age or illness deprive the person of it. The loss of them has no retroactive character. Moral and religious virtues, on the contrary, always have even objectively a certain provisional character because they are by their very nature directed toward the final state of the soul and imply perseverance in the good as an indispensable condition. They belong to the person on the condition that they subsist until the end. It is very characteristic that the holy Church canonizes no one before his death. Thus, feeling a false security and considering our moral standing as settled is absolutely incompatible with the possession of moral and religious virtue.

The proud man has, as we saw before, no interest in values for their own sake, they are for him mere means for his self-glory. He takes it for granted that the values are something that exalt the man who is endowed with them. Without understanding the true intrinsic importance of them and without the inner disposition to conform to their call for their own sake, he sees in them merely a means to exalt his self-glory and to draw out of them a consciousness of grandeur, of exalted being and superiority. The proud man is therefore interested only in the values of his person, whereas the humble moral man never even looks at his own values but is always concerned with all values on the object side, and in his own moral perfection, for the sake of glorifying God.

The higher the value ranks, the worse is the abuse of them that this approach implies. The beauty of one's own face or the skill of one's own

---

18. [Luke 23:43. Editor.]

hands calls for no response but gratitude because God endowed one with this gift. And even this is not morally necessary. The most perfect attitude is to ignore it or not to be concerned with it at all.[19]

In the case of one's own intellectual values, the response of gratitude toward God is required, but above all the response to the goods on the object side to which this capacity is ordered. In considering one's intelligence as a mere means for one's own superiority, one necessarily considers these goods on the object side as a mere occasion to display one's intelligence and intellectual gifts that convey the consciousness of superiority and grandeur.

Thus, the proud man abuses the values on the object side and the call of them by making out of a high task a mere occasion for self-glorification. Whereas the man who draws his consciousness of superiority out of his exterior perfections does not thereby counteract the call of a value on the object side, the proud man whose object is his intellectual values does so necessarily. As morally bad as any self-glorification is, as immoral as the pride that refers to exterior perfections undoubtedly is, quite apart from its ridiculous and silly character, the refusal to respond to the values on the object side, in the case of the pride referring to intellectual values, adds still a new element of immorality to it and forms thus a graver moral fault.

The following sixth reason refers especially to the most decisive difference in this respect: the difference between the moral and religious values, on the one hand, and all other values of the person, on the other hand.

We have already stressed that whether the possession of a value presupposes the intervention of our freedom or whether it has the character of a pure gift plays an equally decisive role concerning the nature of the respective pride. We have now to inquire into the reason for the specific paradox that pride about something that objectively implies merit on

---

19. This already explains why the relishing and self-glorifying in moral or religious values is the worst kind of this pride. But apart from that, an analysis of the difference concerning the situation that obtains with respect to exterior perfections, to intellectual values, and finally to moral and religious values, will reveal clearly the increasing abuse.

our part is worse than pride referring to values for which we are in no way responsible. The paradox reaches here its climax. To exalt ourselves in values of our own person for the existence of which we are responsible seems much more reasonable than doing so with respect to values that are a pure gift. Still, the pride of the Pharisee is obviously morally much worse than any other pride, with the exception of the satanic one.

Precisely because God has granted man the ineffable privilege of freedom and of a free spontaneous conforming to the morally relevant values and to Christ, self-glorification is an incomparably greater abuse than in all the cases in which the glorification refers to values that are pure gifts and in which the self-glorification is an obvious stupidity. The more God exalts us, the worse it would be for us to relinquish the attitude of *religio* and the humble confrontation with God. The more God calls us to collaborate with Him, the worse it is when we glorify ourselves and want to feel superior and grand. The greater the generosity of God, the worse it is when, instead of understanding the call for humility that this condescendence implies, we glorify ourselves. Because the moral and religious values implying our freedom are objectively much more our own and reach into another depth of our being, the poison of pride in the self-glorification penetrates our person to a greater degree. This refers not only to the degree of penetration but equally to the quality of our pride. The Pharisee is much prouder than the man who glorifies himself because of his intelligence, and all the more so than the man who is proud because of his exterior perfections. The very fact that he understands that moral and religious values confer on a man a greater glory than any other values reveals that his thirst for grandeur, exalted being, and superiority is much deeper, much more serious, much more refined. The glory of exterior perfections and even of a genius does not satisfy him. He aspires to a more substantial self-glory.

And his pride has thus a much more dangerous character, it is a deeper and greater degree of pride, approaching satanic pride much more than pride referring to the other values. It is in some way an analogy to the difference between the satanic type, who already sees in every value as such and in its mysterious metaphysical power a detraction from and an impediment to his self-glory, and the man whose pride is satisfied by exterior power, influence, and domination of other persons. The Pharisee is not satisfied with being considered as good and honorable by his fellow man, he wants to take delight in being glorious in the eyes of God, he aspires to a deeper metaphysical self-glory. He does not yet want to dethrone God as Lucifer and, in an analogous way, the satanic type of pride does, but he already wants to use being pleasing to God for his self-glory. The higher the aspiration for self-glory reaches, the worse the pride is morally, the deeper the perversion in our relation to God and the reign of values. Finally, we must state that the higher a value of the person ranks, the more a participation in the reign of values and in God is at stake. The value-response attitude underlying the moral and *a fortiori* the religious values makes us, as it were, into citizens in the city of God and lets us in some way share in the sovereignty and freedom of the world above us. Already, the great artist is in some way in his creative process elevated to "giving birth" in beauty, as Plato says, elevated above himself.[20] But in freely conforming to the morally relevant values and above all in the charity of the saint, this being elevated above ourselves and sharing in the freedom of the children of God is still incomparably more obvious.

To abuse this sublime and humble sovereignty in using it as a means of self-glory is obviously a much deeper form of pride and a specifically horrible attitude. It is a betrayal, and in somewhat an analogous gesture to the sin against the Holy Spirit; it is a sin against the mercy of God. The more God grants us elevation and a share in His sovereignty, the worse the perversion of pride.

We see thus why pride assumes a worse character the higher the values rank to which it refers; and the more our freedom is involved, the more the values are our own and the less stupid and superficial it is to be proud of them. This paradox is no longer surprising; when we analyze the problem in more detail, it even ceases to be a paradox. The higher our own personal value ranks, the more, in a higher and deeper sense, the element of a

---

20. [Plato, *Symposium* (206b7–8, e5), Editor.]

gift of God becomes obvious. Freedom itself is a much more sublime gift of God, much more surpassing the realm of impersonal creatures than any exterior perfection and even intelligence. And concerning the religious virtues, the character of an unmerited gift reveals itself in an incomparably higher sense, grace being essentially a *donum gratis datum* (gift freely given). But the analysis of this apparent paradox has revealed to us many essential features of the type of pride that we called self-complaisance[21], as well as essential features of pride in general. This shall allow us to understand the full impact of this primary root of moral evil.

III.viii. *Static and Dynamic Pride*

Apart from the determination of the nature of pride by the rank of the value to which it refers and by the role that the freedom of the person plays in the possession of this value, pride also differs greatly according to whether it has a static or dynamic character.

We saw already above that the vain man in the strict sense differs from the ambitious man insofar as the vain man relishes his own perfection that he believes he possesses, whereas the ambitious man craves always some new nourishment for his consciousness of grandeur. The vain man believes himself to be grand; the ambitious man wants to become it. General elements must be distinguished here. Firstly, the vain man believes himself to be grand, admirable, extraordinary and does not thirst for more because he believes himself already to possess everything that he needs to be grand. By contrast, the ambitious man does not necessarily believe himself to be already grand, but he wants to become so and believes he is able to become superior. Secondly, the vain man has an ethos of bourgeois, satiated, static relishing in his grandeur, whereas the ambitious has a tense, insatiable drive to climb higher and higher. Even when he has attained a certain degree of apparent grandeur, he will always strive for more. But the principal difference between static pride and dynamic pride, which are typically manifested in the vain man and

---

21. [Hildebrand uses the term to refer to pride concerning moral and religious values. However, it does not appear in his previous analysis of pride included in this edition. Editor.]

the ambitious man, respectively, is a general distinction in all forms of pride, without necessarily implying other characteristics that are proper to the vain, on the one hand, and to the ambitious man, on the other hand. Satanic pride is essentially dynamic as it aspires to a grandeur and sovereignty that it can never attain and that implies a gesture of impotency. As the thirst for grandeur of satanic pride tends toward the absolute and infinite, it is essentially insatiable.

But the difference between static and dynamic pride applies also to self-complaisance, and both dimensions are to be found in the realm of this type of pride. The Pharisee is not only convinced of his glory in the eyes of God, but he also wants to climb always higher, he rejoices in the unworthiness of his fellow man in order always to feel himself higher. He does not have the smiling self-satisfaction of the vain, but the insatiable driven ethos of the ambitious. But there exists also a mere static type of pride concerning moral and religious values. It is found in the man who is completely satisfied with his moral perfection and his piety, who rejoices in every situation for how well he behaved, who naïvely always speaks in some way about himself, who refers to his moral excellence but has no thirst to climb higher and no hard and hostile ethos.

The same difference is to be found in the pride concerning intellectual values. There exists the man who believes he is a genius but who nevertheless is not satisfied with the grandeur he draws out of this conviction. He wants to excel more and more, not only concerning exterior success and reputation but also in the consciousness of his own intellectual standards. On the other hand, the self-satisfied type also exists in this sphere, the one who thinks himself to be so great that there is no need to climb higher.

The same applies even to the pride that refers to exterior perfections. On the one hand, we find the person who relishes the beauty of her face, thinking herself to be incomparable to others, satisfied with the superiority that she draws out of that, without an insatiable thirst for more. On the other hand, we find the ambitious type who, though convinced of her beauty, nevertheless always lives in unrest, in fear that someone could be more beautiful, have more success, fearing to lose her beauty, eager to increase it.

This difference, the static and the dynamic, are two general dimensions of pride and pervade the whole scale of the different values to which pride can refer. And this difference deeply affects the nature and quality of pride. A different general ethos manifests itself according to whether the one or the other dimension prevails, and the dynamic type is generally a more dangerous type of pride. The question arises whether the dynamic type is not necessarily such that he does not restrict his pride to a certain sphere of his personal values or, as we may put it, that *a fortiori* he will not be satisfied with the possession of lower values because his insatiable thirst for grandeur pushes him forward not only with respect to the degree and amount of a certain value but also concerning the superior grandeur that only a higher-ranking value can convey on him.

It must be said: it is true that the dynamic type is formally more directed toward grandeur as such and that the very nature of his pride tends to seek always a higher degree of grandeur. He will not only aspire for exterior perfections but also try to be in every respect above the others, and will resent it if he finds anybody who is superior in one or the other respect. Nevertheless, it also may be that he does not crave the possession of values that he does not consider indispensable means for his grandeur. He may, for instance, ignore moral values and consider them as negligible for his consciousness of grandeur and superiority. The man who craves being intelligent and superior in this respect to all other men may, for instance, not care for a consciousness of moral superiority because moral values seem to him no real basis for superiority and grandeur. He is so blind to them that he does not grasp the metaphysical power connected to them. Unlike the satanic type, he does not want to dethrone them, but he considers them as a concern for lesser, limited persons; he believes himself to be above them. He is too much fascinated by the values that he considers the basis of grandeur and that he believes himself to possess, or at least able to acquire, to care for moral values. Thus, we must say, though the dynamic type of pride has a general tendency not to limit himself to one inferior type of values and not to thirst only for an ever higher degree of one type of values but also for a superiority in every respect, there exist also dynamic types who exclude certain higher values from their striving for grandeur and superiority.

Understanding that dynamic pride is always worse than the static one is what matters from the moral point of view. Not only because it is a higher degree of pride, aspiring for higher grandeur, but also because of the general ethos that it determines. As we saw, the dynamic type has a tense, insatiably driven ethos that implies a hostile attitude against his fellow man and forms a typical antithesis to charity. People who have this type of pride are laden with rivalry, envy, and even hatred. Their insatiable thirst for grandeur and superiority closes their heart to any compassion, generosity, and charity, whereas the static type may have a certain generosity and compassion as long as he feels himself not threatened or hurt in the relishing of his own perfection. We shall analyze later on the nature of the dynamic pride when we shall inquire into the roots of hatred, envy, and malicious joy. For the moment it may suffice to state that besides the role of the rank of values and of the three stages of pride (the conviction of our perfection, the relishing of it, and the self-glorification) for the nature and the moral impact of pride, whether pride has a dynamic or static character is also of paramount importance.

III.ix. *Conceit*

We have now to examine the following factors determining the nature of pride in the realm of the pride that refers directly to our own person.

Firstly, we must distinguish whether the value that forms the object of our pride really inheres in the person or whether the object of our pride is a mere illusion. Not only persons who really are handsome are vain and convinced of their beauty but also persons who are in no way beautiful. This is the man whom we characterize as conceited. He takes it for granted that he possesses a certain perfection, though there is no objective reason for doing so. How many people believe themselves to be intelligent or gifted in certain ways when in reality they lack intelligence or the particular gift! Someone believes he is a great painter or a great poet or a great musician though in reality he is lacking any artistic capacity. Or someone thinks he is more intelligent than his fellow man, he relishes his intelligence, but he speaks and judges without any competency. He believes himself to penetrate and understand every problem, though he is in reality shallow, stupid, and deprived of real intellectual power.

This conceited type of pride is specifically stupid and ridiculous. But from the moral point of view the conceited man is less dangerous than the man who bases his pride on a real perfection. As repulsive as this type is for us because of his ridiculous illusion, from the moral point of view the abuse of being endowed with a value is not found. Pride and static self-satisfaction have the effect of blinding us to reality. Because we want to be beautiful, intelligent, elegant, or gifted, we fool ourselves unconsciously into believing that we possess these perfections. Our self-satisfaction is such that we are not able to grasp reality. But this pride, because it refers to merely imaginary perfections, has a less serious character. The man who abuses the possession of authentic values by considering them as mere means to his grandeur and superiority is more responsible because he is at least able to grasp a real value and, nevertheless, instead of gratitude to God in the case of exterior perfections or of the consciousness of his insufficiency with respect to the tasks to which his capacities are ordered in the case of intellectual values, he turns back to himself and uses these values as means to his grandeur. The conceited man who glorifies himself in imaginary perfection, by contrast, is already disabled by his naïve self-satisfaction from distinguishing the presence of a real value. This pride, though obviously immoral as such, as any pride, above all affects his intelligence and his capacity to grasp reality, and renders him more ridiculous than wicked. The more we are confronted with real values, the more we have really received a gift from God's bounty, the worse and more serious is the attitude of pride.

III.x. *The Pharisee*

But here we must make a distinction in order to avoid a misunderstanding. Self-glorification based on something that in reality does not exist, does not always assume the character of the conceited type whom we have just characterized. The Pharisee glorifies himself also in moral and religious values that, as we saw before, are destroyed by his pride and that cannot come into existence on the basis of this proud attitude. But he obviously differs from the conceited man.

This difference is based on the fact that he does not naïvely presume to take his moral and religious standard for granted, though he is in reality immoral. On the contrary, he glorifies himself in a pseudo-morality, in the fact that he conforms *de facto* to the commandments of the moral law but in a merely exterior way and with a wrong motive. It is not as with the stupid man who believes himself to be intelligent, a mere illusion, but it is a morality the soul of which is destroyed, a pseudo-morality, not a merely illusionary one. And conforming to this basic difference, the Pharisee differs completely from the conceited type in his ethos, aside from the role of the values in question.

The Pharisee, as someone who is completely dominated by pride, can obviously never possess true moral and religious values. He glorifies himself *a fortiori* always in non-existent values, in contradistinction to the man who is proud about intellectual values or exterior perfections.[22]

Nevertheless, he clearly differs from the conceited man, who takes his perfections simply for granted, though they do not exist in reality, because he refers himself to an apparent or a pseudo-morality. His whole ethos manifests this difference. A hardheartedness, a dynamic character of his pride, a dark hideous note, rejoicing in the inferiority of his fellow man, a disposition to envy and hatred, characterize the Pharisee, whereas the conceited man in no way necessarily possesses this ethos. There even exist cases of conceitedness that are restricted to the first stage of pride, that is, the simple presumption of being beautiful or intelligent without relishing it or glorifying themselves in it. The conceited type who takes his moral perfection for granted is the type whose pride frustrates his self-knowledge, the man who is not aware of his moral faults and failures, who lives in the illusion of being faultless. Imprisoned in his pride,

---

22. It must be stressed that this applies only to the type who is predominantly determined by pride. As mentioned above, we are not yet dealing with the cases in which a value-response attitude coexists with pride. This shall be our concern later on.

everything appears to him different as soon as his own person is at stake; he is the man to whom the word of our Lord applies: "Why do you see the speck in your brother's eye, and yet do not consider the beam in your own eye."[23]

But he does not glorify himself in his morality. He is the naïve egoist whose pride blinds him to the faults of his own person. In order to glorify himself he must have an interest in adorning himself with moral values and the acquisition of a pseudo-morality. This is then no longer the conceited type but the Pharisee.

III.xi. *Pride Referring to Disvalues*

The object of pride is not only a real or imaginary value but sometimes also qualities that convey no superiority or grandeur whatsoever. We mentioned already the childish pride about a beautiful moustache or tallness of stature. These perfections are obviously too unimportant to draw any consciousness of grandeur out of them. It is presupposed that one has a childish and ridiculous mind if one is proud about such secondary items. But sometimes we find persons who glorify themselves over their effectiveness in actions associated with outspoken disvalues. A thief may be proud about the slyness and ruthlessness with which he succeeds in his stealing. Another man may be proud of his hardheartedness, that no man will succeed in moving him or receiving any almsgiving from him. His attitude appears to him as a virile strength, a realistic sense, being immune against any trap, any being fooled. That which is in reality a moral disvalue appears to him as a symptom of his superiority, and thus he glorifies himself in it. The well-known type of an adolescent who feels himself great and superior because he has no reverence for anything, because he refuses to admit any obligation, because of his apparent independence and virility, though he copies in a ridiculous way certain persons who incarnate his ideal of independence and depends in reality completely upon this "ideal," is another typical example of this form of

---

23. [Matthew 7:3. Editor.]

pride. Dostoevsky has described this type in a masterly way in Kolya Krasotkin in *The Brothers Karamazov*.

Another may pride himself in how many hearts he has broken, how many immoral relations he has had, whereby the quantity plays an important role in constituting his consciousness of superiority and grandeur. Another man again will glorify himself in his "realistic" mentality that does not care for sentimentality (whereby he in reality means charity, compassion), that shuns every romanticism (whereby he means the reign of beauty and aesthetic values), in a word, who glories in his unsusceptibility to certain moral and aesthetic values even if what he terms "realistic" means in reality to be a mere bureaucrat or a *banausos*. There is no doubt that there exists a form of pride in which the consciousness of grandeur and superiority is drawn out of elements that are no values whatsoever but, on the contrary, outspoken disvalues. Certainly, the disvalue as such is not the formal object of pride but some quantitative element connected to it, some idol, or some technical efficiency or some conventional standard. We have now to inquire into the nature of this pride and its rank on the scale of moral evil.

Consider cases such as the adolescent craving independence, the Don Juan, or German *Corpstudent* who prides himself in his illusionary "honor" and "virility," and does not allow anybody to look down on him, always eager to show off his power to dominate.[24] In such cases the proud person bases his consciousness of grandeur on an idol which is itself already a mere outgrowth of his pride. It is not an abuse of a real value, a turning back to oneself, but the conviction that such qualities invest him with any grandeur is already a result of his pride. He is suffused by pride to such an extent that he is unable to understand that only real values can objectively invest us with glory, that a mysterious metaphysical power is found in moral values. He believes that he can find the grandeur and superiority in such things that are in themselves only the result of pride. He does not consider the values that his fellow man who is not proud considers to be an objective good for himself, to be advantageous for his

---

24. ["Corps students" were members of the German student fraternities called "corps." Editor.]

pride, but he seeks to satisfy his pride in such things that are important only in relation to his pride and he aspires to grandeur and superiority in a more direct way.

The following marks characterize this form of pride: firstly, it has always a dynamic character. There is no satisfaction with that which one possesses; he wants always to increase in his grandeur. Secondly, the ethos is specifically hard, tense, and laden with a hostile attitude toward one's fellow man and an irreverence toward the reign of morally relevant values. It is not yet the satanic metaphysical rebellion and *ressentiment* against the values and God. Acting against the call of the values is not the source of their proud satisfaction; they do not attempt to dethrone them. They glory in an idol such as independence, virility, efficiency in evildoing, and ignore the morally relevant values as something valid only for lesser minds. The case of the adolescent who glories in his independence, in his irreverence and impertinence, apparently has the greatest affinity with the satanic type, but is, in fact, utterly different from the satanic type by his childish and unserious character. He only plays the role of satanic pride, but he does not really possess it. He is in reality unsure of himself, immature, and wants to conceal his inferiority complex. He does not grasp the metaphysical power of values and does not attempt to dethrone them, but he speaks and behaves as if he would despise them, and he does this only in order to show off his independence. He moves still in a social order and not in the metaphysical one as the satanic type does.

We must further distinguish whether the motive for their evildoing as such is pride. The one who glories in his slyness and his skill in stealing does not steal in order to glorify himself, but rather because of his concupiscence. The self-glorification is thus more accidental, and he cannot be considered as a type who is completely dominated by pride. Self-glorification is not the center of his preoccupation. The same applies to the man who glories in his hardheartedness. On the other hand, he reveals in his cynical attitude toward moral and morally relevant values a complete absence of the value-response attitude. As far as his pride is concerned, he is not as evil as the Pharisee; as far as his general attitude toward the reign of morally relevant values is concerned, he is worse than the Pharisee. He is so indifferent toward the morally relevant values that he even glories in doing something morally evil.

His glorying in his technical efficiency in performing immoral actions adds a moral disvalue to the immorality of stealing as such. And this moral disvalue is again twofold. Firstly, the morally negative value of self-glorification as such and, secondly, the profligacy manifesting itself in the degree and kind of bluntness toward the morally relevant values. Whereas the normal thief, in his being dominated by concupiscence, simply ignores the morally relevant values and has a more obtuse bluntness toward them, the one who prides himself in the efficiency of his stealing discloses a new, cynical indifference toward them. The same applies to the Don Juan, who glories in the large number of broken hearts, in the success of his impure life.

In the case of the stingy egoist who glories in his imperturbability and insensitivity to the misery of his fellow man, which he regards as self-control, an ability to resist, being shrewd enough in order not to be fooled and so on, again pride is not the motive of his stinginess and his egoistic lack of charity. Rather, this is conditioned by concupiscence. But by glorying in his evil attitude he adds, in contradistinction to the blunt egoist who does not pride himself in it, the aforementioned twofold disvalue: the negative value of self-glorification as such, and the profligacy of a new and worse type of indifference toward the morally relevant values. It is a more conscious and outspoken indifference, a more radical and more outspoken antithesis to the *religio*.

But these three types need not be primarily dominated by pride. Above all they need not be possessed by dynamic pride. We find a combination of pride and concupiscence in them whereby concupiscence obviously is the predominant factor. On the other hand, the value-response attitude has been extinguished in them in a certain respect to a greater extent than in the Pharisee, a fact that is manifested in their self-glorification because of something evil.

A completely different situation is to be found in the cases in which someone glories in an evil idol. We think of the idol of a pseudo-virility (which is in reality a proud master-position) or of the idol of the master-morality.[25] Here the idol itself is already an outgrowth of pride that has an affinity with satanic pride. A predominant role of pride is here presupposed and also a dynamic one. In sum, we may say that the nature of pride referring to something morally negative completely differs according to the different cases.

The fact that the self-glorification refers to elements that are intimately connected to moral disvalues does not determine a homogenous type of pride. Sometimes the role of pride is secondary, sometimes it is fully presupposed as in the case of an idol, sometimes it has the character of an unserious and immature copy of the satanic type. But pride is always characteristically different when the self-glorification is based on apparent values or on true values, as in the case of the Pharisee or of intellectual pride.

III.xii. *Pride Referring to the Absence of One's Personal Values*

Pride does not manifest itself only in the three aforementioned stages: the conviction of possessing a perfection, the relishing of this value, and self-glorification. It manifests itself also, as we saw before when we discussed the dynamic dimension of pride, in the thirst for acquiring values that convey to us the consciousness of grandeur and "exalted being." Moreover, it manifests itself also in the attitude concerning the experience of a lack of perfections and values. There exists also the proud man who, unlike the conceited man, is fully aware that he is ugly, not intelligent, or at least less intelligent than his fellow man, that he is lacking certain gifts and talents. The way in which he reacts to his insufficiency is very characteristic of the nature of his pride. But because of his thirst for grandeur and superiority, his inferiority will always be unbearable for him, and he will never simply accept it. We have now to inquire into his different reactions.

25.[Notoriously, in his *Genealogy of Morals* and elsewhere, Nietzsche opposes the supposedly genuine, authentic "Herrenmoral" to the servile "Sklavenmoral." Unlike Nietzsche, Hildebrand uses this term as a title for a specific moral idol. Editor.]

The first distinguishing factor here is the question of which values he considers the source of grandeur and superiority, and, accordingly, which kind of insufficiency hurts him most. The higher his aspiration for grandeur, the more he will crave the possession of higher values and, consequently, the more the consciousness of being deprived of the source of his grandeur will hurt him.

The person who resents above all her small figure or her ugliness has a lower aspiration than the one who resents his intellectual inferiority. What we stated concerning the nature of the pride of self-glorification through the possession of values applies to the *ressentiment* based on one's insufficiency. We abstract here from the various inferiority complexes that obviously also presuppose the intervention of pride. This much more innocent form of reaction to one's own insufficiency shall be examined later on as it presupposes neither a predominance of pride in general nor the absence of a true value-response attitude in general. It belongs, rather, to the vast field of coexistence of pride and the value-response attitude that we mentioned at the beginning as the state of a struggle between both. It occurs also in the man who may have a predominant value-response attitude that however did not yet penetrate his whole personality and did not overcome pride in every *Schlupfwinkel* (hidden place) of his being. It applies to the situation of the normal morally good man who is not yet a saint.

The question arises whether the absence of moral values also may hurt pride. Does there exist a counterpart to the Pharisee, that is, someone who is hurt in his pride because of his immorality, as the pride of the Pharisee revels in his moral glory? This seems impossible as this immorality is a result of one's perverted will. To resent one's immorality because one cannot make it an object of self-glorification presupposes the aspiration to the glory of a pseudo-morality, and this would mean that one strives for this pseudo-morality as the Pharisee does. Immorality is not an imperfection that we cannot change, unlike a lack of intelligence or the ugliness of our face.

The satanic type aspires to metaphysical grandeur and sees in moral values as such a rival. He thus wants not to possess them but to dethrone them and to deprive them of their intrinsic metaphysical power. He hates every man who possesses moral values, but he does not want to glorify himself in them. He has declared war on God, on all the moral and morally relevant values, and seeks a metaphysical grandeur by dethroning the values.

The Pharisee, on the contrary, wants to glorify himself through the possession of moral and religious values, and although he deceives himself since it is only with a pseudo-morality that he can possess this attitude, he nevertheless believes himself to be good and adorned with moral glory. He will resent any confrontation with a person of a high moral standard and react with hatred and envy when he is confronted with his own inferiority. But he is obviously not the man who, conscious of his immorality, is hurt in his pride by this insufficiency. The man who ignores the call of moral values because of his concupiscent pride will not look at it as an insufficiency that wounds his pride. He will not consider it an inferiority.

In sum, we may say: whereas the absence of every other perfection may hurt the pride of a man who is primarily dominated by pride, the absence of moral values will not hurt him. The only type of proud person who aspires to grandeur by adorning himself with moral values is the Pharisee. And the Pharisee believes himself to be morally good. Only in being confronted with a person possessing a high moral standard will he respond with envy, hatred, and the desire to minimize the virtues of his rival. He may even subconsciously resent his objective inferiority compared with his fellow man but without admitting even to himself his inferiority.

We have now to examine the different ways of reacting to the consciousness of inferiority. Firstly, we have the proud man who is bitter and hardened by the fact that he is ugly, deprived of certain gifts, inefficient, or unintelligent. To be inferior is unbearable for him, and the absence of certain values and perfections incites his dynamic pride. He has envy and a hostile attitude toward his fellow man. His ethos is even more poisonous and virulent than the ethos of the man who glories in his grandeur and feels he is the *beatus possidens*.[26] It obviously is much more dangerous than the static pride of the vain man who relishes his glory and is satisfied with that which he possesses. But he even surpasses with respect to the hard, bitter character of his ethos the dynamic type who glories in his values.

Obviously, the pride manifesting itself in resenting one's own imperfections and the pride manifesting itself in the glorification of one's own values are mostly found in one and the same person. Although they feature two types of reactions to two different objects, they grow from one and the same root. Thus we examined them in different types in which the one or the other prevails according to the situation with which the person is confronted.

The proud man who glories in his perfections and values will necessarily find it unbearable to feel inferior and lack some perfection only if he considers this perfection indispensable for his consciousness of grandeur and superiority. But notwithstanding this fact, there is a different note in the pride manifesting itself because of an insufficiency, and the pride of self-glorification. For it is only in the former case that pride engenders envy, hatred, and *ressentiment*.

There are two main ways in which the proud man may react to the consciousness of his own inferiority. The first is a desperate effort to acquire the perfections he lacks and a hostile attitude toward those people who appear to him to be his superior. Envy, jealousy, and hatred of those people will arise in him. He is at war with everybody whom he believes to be superior. He will not admit that the others are superior to him but, rather, will minimize their value and always seek to find some imperfections in them. He will slander them. An inner interest, an embittered approach to the world, and a rebellious attitude against providence characterize this man. He has a spirit of contention toward God.

The second type of reaction is the attitude of *ressentiment* that has

---

26. [The phrase "blessed those who possess" originally refers to a legal principle. Whoever owns a thing has an advantage. For example, in a dispute over ownership, it is not the owner but the person claiming the thing who must prove his right. Editor.]

been analyzed in the work of Max Scheler.[27] It is the attempt to overcome one's own inferiority by minimizing or devaluing the values that one's fellow man possesses and that one does not possess. The notion of *ressentiment* was originally introduced by Nietzsche.

If one is ugly, he will declare that exterior beauty is an effeminate concern of lesser people, a mere appeal to sexuality, or that beauty is something completely relative, depending upon the subjective taste of an individual. If he is less gifted, he will pretend that these gifts that he does not possess are useless and despicable. If he is not gifted for philosophy, he will declare this kind of intelligence to be the enemy of vitality—a symptom of a destructive attitude, as for instance the Nazi concept of "*Intelligenzbestie.*"[28] But above all he will try to replace true morality with certain idols, such as the master-morality, or with the theory that all moral values are merely relative, conditioned by a certain society.

It is the insidious, hideous attempt to do away with superiority of one's fellow man by undermining, so to speak, the values at stake and creating a new standard of pseudo-values that deprive one's fellow man of his superiority. This process of undermining is a half-conscious one, and the ensuing deception is partly a self-deception. It is not a simple conscious calumny. Calumny is a conscious lie, spreading rumors about moral faults of our fellow man in order to wrong him by destroying his reputation. This may satisfy, to a certain extent, the first type of pride. The *ressentiment* type could not be satisfied by a mere exterior dethroning of the superiority of his rival. Destroying his social image does not quench his aspiration to do away with the superiority that is unbearable for his pride. He wants to undermine it in a deeper way. By replacing true values with a scale of pseudo-values, he wants even in his own eyes to deprive the other of his superiority. *Ressentiment* is obviously a still deeper and morally worse type of pride. It approaches the satanic type. But what still distinguishes it from the satanic type is that its dethroning of values

---

27. The notion of *ressentiment* was originally introduced by Nietzsche. Scheler in his work *Das Ressentiment im Aufbau der Moralen* has refuted Nietzsche's application of *ressentiment* to Christianity and deepened the notion of *ressentiment*.

28. [A swear word invented in Nazi propaganda with the purpose of defaming, among the "*Volksgenossen,*" leftist and Jewish intellectuals. Editor.]

refers to one's fellow man, whereas the satanic type already sees in values as such an unbearable injury to his grandeur, that he tries in an impotent gesture to tear away from values their metaphysical power. The satanic *ressentiment* is of a metaphysical order. The person possessed by it not only hates the good man and tries to deprive him of his superiority by reversing the moral order, but she also hates values themselves, she wants to destroy them as such, she wants ultimately to dethrone God.

Thus we see that the typical *ressentiment* type, though analogous to the satanic type, is not as bad as this ultimate wickedness, because it restricts its dethroning of values to the human order and does so in order to do away with one's inferiority. By contrast, the satanic type hates the light as such, and sees in every value a rival, and wants ultimately to dethrone God.

In sum, we may say that there are two main ways in which people dominated by pride in their fundamental attitude may react to the insufficiency of themselves and to the superiority of other persons. Firstly, one may react with a deep rancor, a poisonous unrest and irritation, an open hostility to the superior fellow man, manifesting itself in jealousy, envy, hatred. In this attitude we find an attempt to do away with the superiority of one's fellow man by denying that he really possesses the values in question, to slander him, to deprive him of these values.

Secondly, there is the much worse reaction of *ressentiment* in which one attempts to do away with one's own inferiority and the superiority of the other by attempting to reverse the order of values. One does not deny that the other really possesses these perfections, but one denies that they are values. One discredits not only the individual person of the rival but also the values themselves. One goes a step further and proceeds in a much more insidious and perfidious way. This *ressentiment* type approaches satanic pride, with the difference being that the *ressentiment* in satanic pride displays itself in the metaphysical order and thus goes yet a step further. Moreover, satanic pride is a more conscious war with the reign of moral values and God; it relishes every moral evil as a weapon in the attempt to dethrone God, expressing the pure hatred of God.

The reaction that is called "inferiority complex" will be treated when we deal with the role of pride in the cases in which pride does not predominate but coexists with a predominant value-response attitude.

III.xiii. *Pride Referring to Exterior Goods*

We do not need to explore in detail how the pride of self-glorification displays itself in the field of our different activities. All the distinctions we made concerning this dimension of pride in the field of one's own personal values apply also to the glory that this pride draws out of the perfection in the accomplishment of any activity. As soon as an activity is such that its accomplishment may allow the predication of a perfection, and thus may invest us with some excellence, it can become an object of self-glorification for this pride.

We find here again all the analogous distinctions concerning the nature of pride according to the rank of the value that is abused for our self-glorification, the distinction of the three stages, as well as the distinction of the static and dynamic character of pride. We shall examine later on and in more detail the way in which pride displays itself in the field of our activities when we analyze the role of pride in the man who is not predominatly determined by pride, that is, pride as a factor in every human being.

We now have to inquire into the role of pride concerning goods on the object side that represent a new field of pride and obviously imply completely new problems. We have hereby to examine, firstly, which kinds of goods are an object of pride and, secondly, to which dimension of pride the different goods appeal. Obviously, this will include the role not only of the different positive goods but also of their respective evils. Firstly, we have to state that all goods possessing a morally relevant value, as the life of other persons, the dignity of man, the conversion of a fellow man, a just social order, the rights of our fellow man, mean nothing to pride. Or, as we may put it, the value as such of any good outside of our own person is for pride either a scandal or something indifferent, depending on the nature of the good and on the specific dimension of pride. Insofar as they have a value they can never positively appeal to pride, but they may do so because of another kind of importance that they may simultaneously have. The just social order may interest the pride that seeks its satisfaction in exterior power, not insofar as it possesses a value but as a means to come to power. Obviously, this pride abuses this good, it has no sincere interest in this good as such; to become an advocate for it is a mere strategy on the part of the person possessed by this type of pride in order to acquire power. Or the intellectual values of a relative—a child, a husband, and so on—may appeal to the vain because he considers his relatives an extension of his own person. The same applies to certain types of the pride of self-glorification. We have thus to eliminate all the goods endowed with a morally relevant value from our analysis, insofar as their value as such is concerned.

Firstly, we shall examine the sphere of subjectively satisfying goods. The agreeable: good food, sexual pleasure, things that make our life comfortable, amusement, all that which, as we saw, plays such a predominant role as an object of concupiscence, does not appeal to pride. It may become an object of pride only in an indirect way, as a symbol of something else. Not the enjoyment of the pleasure that good food conveys but the fact that one has exquisite cuisine at home may become an object of pride—as a symbol of one's distinction, of one's high social standing. It refers, then, not so much to what we eat ourselves but, rather, to what we are able to offer to our guests. It may eventually also refer to our own meal insofar as it conveys to us the consciousness that only the best is good enough for such outstanding people as we are.

For a king it may have been an object of pride to have the best cook, and he may have resented the idea of another king or even another less distinguished person having a better one. Excellent cuisine assumes, then, the character of a symbol of one's grandeur. The dimension of pride in question is thus the craving for exterior lordship or vanity. For satanic pride, for the Pharisee, and for haughtiness, it means nothing. Eventually, it may appeal also to certain forms of self-glorification.

The same applies to exterior comfort. It does not appeal as such to pride, but as a symbol of an exterior splendor and grandeur it may become an object of vanity and of certain kinds of self-glorification.

A specific element of supremacy is the presumption obvious to them that as such important people as they believe themselves to be, they may arrogate to themselves always that which is most comfortable. This supremacy may also be found in the haughty, not so much with respect to craving the comfortable, but with respect to their obviously deserved arrogation of these things—a consciousness that one has an indisputable right to claim them for oneself.

In sum, we may say that subjectively satisfying goods, as far as the specifically agreeable and the comfortable are concerned, only indirectly appeal to a certain dimension of pride when the possession of them functions as a symbol or a manifestation of one's own grandeur. The dimensions of pride to which they may appeal in this way are vanity, the craving for exterior lordship, and, in a modified way, haughtiness.

Other subjectively satisfying goods, for instance, elegant clothes or jewels, appeal in a more direct way to a certain vanity. Vanity is drawn to their character as adornments of our exterior appearance, increasing our elegance or beauty, insofar as it is directed to exterior perfections. We do not want to relish the naïve and innocent enjoyment of the charm of beautiful vestments and jewels but rather have interest in them as means for increasing our own beauty, a manifestation of the gesture of self-adornment. These goods then play a disproportionate role in our life. Our thoughts and our will center on them and blunt our regard for higher goods.

Amusement: a party, a game, a sensational movie or detective novel, chatting with other persons, have as such no appeal to pride. The game may become an object of pride insofar as we can manifest, in playing it well, our superiority. It may not have this function because of its specific game-character, the unserious relaxing element that appeals to concupiscence, but has it insofar as excelling in it flatters our vanity, our pride of self-glorification, our ambitious craving for exterior lordship. It forms thus no new problem with respect to the general role of any activity in which we can manifest our superiority.

A party may appeal to pride not because of its amusing character but as an occasion for the vain man to expose his beauty, to display his intelligence and to receive admiration, or for self-glorification by manifesting his superiority and engendering admiration or enthusiasm in his fellow man.

Sexual pleasure as such does not appeal to pride. But the domination of other persons in a sexual relation, the success in fascinating other persons, or the quantity of one's victims may appeal to the pride of self-glorification and even to the pride of craving exterior lordship.

It is always the same picture. Everything that is primarily an object of concupiscence may become indirectly, from another point of view, an object of pride. Here we touch a specific mark of pride in general that manifests itself also in the role of pride in the life of every human being (which we shall examine later on). Everything can be abused by pride: whether it is a good possessing a high value or something merely subjectively satisfying, it can become an object of our pride. Pride is a poison that may infect and pervert the relation to everything. But this does not efface the difference between the immediate and specific object of pride and the goods that may only indirectly become an object of pride while they as such appeal to concupiscence or even only to the true value-response attitude.

Before turning to other groups of goods in order to examine their role in different dimensions of pride, we must state the following: possession as such, independently of the content of what we possess, is always an object of pride. To possess something that belongs to us, that we are free to dispose of according to our arbitrary mood, includes a master-position that appeals to pride. While the concupiscent man cares more for the content of what he possesses, pride finds in the very fact of the ownership as such a satisfaction. Or, as we may put it, the concupiscent man relishes the ownership of something insofar as he wants as much as possible of that thing for himself; his concupiscence implies the greedy gesture of appropriation, to lay his hand on it, whereas the proud man relishes the ownership insofar as it gives him the consciousness of a master-position. The dimensions of pride to which ownership appeals are the craving for exterior lordship and haughtiness. For satanic pride it does not mean much; the master-position resulting from ownership as such is far below its aspirations. For the Pharisee or any form of self-glorification, it also does not mean much. The formal nature of ownership appeals not to vanity but only the aforementioned fact that the possession of certain goods may be a symbol of our outstanding social position.

III.xiv. *Pride Referring to Wealth and Money*

We saw before that wealth and money are a specific object of concupiscence. We have now to inquire whether they also appeal to pride and, if so, to which dimension of pride. Insofar as wealth and money are means for might and power, they are a direct object of pride in the sense of craving for might and exterior lordship. Though the approach differs completely from concupiscence, wealth and money are as much an object of this type of pride as of concupiscence.

It is in this sphere that pride and concupiscence most often create a real symbiosis. The man who craves exterior might sees the means for might and influence in wealth and money. He needs money to attain his goal, but mostly he is also concupiscent, and his interest in money also refers to the possibility of procuring for himself all the goods that satisfy his concupiscence.

Wealth and money may be attractive even for satanic pride as an instrument to wage war against the moral order, to corrupt other people, to lure them into moral traps, not to dominate them for the sake of exterior domination as such but for the sake of having them morally in one's hands.

Wealth and money do not appeal to the pride of the Pharisee. They are no specific object of his interest. But for other forms of self-glorification, wealth and money may mean something. They may even become the primary source of one's consciousness of grandeur and glory. The position that great wealth conveys, the respect from others, the consciousness of independence and security may be the very source of one's feeling superior and grand. Certainly, this source alone will not suffice to satisfy the pride of self-glorification that dominates the entire life of a person. Other objects must equally nourish this consciousness of grandeur and glory. But it may be the primary object and especially the root of this consciousness of superiority. People possessed by this form of pride may be neither beautiful nor intelligent, but their wealth as such gives them the consciousness of being important and superior, and they look at other people who are not wealthy as *quantité négligeable*, with a kind of contempt, a mixture of disdain and compassion. They relish the superiority that their wealth confers on them; they may even boast about their money.

This function of wealth and money for pride becomes still more obvious with haughtiness. But here it assumes more a character of an unconscious presupposition, a basis that endows the haughty man with a consciousness of independence and a superiority obvious to himself. The haughty man will not glory in his wealth, he will not draw his consciousness of superiority out of it, but wealth will mean much for him because it makes him independent, because it gives him *a fortiori* a strong position and spares him from serving others, asking them for help, being dependent on them.

The haughty man will not crave money if he is poor because this would already be incompatible with his dignity and independence. He will accept many hardships rather than admit his weak situation, his need. In such a situation, he would prefer to become a Diogenes and make of his poverty a title of independence and autarchy.[29] But if he is wealthy, his wealth will become a basis for his autarchy and his haughtiness. Even for vanity, wealth and money can become an object of pride. The *nouveau riche*, the *parvenu*, may relish his money as a means for higher social position and look at himself as more perfect, take delight in his belonging to the "honorable class." We see thus that, in various ways, wealth and money are a specific object of pride. The same applies analogously to titles, nobility, and any high social position.

We now must inquire into the role of goods such as an influential position, might, high reputation for the pride of exterior lordship, the

---

29. [Allusion to Diogenes the Cynic, a Greek philosopher, contemporary of Plato, one of the founders of the Cynic school, famous for making a virtue of his poverty. Editor.]

specific object of which is might. Insofar as might is concerned, we need not examine its role for this dimension of pride, as it is the object of this pride *par excellence.*

Haughtiness does not seek might, but if the haughty man possesses it, he will defend it and consider any attempt to deprive him of it as an injury to his honor and his right. It is not the object out of which he draws his consciousness of grandeur, but once he possesses it, it becomes an obvious element of his grandeur and belongs to the things that his virile strength has to protect. Any yielding would appear to him to be a weakness and is thus incompatible with his haughtiness. He does not relish it, but it flows in an unexamined way into the consciousness of a strong position that is the starting point of his pride.

For the Pharisee it has no direct appeal. Equally, for the other types of pride of self-glorification it is not might as such but eventually their ability to acquire it that may become an object of their glory. Might as such does not appeal also to the Pharisee, but the fame, the high reputation connected with it, or the ability to acquire it may appeal to him. A vain king may consider his high position a satisfaction of his pride; he may relish being admired and praised. Obviously, might as such does not attract the ambitious man. He does not seek it for its own sake, as the specific nourishment of his pride that satisfies vanity, but only a secondary element connected with pride.

For satanic pride, exterior might is only a weapon to wage its war against the reign of moral values on earth, similar to money and wealth. In contrast, high reputation appeals above all to the pride of self-glorification. The Pharisee relishes a high moral reputation, his specific aspiration is the moral glory in his own eyes and above all before God.

The man who glories in his intellectual grandeur obviously craves a high reputation and glory among his fellow man. He needs this glory as a confirmation of his grandeur, as an echo of his superiority. The thirst for glory, for great fame, for the immortality of his name, belong essentially to this form of pride. The nature of glory and fame to which he aspires will vary according to the degree of his aspirations and the specific field in which he feels himself outstanding. The high reputation is, so to speak, a mirror of his own perfection, and he relishes it and glories in it by relating it to his own excellence.

High reputation and fame are also an object of delight for vanity. The vain man does not crave it as the person possessed by the dynamic pride of self-glorification does, but he expects it as a given and tends to imagine fame and a high reputation even when in reality it is not present. He looks at these as an obviously deserved tribute to his excellence and relishes them in a soft and quasi-concupiscent way. When he realizes that this tribute is not paid to him, he will tend to blame his fellow man as stupid or incompetent.

For the haughty man, exterior glory and a high reputation will assume the character of an element of his honor. He does not crave it because the source of his consciousness of superiority is not based on it and to depend upon it would already be incompatible with his sense of independence and autarchy. But if he possesses it without seeking it, he will look at it as an element of his honor that he will defend. The haughty man refuses to admit that anything coming from outside could add something to his glory because this contradicts his ideal of autarchy. We must here distinguish two degrees or types of haughtiness. One considers everything that he possesses without striving for it as an obvious element of his superiority, and he will defend it because he believes that to give anything up would be a sign of weakness and a lack of virile strength. He will be always on the *qui vive* concerning his honor and his right. He will suspect in everything an offense without realizing that in this attitude he already admits a dependence upon his fellow man.

The other type of haughtiness is more consistent. His desire for autarchy goes so far that he does not want to admit that anything could hurt or perturb him. He feels so superior in his dignity that he does not care for a high reputation, he is not interested in what other persons think of him. He despises his fellow man, and he would consider it already a weakness to let himself be offended by another person's attitude. This second type of haughtiness, incarnated in the Stoic, despite being more consistent, is nevertheless less typical of haughtiness than the first.

The refusal to bow before any other person, the spasm of virility, is still more outspoken in the man whose idol is honor and his right. For satanic pride, high reputation does not mean much. It does not take it seriously, but it may be considered useful as a weapon in the war for the triumph of evil.

The way in which different attitudes of other persons directed to our own self appeal to pride is equally characteristic of the different kinds of pride. To be admired appeals to the different forms of self-glorification and to vanity. The pride of self-glorification craves being admired, vanity relishes it according to the dynamic character of the first and the static of the second. To be held in esteem appeals to haughtiness, to be respected in one's honor and in one's rights. Admiration, obedience, submission, even to be feared by one's fellow man are sought by pride craving exterior lordship. For the person possessed by satanic pride no attitude of other persons matters, she is interested only in the triumph of evil and in the destruction or seduction of mankind, without expecting any satisfaction of her own grandeur by the attitudes toward herself. All she may ask of her fellow human beings is to be influenced by her, to yield to her corruptive action.

III.xv. *The Reaction of Pride to Being Loved*

What is the reaction of pride to being loved? The true bliss of being loved is unknown to pride, since this bliss presupposes, firstly, the value-response of true mutual love given by each to the other, and secondly, an appreciation of the preciousness and intrinsic beauty of love. Both are alien to pride. But being loved may become the object of pride through an abuse of it.

The pride of self-glorification relishes being loved as a tribute to one's glory. People possessed by this form of pride do not care for the true character of love as such, but they care for love only insofar as it implies admiration for themselves, a looking up to themselves. It does not move and delight them; it only flatters them. The effect of their perfection and excellence on other persons, the tribute paid to their grandeur, flatters their pride. Vain persons react to being loved similarly but in a more sentimental way. Being loved is for them the mere flattery of their sense of perfection. Both the vain and the one seeking self-glorification are unable to love. They are incapable of any value-response, and hence they are *a fortiori* unable to give this most central value-response that is a self-donation.

In their self-centeredness they abuse this priceless gift of being loved as a mere means for their self-glory. Obviously, a Christian love of neighbor means nothing to them as they cannot draw out of this love a flattery of their perfection. They want to please their fellow man, to be admired. Charity offers no nourishment of their self-glory for there is nothing to boast of about this gift that flows out of the love of Christ. Any kindness that they receive as a fruit of charity will either be misinterpreted as a symptom of another type of love which will then be relished; or, when they understand it in its true nature, they will not appreciate it and instead react in an unfriendly way. The infamous character of pride manifests itself in a specific way in its abuses of the noble and priceless gift of being loved and its rather hostile reaction to the sublime gift of charity.

The pride that craves exterior lordship will see in being loved a mere occasion for the domination of other persons and thus will relish it. The equally horrible perversion is obvious. Charity will appear as a symptom of weakness, and the seeker of the exterior lordship will welcome it as a means, using the other person for his aims.

The haughty man will be indifferent to being loved, and charity will irritate him as a gift that alters his autarchy. Moreover, he will see in this specific embodiment of goodness and bounty something soft and deprived of virility. He despises charity and sees in it a kind of condescension that his haughtiness rejects.

Satanic pride obviously shuns love and charity as such. But being loved may be a tool for spreading evil in the soul of the lover, an open door for seducing and corrupting him. But charity will foster hate in this prideful person and engender a specific hostile venomous attitude toward the charitable, as indeed any manifestation of the spirit of Christ does.

Here we touch on a specific characteristic of pride and its different dimensions. Every man has different fields of susceptibility according to his basic attitude, that is to say, according to whether it is the value-response attitude or pride and concupiscence.

The way in which someone is affected by attitudes toward him and by events or goods characterizes the respective field, or, as we may put it, the specific fields of susceptibility determine which attitudes, events, or goods affect him and how they affect him. The affective attitudes toward persons are directed toward certain fields in the person; their specific content of the affective response intends to affect a certain field in the person to whom it is directed and to engender a specific effect in this field. But depending on whether someone is dominated by the value-response attitude or by pride or by concupiscence, the nature of the fields of susceptibility will vary, and again, according to the nature of these fields, people will react in specific ways to the attitudes directed to them. We can grasp the nature of these fields by examining someone's specific vulnerability, the point where he is vulnerable and how he reacts to being hurt.

IV

Hatred[1]

IV.i. *Hatred as the Attitude Rooted Not Just in Concupiscence and Pride but Also in Certain Particular Situations and Experiences*

We raised the question in the beginning of this chapter whether all morally evil attitudes and immoral actions derive either from concupiscence or pride or from a combination of both. Is every kind of immorality or moral evil rooted in these two centers, or are there still other roots? (Above we saw for which types of immorality concupiscence is responsible.)[2]

In order to answer this question, we have to distinguish between the basic attitude of the person and the factors in the exterior world that may influence the development of moral evil because of the disposition of the will in the person.

The dialogical situation of human life always implies two factors: our

---

1. [Ana 544, 14, 5. Editor.]
2. [This seems to be a reference to the manuscript and/or typescript dealing with concupiscence, that is, a text included in the present volume. Editor.]

basic attitude, on the one hand, and the situations, influences, education, events that we experience, on the other. Though the role of these experiences in no way removes our responsibility for any moral evil on our part, they play undoubtedly an important role in the development of many morally negative attitudes.

Concupiscence and pride are the roots of all moral evil insofar as they pervert our relation to God and all the values reflecting and announcing Him, as well as our relation to the call of God that morally relevant values imply. These two centers falsify our relation to God and the world, and in the measure that they dominate us, they cut us off from any morally good attitude.

But many evil fruits of concupiscence and pride, many immoral actions will develop only under the influence of certain situations and through certain experiences; thus, in order to see that pride and concupiscence are the roots of every moral evil, we must also take into account the specific reaction of concupiscence and pride when confronted with certain situations and exposed to certain experiences. Many morally evil attitudes and actions that seem at first glance not to be rooted in concupiscence and pride will reveal themselves as based on one or both of them when we take the role of the exterior situations and experiences into account.

The proverb "occasion makes thieves" hints at the role of a situation and its immanent temptations. A concupiscent man may not steal as long as he is not exposed to a certain temptation. And obviously pride engenders different attitudes in the *beatus possidens* than in the outcast.

We have thus to distinguish, firstly, those attitudes that are the result of concupiscence and pride as such and that will be found in every man who is dominated by them because they result from the response to the objects that are always present for all men as men, and secondly, those attitudes that result from the reaction of concupiscence and pride to certain particular situations and experiences that belong to the specific history of an individual. The first kind of attitudes we have already examined. We shall now inquire into the second kind and proceed thereby in such a way that we analyze the main morally evil attitudes that were not included in the analysis of pride and concupiscence in order to discover whether they are rooted in pride, concupiscence, or a combination of both. We begin with the analysis of the attitude that forms a unique embodiment of moral wickedness: hatred.

IV.ii. *Hatred as the Antithesis to Love*

Hatred is the exact antithesis to love and charity, and as love and charity form the summit of moral goodness, hatred is the climax of moral wickedness. Hatred is not the negative counterpart to love in the same way that indignation is to enthusiasm, sorrow to joy, or contempt to esteem. Indignation may be a value-response as well as enthusiasm. The same basic value-response attitude conditions both a "no" to moral disvalues, as well as a "yes" to moral values in enthusiasm. They issue both from the same center in the person, and their antithesis is conditioned by the difference on the object side.

Hatred, on the contrary, is not only opposed to love concerning the object; it is not only a "no" instead of the "yes" in love, but also its content is a much more radical antithesis to the content of love, issuing from a center in the person that is incompatible with one from which love issues. We have spoken of this deeper incompatibility in the beginning of this chapter.[3] Hatred in the strict sense is never a value-response attitude. Its venomous, dark character is qualitatively the very antithesis to the victorious intrinsic goodness of charity.

The so-called hatred for sin that is a value-response has a completely different quality and must be clearly distinguished from real hatred. After having examined the nature of true hatred, we shall briefly examine the hatred of sin, and it will then become obvious that the term "hatred" is equivocal when applied to both. The analogy between both refers not to the essential point of hatred but merely to a secondary formal element.[4]

Let us first begin with the most venomous and terrible of all hatreds, the hatred of God. It is, as we saw before, an essential element of satanic

---

3. [This seems to be a reference to *Ethics*, 432–33 (408–09). Editor.]
4. [Cf. section IV.viii. Editor.]

pride. The result of this metaphysical desire for "exalted being," when directed to God, the infinite being and infinite goodness, is an impotent gesture to dethrone God.

Satanic pride is the incarnate ultimate hatred, and it extends itself, as we saw before, to every value reflecting God and to every human person. The intrinsic connection between hatred and satanic pride is obvious, and so far as this pride is concerned the question about what is the source of hatred forms no problem. Hatred is equally an essential element of satanic pride in its analogous human form. This becomes especially obvious in the hatred directed to all morally good men. Cain hates Abel because of his goodness. Rakitin hates Alyosha and the Staretz Zosima. This hatred is, as we saw, primarily directed against the reign of values and, ultimately, against God, even if those men deny God. In hating the morally relevant values, these rays of God's infinite glory, man implicitly hates God.[5] His soul is entirely pervaded by hatred. The *ressentiment* that characterizes him, as we saw before, is the most venomous form of hatred, and the one that has the most habitual character. But there exist many other forms of hatred apart from this constitutive general hatred of satanic pride, and here the connection with pride is not so obvious.

IV.iii. *The Relation between Pride and Hatred*

Whereas in satanic pride the most venomous, deadly hatred is an inevitable consequence of this pride, whereas it is even implied in the basic gesture of this pride as a habitual element that directs itself against every light, to being as such and to every value, hatred is more or less accidental in the other forms of pride and does not form a constitutive element of them.

The pride of the Pharisee implies no hatred against God, nor any against the morally relevant values as such. He hates neither the sinner nor the man whom he considers morally inferior to him. He despises him and relishes his superiority over him. He obviously lacks charity; he

---

5. Satan hates every human person, and the higher one ranks morally the more Satan is eager to corrupt and destroy him.

is hard and indifferent toward his fellow man. He even rejoices in the sins of his fellow man because they favor his own glory. He rejoices in being able to become indignant over him. But as soon as he is confronted with a man endowed with high moral values whom he can no longer consider inferior, hatred arises in his soul. This hatred reaches its climax vis-à-vis the saint, vis-à-vis his charity and sublime goodness, which throw into confusion the pseudo-morality of the Pharisee and make him aware of his inferiority.

He does not hate God, because the notion of an infinite, mysteriously hidden God does not force him into a concrete confrontation with divine goodness. But he hates Christ because the epiphany of God in the sacred humanity of Christ forces him to this confrontation. He may no longer hate Christ as soon as he is no longer directly confronted with Him, that is to say, as soon as Christ no longer as man dwells among us.

He may accept Christ as God in heaven without hatred, working himself into the illusion that he is glorious in the eyes of Christ, of a Christ falsified according to his wishes. But he will necessarily hate every saint, every true manifestation of Christ that forces him into a real confrontation with the real image of Christ.

We can thus clearly see that in the Pharisee hatred is not yet actualized in his pride as such, as it is in satanic pride, but that hatred arises necessarily in him as soon as he is confronted with a person who embodies the true morality and goodness that put his own grandeur into question; and his hatred will be the more venomous and deadly the higher this goodness ranks, reaching its climax in the hatred of Christ and the saint.

In the other types dominated by the pride of self-glorification, hatred assumes a still more accidental character. The decisive factor here is whether someone considers himself a genius, intelligent, endowed with perfections, or whether he is aware of his inferiority, whether his thirst for grandeur is continually cut down by his awareness of inferiority.

The pride of self-glorification assumes a different character according to whether someone is a *beatus possidens* or whether he is filled with the consciousness of his inferiority. In the first case, hatred is not necessarily an element of his pride. It will arise in him only accidentally vis-a-vis a rival. Though he will lack charity because of his self-centeredness and will not be able to love someone in the true sense of the term, he may look in a friendly way at his admirers and have no hatred for someone unless it is a rival who has more success and makes him feel uneasy in his rival's superiority. This is then a hatred born out of jealousy. But in the second case in which he is aware of his inferiority and is disparaged by his fellow man or exposed to continuous humiliations, he will become bitter and develop *ressentiment*, which makes hatred into an element of his general approach toward his neighbors, to humanity, to society. It is the hard, tense, ambitious man in whom a habitual hatred lives, actualizing itself in a specific way toward all those persons towards whom he experiences his inferiority in a more drastic way.

Something analogous applies to the haughty man. As long as he does not feel attacked in his honor or right, as long as he remains undisturbed in his consciousness of autarchy and independence, he will not manifest hatred. His haughtiness bars him from charity and even from true love. But he does not have to hate anyone. Only as soon as he believes that someone disrespects his honor or his rights, or wants him to bow, will he hate him. It is the hatred directed against the offender, the man who wants to humiliate him.

He may even hate someone because he is indebted to him, and the benefit received from him calls for gratitude, which is incompatible with his consciousness of autarchy. But apart from this more accidental hatred, the haughty man who has been often humiliated in his life, who has been forced to bow before other persons, who has experienced continually a state of dependence on others, develops *ressentiment* and becomes bitter, which implies hatred. He will also extend his hatred to every man, to society, to any authority. Habitual hatred will become an element of his approach to the world.

In a similar way, pride craving exterior lordship does not imply hatred. A hereditary king possessing might and influence may show, though exterior grandeur is the center of his interest, no specific hatred. He will lack charity and be unable to love, but he will hate only such people who are rivals or a danger to his might. Hatred will be of a more accidental character in him. But the ambitious man who has not yet attained power and might, who is a neglected, unimportant man, without any influence—whereby the enemy assumes more the character of an obstacle—will be disposed to hatred in his striving for power. The demagogue, the politician, the ambitious common man, who is devoured by the ambition to climb higher, has habitual potential hatred of anyone who stands in his way. But if he does not succeed in his striving for influence, might, and power, he will develop *ressentiment* toward anyone, and his embittered attitude will degenerate into a habitual hatred of any individual, humanity, society, and ultimately of providence.

If we saw before that besides satanic pride, pride assumes a morally worse character in the man who is deprived of the basis of his self-glory than in the man who believes himself a *beatus possidens*, we now can state that this manifests itself in a specific way with respect to the role of hatred in his ethos. We could say that the dynamic character of pride, insofar as it is rooted in the fact that someone has not yet attained the object that satisfies his pride, endows his ethos with potential hatred. The tense, ambitious form of pride has more affinity with hatred than the static, satisfied one.

But hatred assumes still another role in dynamic pride that does not succeed in its striving, that has undergone many humiliations in which pride has been repressed. It degenerates here into habitual hatred that flames up towards every person who is directly or indirectly the cause of humiliation, of the failure of attaining the desired goal, or of any wounding of the respective dimension of pride.

In vanity, which is essentially static and thus presupposes the consciousness of possessing a perfection, hatred plays no essential role. The ethos of vanity implies no potential hatred. Though the vain man will lack in his self-centeredness real charity and even true love, his satisfied and soft ethos does not tend toward hatred, but toward a superficial friendliness. Even toward the persons who do not pay tribute to him, which he believes his due, he will not feel real hatred; rather, he will despise them as incompetent fools. The vain person may feel hatred only toward a rival who robs him of his success or toward someone who has humiliated him. It is obvious that in this dimension of pride, hatred assumes a merely accidental role.

IV.iv. *Hatred That Is Not Based on Pride; and Its Roots, Revenge*

After having examined hatred in the frame of the different dimensions of pride, in also taking into account the role of the factors that are coming from without, as experiences of all kinds, humiliations, situations, obstacles for the satisfaction of pride, we must now inquire into other types of hatred in order to discover their roots.

Obviously, we also encounter hatred in persons who are not dominated by any one of the dimensions of pride. Firstly, we find a certain hatred in the man who is dominated by concupiscence. Though concupiscence as such does not have the affinity with hatred that we found in pride, concupiscence not only excludes charity and true love but will also engender a certain hatred of people who are in some way an obstacle to the satisfaction of concupiscence. It may be someone who contests an object of one's concupiscence, or someone who deprives one of such an object, or someone who has in some way frustrated the satisfaction of one's concupiscence. The character of this hatred differs completely from the hatred of pride. It is not the outspoken, venomous, gloomy hatred that wants to pierce the soul of one's adversary. Rather, it is a brutal hostility, an anger that wants to do away with this obstacle, a hatred that treats the other person as an object. Only in the case of typical revenge is real hatred to be found in the realm of concupiscence. Only then do we find this superactual, devouring fire of hatred that not only wants to destroy the adversary, but is simultaneously always a self-destruction, filling one's own soul with a deadly disharmony and a corrosive poison. (It is a brutal destructive gesture, a slapping of the enemy, more akin to wrath than to outspoken hatred.)

A gangster has been betrayed by his companion. He hates this companion and waits for the moment to take dreadful revenge. We have to raise the question: is this hatred exclusively rooted in his concupiscence, or, as we may put it, is the hatred a pure reaction of his concupiscence to the injury that he received?

Obviously, this case differs from what we encountered in the realm of pride. Also, it is not the frustration of the satisfaction of concupiscence that engenders this hatred.

The frustration of the satisfaction of concupiscence was the root of the wrathful hostility that we described as not being real, full hatred. But in this case of revenge, the injury is not a mere frustration of our concupiscence, not a mere obstacle, but an injury that is beyond question.

Revenge presupposes the consciousness of being wronged by someone. Obviously, the question whether it is a real *injuria* inflicted or whether one only considers it a wrong inflicted on him, when in reality it is either a just punishment or something in itself just, will influence the character of revenge. But we shall abstract from this difference for the moment and concentrate on the general features of revenge. It necessarily presupposes the consciousness that someone has wronged us. It may also direct itself against someone who, without intending it, is objectively only the instrumental cause of an evil that we suffered. But in order to engender revenge in someone, it must at least appear to him that someone else is responsible.

It is notable that even a man who has been blinded to all morally relevant values by concupiscence still knows the category of a "wrong" inflicted on him. He may do the same to his fellow man without any scruples, but as soon as it is directed against him he will experience it as a "wrong." In revenge, the adversary is no longer a mere obstacle to the satisfaction of concupiscence; he becomes himself the aim of our hatred, and to hurt him, to take revenge on him is a satisfaction in itself, independently of the question whether taking revenge is of any use in order to attain the object that was originally at stake in the "wrong" we suffered. The question thus arises in which center of the person revenge as such is rooted.

Independently of the question of what center has been hurt by the "wrong," whether it is concupiscence or something else that is itself the root of revenge, and of finding in hurting one's adversary a satisfaction as such, the value-response attitude certainly is not the root of the desire of revenge.

After having analyzed the hatred that is a constitutive element or a result of pride when confronted with certain situations and experiences, we must now inquire in which center of the person the other types of hatred are rooted. Obviously, hatred is not found only in persons who are dominated by one or the other dimension of pride. We have first to inquire about what other types of hatred exist and then try to trace their roots in the person.

Firstly, there exists a hatred that is an element of revenge. It presupposes the consciousness of being "wronged" by someone, independently of the question whether this consciousness is founded in an objective *injuria* inflicted or not. It is a typical form of hatred implying a venomous, virulent content, a superactual, hostile, destructive intention toward another person.

Secondly, we find hatred in different forms of enmity. It does not necessarily flow out of the respective enmity, but it can do so, as in the hatred of members of a family that has an old enmity with one's own, such as in the case of the Montague and Capulet families in Shakespeare's *Romeo and Juliet*; or the less individual hatred of members of a nation with whom we are at war; or the hatred of a person with whom one lives in an old enmity, be it an old lawsuit or any struggle about an object that each claims belongs to him; or the hatred of members of a political party that is the enemy of our own party.

Thirdly, hatred can arise for people who profess ideas and ideals that are wrong and evil, and the fight against their ideas may degenerate into a hatred of the persons themselves. This is, for instance, the case in religious conflicts, and fanaticism is the specific manifestation of this hatred.

Fourthly, there exists a hatred that is based on indignation about someone's moral meanness and depravity. The morally good indignation about the wickedness of someone who has not wronged us personally and is not our personal enemy degenerates into hatred of the person himself. The spark of indignation about the immorality of this man springs over into the fire of hatred of the sinner. Obviously, the nature of hatred varies in these four types. We shall examine this difference by inquiring into the roots of hatred in these four main types of hatred.

Revenge: many philosophers see in revenge a kind of natural, pre-rational prelude to the consciousness of the basic fact and elementary truth that punishment for moral guilt is due, or, as we may put it, that moral guilt calls for punishment.

This theory seems to us to be fundamentally wrong. The dark, passionate character of revenge differs essentially from the consciousness that a crime deserves punishment. Firstly, revenge always refers to an evil inflicted on one's own person and such persons whom we consider an extension of our own person, for instance, relatives, members of our own party, our nation, and so on. It never refers to a moral evil as such (for instance, a blasphemy or pride as such) nor to evils inflicted on persons whom one does not consider as belonging to one's own person. The anarchist who wants to punish moral evils because of a wrong conception of justice, who arrogates to himself the right to replace the state in its function of punishing certain moral evils, must not be considered as taking revenge. His attitude is a completely different one; he shares with the avenger only the bypassing of legitimate authority, the function of which is to punish certain crimes. But the motive of the avenger is another one; he wants to punish the crime not in order to make justice triumph but to hit back when he has been injured.

But revenge presupposes, on the other hand, consciousness that the offender is responsible for the injury inflicted on one's own person. An evil that is obviously not intended, whereby the other person is, without any question, merely an instrumental cause of the injury we suffered, cannot engender revenge. A man who, falling from a window, injures us cannot become the object of our revenge. The object of revenge is thus always a man whom we believe to be responsible for a wrong inflicted on us or on persons whom we look on as an extension of ourselves.

Revenge always implies hatred. The man who thirsts for revenge thus sees in injuring or killing the object of his hatred an end sought for its own sake and not merely a means for acquiring something to which his pride or concupiscence aspires. The murder of Duncan by Macbeth is no act of revenge; it is only a means to ascend to the throne. The robber kills his victim merely because he wants to have his money. The killing of his victim implies no satisfaction as such for him. The vengeful, on the contrary, finds satisfaction in the very act of harming his object. Even if it endangers or ruins him, he cannot abstain from it. Revenge is the specific satisfaction of a certain kind of hatred and differs thus from any injustice inflicted on other persons that has the character of a means to another end.

Secondly, the vengeful person desires *himself* to inflict directly or indirectly the evil on his object. It does not suffice to quench his thirst for revenge that the person whom he considers to have wronged him suffers through others or that he dies because of illness. He wants himself to be the initiator and free cause of the evil that is the retribution for what he endured. It is different with the hatred implied by envy; here it may suffice to see the hated person suffer or perish. For the vengeful person, however, he himself must be the one who inflicts the blow on the hated person in order to satisfy his thirst for revenge and to consider the wrong inflicted as expiated. Thus, the hatred of revenge is characterized, firstly, by the fact that it is engendered by the consciousness of being "wronged" by another person. It is not the superiority of the other person as such that incites the hatred of pride; it is neither the hatred caused by rivalry as such, but it presupposes the consciousness of being "wronged" by him, implying the responsibility of the person for this injury.

IV.v. *The Center of Irascibility and Its Reactions to Offenses*[6]

We saw above the role of the factors residing outside of the person, that is to say, the different situations and experiences that engender hatred in persons dominated by pride. In order to understand the origin of hatred in persons who are not dominated by pride, we have to concentrate on a certain field in the human person that we could term the "irascible

---

6. [Ana 544, VI, 14, 2. Editor.]

center." Our nature resents everything disagreeable with a gesture of repulsion. Every evil that is inflicted on us by other persons—an unfriendly attitude, an offense, an insult or a frustration of our legitimate interests, an injustice, a persecution—hurts in a specific way that differs from being hurt by an impersonal evil.

The hostility of other persons directed to us normally engenders hostility on our part towards the offender. It may be anger, irritation, wrath, or any hostile impulse, according to the nature of the hostility that we have endured and according to our temperamental disposition. This center is a legitimate one. As such it does not presuppose domination by concupiscence and pride. This vulnerability of the human person to any hostility on the part of other persons is a constitutive feature of our fallen human nature. But the decisive moral difference manifests itself in the attitude of our free spiritual center toward these experiences and toward the moral impulses arising as a natural reaction to the experience of a hostility on the part of other persons.

The morally unconscious man who has not yet discovered the capacity of sanctioning and disavowing his own spontaneous attitudes and has not grasped the obligation to do so is in danger of letting these natural impulses and hostile reactions develop according to their immanent logic.[7] He will not counteract them with his free spiritual center. Though not lacking a certain value-response attitude, he follows the tendency of his nature, having the consciousness that injustice has been done to him and that he has the right to react in this way. We abstract here from the types who are dominated by pride or concupiscence and were thus deprived of any value-response attitude. We think of the man who would not yield to any temptation of dishonesty, who submits to the call of morally relevant values insofar as he grasps them. But in enduring a hostility from his fellow man, he experiences his natural hostile reaction as something completely legitimate. He will perhaps examine whether a real wrong has been done to him, the situation on the object side will

---

7. [Sanction and disavowal are terms of fundamental importance in the moral philosophy of Hildebrand. For the fullest account of this distinction given by Hildebrand see his *Ethics*, Ch. 25. Editor.]

preoccupy him, but as soon as he believes himself to be sure of the undeserved hostility, he will let his reaction unfold itself according to its immanent logic. The hostile impulsive reaction—not yet illegitimate as such—will then degenerate according to his temperament into an outspoken hostile attitude of his entire person. It may be a soft closing up oneself, a rancor that poisons one's soul, it may be a fit of anger manifesting itself in insults to the offender. Whereas the morally conscious man will disavow these impulses with his free spiritual center and counteract them, this morally unconscious type will fall prey to the immanent logic of his hostile impulses. His image of the offender will be increasingly falsified: everything that the offender does will be interpreted in a negative light, the offender will appear to be increasingly hideous. Whether the injustice inflicted seems very grave to us or whether an unimportant offense develops by this process of accumulation of offenses to something apparently grave, the decisive point is that the morally unconscious man lets the as such normal and legitimate impulsive reaction unfold itself according its immanent logic and thus is in danger of opening the floodgates of passions—and hating his offender. He looks at his hatred as something morally legitimate because he has preserved the original consciousness of the legitimacy of his hostility during this entire process of degeneration. Because he is convinced of the injustice on the part of his offender, every hostile attitude on his part seems to him justified. First, he looks only at the object side and does not bother about the moral character of his own attitudes, that is, he is not aware, because of his spiritual laziness, of the process of degeneration that has taken place in him. Secondly, he does not realize the falsification of the moral image of his offender that took place under the impact of his passion. Thus, we observe in those persons that they may continue to be responsive to many moral obligations, may continue to be generous and kind to other persons, and simultaneously hate the offender.

Nevertheless, even in this case, the hatred is rooted in concupiscence and pride. The dark depths of passion that he has allowed to unfold are the reign of pride and concupiscence. The hard, venomous content of hatred manifests the cooperation of pride, while the overwhelming blinding impetus of hatred, the gloomy, passionate fire manifests the cooperation of concupiscence.

But the person is not necessarily under a general dominion of pride and concupiscence in having, by this process of degeneration that lies between the normal and legitimate impulse of hostile reaction and the conscious hatred implying a silent sanctioning on our part, yielded to concupiscence and pride concerning this one person. The hatred may pervert her completely and eliminate every value-response attitude, but it need not be so. It is a specific case of the mysterious coexistence of a general value-response attitude and a single attitude that grows out of pride and concupiscence.

There are two ways in which the morally conscious man can avoid the degeneration into hatred of the legitimate impulsive reaction to injustice and offenses committed against him. Or as we may put it, two ways in which he counteracts and controls these impulsive reactions. The first is the only possible way for a merely natural morality or a morality separate from knowing or following Christ. It is abstaining from passions by the predominance of reason. He will firstly try to control these reactions with his free will guided by reason. He will not allow these impulses to develop into wrath and, above all, he will not allow himself to act out of his wrath. He will, secondly, through reason, not allow for these impulsive reactions to make the injustice or offense seem bigger than it actually is. He will try to look at them as an inevitable element of human life, and with his reason and self-control resist the immanent logic of these impulsive reactions. Above all, he will abstain from opening the floodgates of the sphere of passions. He will neutralize the whole experience and, in a reasonable way, remain above the situation. Thus, hatred will not arise in him.

The motives of his attitude are the disvalue of hatred as a passion. He grasps the incompatibility of this passion with freedom and reason. He wants to remain free and guided by reason. He also wants to abstain from any injustice toward the other person to which hatred may lead him. We are here thinking of the most noble attitude in the frame of natural morality, as we find it, for instance, in Socrates or Plato. The Stoic attitude may in many respects be similar, but its moral significance is different because here it is an outgrowth of the ideal of *ataraxia*, which is rooted in pride.

The second way to avoid hatred in counteracting the natural impulsive reactions to being harmed by another is the Christian attitude. The basis of Christian morality is, as already mentioned, the love for God. This value-response *par excellence* endows the whole of morality with a completely new character.

Firstly, it is not the mere response to the impersonal reign of values but the response to absolute goodness, who is a person. Moreover, the value-response is not just obedience, submission to an almighty God and Lord, but the love for the God whose infinite goodness and holiness has been revealed in the person of the God-Man, Christ.

This implies, firstly, that the disvalue of hatred, its intrinsic incompatibility with God, is grasped. Hatred is shunned not only as a passion that dethrones our reason and our freedom but also because of its antithetic character to love and charity. The intrinsic disvalue of hatred, its venomous wickedness, is understood. The Christian knows of the indestructible value of every immortal soul, he is aware of the incompatibility of hatred for a human person and the divine love of Christ for this person. He grasps the intrinsic value of forgiving and understands the obligation of loving his enemy and the commandment to reward evil with good. A completely new world of values and obligations has been revealed to him. He will thus fight against the natural impulsive reaction to injustice and offenses. He will expose his soul to the love of Christ and will let these reactions be melted by the confrontation with Christ. He will already see in these natural impulsive reactions something evil instead of taking them as justified. He will always examine whether the offense was really an unjust one. He will resist the immanent logic of his nature because his life develops within the fundamental attitude of *religio*, with a wholesome mistrust of his nature and an awareness of the general obligation to be vigilant. Because of his love of Christ, because of a pure value-response to the evil of hostility, he will fight against these impulsive reactions. In the state of spiritual vigilance, he will be on his guard not to fall prey to the immanent logic of his natural tendencies, and he will do so in an unceasing confrontation with Christ. He will try to develop a full forgiveness of the offense, not by reason and self-control but through his love of Christ—with the help of Christ. He will try to love his offender and, instead of neutralizing his experience, he will dissolve it by love. In the saint, even the natural field of vulnerability undergoes a deep transformation. Not that he becomes indifferent as the pagan sage strives to become. But the nature of his vulnerability is transformed by the value-response attitude, that is, by his love of God and his charity toward his neighbor. It is no longer the natural self-defense against injustice and offenses of all kinds. The hostility directed against him wounds his heart, firstly, because of the offense to God that it implies and, secondly, because of the objective evil that it presents for the offender. Insofar as the Christian lives in a pure value-response attitude, his sorrow is similar to the sorrow over any moral evil, whether it is inflicted on his own person or on another person, or even a sin that is not connected with any *injuria* against a human person, for instance, blasphemy or impiety. But he will also be wounded by the hostility directed against his own person. But it will affect him only insofar as this hostility is an antithesis to charity. It is not the curtailing of his rights, the offense of his honor, not the injuring of his legitimate self-affirmation, nor the humiliation that will make him suffer, but only the lack of charity implied in these attitudes. The field of self-defense of honor, the susceptibility for his rights is surpassed in him. The elements in the hostile attitude that irritate our natural attitude and engender a reaction of self-defense no longer affect him. For instance, an insult which is intended to insult our honor, which tends to irritate and fill our soul with the poison of anger and hostility, does not affect the saint in the way in which the aggressor intends it. The saint is susceptible only to the uncharitable element that it implies. It wounds his heart and engenders only a sublime sorrow.

Suppose a thief steals someone's money. If this victim is dominated by concupiscence, such as Harpagon, he will above all resent the loss of this money.[8] Certainly, he will be furious with the thief, but the difference

---

8. [The protagonist of Molière's comedy *The Miser*. Editor.]

between losing the money by speculation or by theft is not very great for him. The main theme of his grief is the loss of the money. The man in whom pride is more or less predominant will resent the offense of his rights more than the loss of the money. The difference between losing the money through his own fault and by theft will be significant. By contrast, the saint will worry about the sin of the theft and the evil that it represents for the thief himself.

Thus we see in the saint in whom the transformation into Christ has fully taken place, whose nature is victoriously transfigured by the love of God and the love of neighbor, that even the natural center of self-defense and vulnerability has been transformed and the only way in which he is vulnerable to a hostile attitude of his fellow man is, besides the sorrow about the offense of God and the objective evil for the sinner implied in this offense, that his heart is wounded by the uncharitable attitude, by the antithesis to charity that it implies. It is the sublime vulnerability of charity itself.

We turn back to the problem of hatred and its origin in self-defense. The morally unconscious man in the frame of a merely natural morality, who is as such not exclusively dominated by pride and concupiscence, is imprisoned in his self-defensive attitude. He knows of no higher ground from which he can regard the offense that he endures. He is not sheltered in a world above which would disclose the relative insignificance of being attacked, which would make him aware that the natural gesture of hitting back does not do away with the evil of the offense but, quite to the contrary, involves us in the evil and risks that we become morally poisoned by hatred. Obviously, it is his own fault not to be aware of that, as he is fully responsible for his moral unconsciousness. He could, in the frame of a merely natural morality, emerge to this moral consciousness, which we observe in such great moral pagan personalities as Socrates or Plato.

In those personalities, this higher ground is given in their conscious response to the reign of morally relevant values. The confrontation with this world of values reveals to them the futility of the reactions of a natural self-defense, the evil that hatred would mean for themselves. They understand that the passion of hatred deprives them of the use of their reason and their freedom. They grasp the indignity of hatred, of being imprisoned in the automatism of their passions.

Being sheltered in the world of values, they understand that no evil inflicted on them from the outside can really affect their true self, that they themselves alone can, in acting immorally, inflict a real evil on their true self. Thus Socrates says: to do injustice is a greater evil than to suffer injustice.[9] His value-response attitude enables him to grasp that immorality is the supreme objective evil for the person. But he has not yet grasped the intrinsic wickedness of hatred, its antithesis to charity, and he does not understand the obligation to love his adversary, to return good for evil. Socrates says in his apology: you cannot affect me in condemning and killing me; I cannot be really damaged as only something better can come for me by that. But you damage yourself in being unjust.[10] This attitude reveals a noble sobriety, the reasonable stand of a man who is firmly rooted in the world of moral values, but it differs completely from the victorious ardent *radicatus et judicatus*[11] in the love of Christ.

The Christian knows that he is sheltered by God. He knows that he is loved by the almighty God who is absolute goodness and charity. His impregnability is completely different from the inaccessibility of the noble pagan. It is not the awareness acquired by reason that no injustice afflicted on us can affect our true self but the blissful awareness that everything turns to good for the one who loves God. It is exposing our unarmored heart to any offense in the imitation of Christ. It is not the self-assurance based on reason but the consciousness that God alone is our strength. It is the expectation that everything can be solved only by Christ from above through the love of Christ. No neutralization is here at stake but a superabundance of love. The decisive antithesis is no longer reason, on the one hand, and the dark currents of passion, on the other

---

9. [Plato's Socrates defends this claim in *Gorgias* and in the *Republic* (358e–359a). Editor.]

10. [It is not clear which passage from Plato's *Apology of Socrates* Hildebrand is referring to here. Editor.]

11. [Hildebrand is likely paraphrasing from Ephesians 3:17 and Colossians 2:7. Editor.]

hand, but the heroic love of Christ, on the one hand, and the law of our fallen nature, on the other hand, including a self-sufficient reason that is not rooted in God. Reason as such is not contradicted but surpassed by the light of the Logos; the *ebria sobrietas* has become a *sobria ebrietas*.[12]

In antiquity, we find in its highest representatives, such as Socrates and Plato, a touching prelude, a longing of advent, an ascension toward the world above, but this prelude ended in the void, unable to reach the fulfillment that only the movement of God toward man can accomplish, that is, the redemption and revelation of Christ.

In sum, we may say: hatred can arise even in persons who are not dominated by pride and concupiscence insofar as they are morally unconscious. Because of spiritual laziness, the impulsive reactions of the center of self-defense can degenerate into hatred. By falling prey to the immanent logic of our nature and especially to self-defense, hatred may develop. But this hatred is always an outgrowth of pride and concupiscence. In hatred there is, firstly, always a gesture of pride insofar as we expect our happiness not from God but from our self-defense. Hatred implies a refusal to accept our situation as a creature. We arrogate to ourselves the right to judge the offenses and the capacity to take care of our fate by our own forces.

It implies, further, a proud manifestation of our own might, a self-assertion of our capacity to destroy something precious and noble, a confirmation of our own privilege and freedom. In hatred lives something of this self-assertion that discloses itself in the nonsensical murder, the satisfaction of our pride in the capacity to destroy a good possessing a high value, the attitude of Herostratus.[13] Also, the specific element of passion in hatred implies pride. The satisfaction of throwing away the bonds of *religio*, putting all one's eggs in one basket, which is the typical

---

12. [*ebria sobrietas* - drunken sobriety; *sobria ebrietas* - sober drunkenness. The expression "*sobria ebrietas*" comes from Philo of Alexandria. In the West, it is known through St. Ambrose (*De fide* 1,135, *In Ps.* 1,33, *In Ps.* 35,19). It appears also in St. Augustine when, in his *Confessions*, he speaks about Ambrose (*Conf.* 5,13,23). Cf. Hans Lewy, *Sobria ebrietas: Untersuchungen zur Geschichte der antiker Mystik*, Geissen: Alfred Töpelmann, 1929. Editor.]

13. [A fourth-century B.C. Greek arsonist who sought notoriety by destroying the second Temple of Artemis in Ephesus. Editor.]

gesture of cursing and of the "flying Dutchman" and is proper to every conscious opening of the floodgates of our passions, is rooted in pride. The abuse of our freedom in throwing ourselves entirely into this dark stream, in cutting the ties that link us to the moral order and to God, is a gesture of rebellion and of a proud masterly sovereignty.

But the perverted satisfaction that consists in allowing oneself to be dominated by a passion is also rooted in concupiscence. Every succumbing to the law of gravity of our nature, every letting of oneself to be drawn down, every relinquishing *religio* and moving without the "burden" of this obligation, is a satisfaction of concupiscence.

The concupiscent man relishes being submerged in an intense stream of his passion. Besides the specific content of the passion that may appeal to concupiscence, as, for instance, a sexual passion, giving up to a passion, giving oneself away unconditionally to its immanent law, even if the passion in its content does not specifically appeal to concupiscence, as in the case of hatred, is a specific satisfaction of concupiscence.

The different types of hatred, such as hatred arising from jealousy, from enmity of all kinds, and especially the hatred of revenge, will be analyzed in the second volume, which will be dedicated to a minute analysis of the different main morally positive and negative attitudes of man such as love, joy, contrition, hatred, envy, jealousy, and so on.[14] In this context it may suffice to trace the roots of hatred in pride and concupiscence and its originating in a spiritual laziness even in persons who are not dominated by pride and concupiscence.

There are, however, two types of hatred that we must examine briefly in this context because they differ completely from all the aforementioned ones in their quality and origin: the hatred implied in fanaticism and the hatred of people because of their objective depravity and meanness—the hatred of the enemy of God.

---

14. [This is a notable remark as it indicates the original intention of the author regarding the purpose of the present manuscript. However, it is not clear what is meant by first and second volume in this context. Editor.]

IV.vi. *Two Stages of Hatred*

But before turning to this problem, we must distinguish two essential stages of hatred, a distinction that is of general importance for the entire analysis of this specific embodiment of moral evil. Besides innumerable degrees of hatred, there are two clearly distinguished stages. The first cuts, as it were, the elementary implicit bond which unites us with every man with whom even no personal relation whatsoever links us. It is the potential friendly disposition that is to be found toward anybody in every man who is not completely dominated by pride or concupiscence.

This stage of hatred speaks to its object: I will never see you again, I cut any bond and relation with you, I cancel you from the list of living men. It is a gesture of pushing the adversary away, of departing from him forever, of repulsing him. It is obviously not only an act of ignoring him in complete indifference. It is an outspoken hostile attitude that expressly severs the implicit bond uniting us implicitly with every human being. It is a gesture of casting the adversary out of the largest frame of community. This hatred is, so to speak, satisfied in ostracizing the hated person, in expelling her from the spiritual space of community that counts for us.

The second stage is not the cancelling of the hated person but, on the contrary, seeking him in order to pour the venomous poison of hatred into his soul, to wound him, to destroy him with this poison. This stage of hatred is not satisfied in expelling its object but aims at his destruction. It does not have to lead to an exterior aggression, but the very content of this hatred wishes every evil upon his adversary. It rejoices in his sufferings; it always again turns to him in a gesture of intentional destruction. It pierces his soul with the spiritual dagger of hatred.

In the first stage, the sufferings and misfortune of the hated one will leave the hating person cold, and she may say: I do not care what happens to him because he exists no longer for me. In the second stage, the sufferings and misfortune of the enemy will be a source of malicious joy and satisfaction, and the hating person may say: it is not enough, he deserves much more. I wish he would perish and go to hell. It goes obviously far beyond the first stage, not just in that it destroys every bond between the two; it seeks an outspoken antithesis of union between them. Not only does it push the hated person back; it tries to reach her with its deadly poison. It stabs her soul. In the first stage, the hating person is not always preoccupied with the hated person; in the second, she focuses on her. In the first stage, the soul of the hating person may not be completely poisoned by the hatred; in the second, it is *devoured* by this poison and hatred fully unfolds its self-destructive effect on the soul of the hating person. Obviously, it makes a big difference in all of our former analysis of hatred whether the first or the second stage of hatred is at stake.

IV.vii. *Fanaticism*

A different situation is at stake in the case of hatred based on the fight against error and evil ideas.[15] Here the fight against error is a pure value-response attitude and a morally obligatory one. The love of God implies as a necessary element the "hatred" of error and specifically of errors concerning values. But this "hatred" has, as we saw before, nothing in common with the real hatred that is the antithesis of love. Besides the immanent "no" addressed to the object, it has not the venomous evil content, the immanent corrosive disharmony that not only wants to destroy the adversary but is simultaneously a self-destruction. The so-called hatred of error and evil ideas is luminous, noble, and has all the features of a pure value-response.

But it can never be extended to the person who professes the errors and evil ideas. The negative value-response directed to the error implies that we realize that the error is as much the enemy of the man who professes it as it is our own enemy. The primary root of our hatred of error is the love of God because error, and especially the error concerning values, is an offense against God, the incarnate truth, because it is incompatible with God.

---

15. [From the formal point of view, the manuscript is here not entirely coherent. However, thematically it turns back to what was announced before the excursus regarding the two stages of hatred, namely, to the hatred implied in fanaticism and the hatred of the enemies of God. Editor.]

But as the love of neighbor issues necessarily and organically from the love of God according to the word of Christ—"and the second is love thy neighbor as thyself and both are *one*"—error is secondarily shunned because it is an objective evil for the man who professes it, because it contradicts the true ultimate interest of any human being and therefore is also an objective evil for the man who is the champion of the error.[16] The love of neighbor also engenders necessarily a negative value-response attitude to error. The words of St. Augustine, *interficere errorem, diligere errantem*, express in an admirable way the deep inner connection of the love of neighbor and the hatred of error.[17] Certainly the first reason for the hatred of error is the love of God. But the "*diligere errantem*" also necessarily calls for an "*interficere errorem.*" A love of neighbor that would not include the hatred of error would not be true love but a selfish, jovial weakness, an indifference toward the true good of the neighbor. But how is it then possible that the value-response we call hatred of error can degenerate into an evil hatred of the person who professes the error? This happens undoubtedly in the case of fanaticism.

It is the result of an oversimplification, of a typical falling prey to the immanent logic of fighting and of spiritual laziness. Human nature is full of contradictions, and, as we have seen again and again, there occurs an unnoticed transition of the value-response attitude to attitudes that are an outgrowth of pride and concupiscence. Although the two are incompatible as such, in fallen human nature the transition from one to another happens easily.

In our case the hatred of error, originally a value-response attitude but in those people not a completely pure one, remains not in the luminous free realm of the value-response but is, as it were, nourished by the full impact of our nature, the overwhelming weight of our natural hostile reaction, so that our fight becomes formally similar to the fight for our own interests. The immanent logic of this fight absorbs us and

---

16. [Paraphrase of Matthew 22:36–40. Editor.]

17. [The sentence "Love the sinner, hate the sin" is a well-known Christian saying. It can be traced back, at least in part, to St. Augustine, who in one of his letters (*Ep.* 211, 11), says, "*Cum dilectione hominum et odio vitiorum.*" This principle can be found also in Aquinas (*Summa theologiae* II-II, q. 34, a. 3). Editor.]

dictates an approach that contradicts the original value-response attitude. It blinds us to the indestructible value of the person who professes the error, indestructible insofar as it cannot be dissolved as long as the person is alive and has not definitively separated herself from God. It extinguishes the value-response of charity toward the person that is called for by her indestructible value. In sinister oversimplification the person who professes the error is identified with the error, and the blow directed to the error is directed with its full weight to the person herself.

This oversimplification is a typical outgrowth of spiritual laziness. One confronts the attitude with God only in the beginning, but once one has begun to fight the error, one yields in an uncontrolled way to the immanent logic of fighting. Instead of repeating in every phase of our fight the confrontation with God, instead of inspiring oneself again and again by the love of God and the love of neighbor, one hands this fight over, as it were, to the automatism of our nature.

The hatred of the person who is the champion of a moral or religious error obviously differs completely from the so-called hatred of the error as such. It is never a value-response attitude because it contradicts the value-response of charity toward the person. It is poisonous, virulent, and evil; in one word, it is real hatred. It hardens and perverts one's own person, it removes one more and more from the value-response attitude. But it differs also from the aforementioned types of hatred. The starting point that was a value-response attitude, though not a completely pure one, endows the hatred of fanaticism with a certain element of objectivity and rectitude that is alien to all other types of hatred. But this moral advantage comes with other grave dangers. The good conscience bars the person who hates in this way from the discovery of her own evildoing and brings her close to pharisaic self-assurance. It is specifically hideous and false in its combination of an original value-response and an outspoken antithesis to charity. The man who makes himself a champion of the cause of God is still more responsible for offending God by hatred.

Besides the lack of moral consciousness that made him fall prey to the immanent logic of fighting, the roots of this hatred are pride and concupiscence. Not only, as we saw before, is the spiritual laziness conditioned by pride and concupiscence, but the hatred as such is an outgrowth of pride. Insofar as we arrogate to ourselves the role of judge of the human person, we, in our hatred, anticipate something that is essentially reserved for God. Second, this hatred implies an element of concupiscence insofar as the overwhelming uncontrolled weight of our nature and the character of passion is at work in this hatred. The satisfaction implied by the spiritual beating of the adversary, letting the immanent law of our nature fully display itself, without confronting it with God and the reign of the morally relevant values, are typical features of concupiscence. It is a satisfaction based on departing from the fundamental attitude of *religio*, and based on a disordered unfolding of our nature outside the bonds and obligations of *religio*, and this with a good conscience, with the consciousness of being a champion of the cause of God.

IV.viii. *The Hatred Directed to the Enemy of God*

Something analogous applies to the situation in which we hate someone because of his wickedness and moral depravity because he really is an enemy of God. We do not need to repeat that the negative value-response to the moral depravity of the person, the indignation about his wickedness, is obligatory, and that this negative value-response, primarily determined by the love of God, is also a necessary consequence of our love of neighbor.

Insofar as the process of a degeneration of indignation into hatred is due to spiritual laziness and to falling prey to the immanent logic of our nature, it is similar to the former case. But there is nevertheless a difference. Firstly, the identification of the person as such with his wickedness and moral depravity is much more difficult to avoid than the identification of evil theories with the person who professes them. The immorality is, so to speak, much more embodied in a man than the evil theories to which he adheres. It is more difficult to preserve the vision of the dignity and indestructible value of the person who is an enemy of God, whose profound meanness and wickedness repulse us, than in the case of the champion of evil errors.

Moral wickedness penetrates his being in a deeper way and makes the nobility and beauty of his immortal soul created by God and destined to eternal community with God more invisible than the profession of evil errors. The identification of the evil with the person himself is thus more tempting here than in the former case.[18]

For every primitive morality the identification of the entire person with his wickedness is more or less inevitable. It is a specific mark of Christian morality to make a clear distinction between the immorality of a man and the indestructible value of his immortal soul. Only Christian revelation makes this ultimate ontological value of the person visible. The love of the sinner is a specific commandment of Christ. In the realm of merely natural morality, we find either no indignation about meanness and moral depravity, that is to say, indifference toward it combined with a jovial, friendly attitude toward the man who does evil. Or we find an indignation about the moral depravity that degenerates into a hatred of the person herself. Only in a morality that is centered on and rooted in the love of God, of the true God who has revealed himself in Christ, can the indignation about moral depravity, the so-called hatred of sin as such, and the love of the sinner be combined. We say "love," because the mere absence of hatred is impossible in this case. As soon as the indestructible ontological value of the person as an image of God, destined for eternal communion with God, called and loved by God, is grasped, the call to love the sinner is equally understood and an indifferent attitude toward him is no longer possible. True love of the sinner may not yet be attained, but the direction of our will toward this love must arise. Or, as we may put it, if the value-response of indignation has been given and the fact that the sin is an enemy to the sinner, that it is the greatest objective evil for him, is understood, then the mere absence of hatred is no longer possible. The pure value-response attitude engenders, then, not only the indignation but also the will to love the sinner. If love of God is not the basis of a morality, there is either a lack of the value-response to the sin or hatred embracing the sinner as well as his sinfulness.

---

18. It may therefore occur even in persons who are morally and spiritually more awakened than those who have fallen prey to fanaticism.

But even after the revelation of Christ in the redeemed, a man lives in danger of hating the enemy of God as long as he is not a saint. He experiences the tendency of his fallen nature to extend the obligatory value-response attitude of indignation and the "hatred" of sin to the sinner. He is exposed to the danger of letting his value-response to the sinfulness degenerate into a hatred of the sinner as soon as he is not morally awakened, as he does not collaborate with grace, that is to say, as long as he does not again and again confront his attitude with the light and truth of Christ and place himself with his free moral center into this light.

The roots of this degeneration in the Christian are analogous to the case of fanaticism: spiritual laziness, the immanent logic of his nature, oversimplification. But the nature of this hatred will have a less virulent and poisonous character. If the hatred of fanaticism already differs in its quality from the other aforementioned types of hatred, this applies to a greater extent to the hatred of the evildoing enemy of God. It does not have the gloomy, dark fire of the hatred of enmity; the value-response that is its starting point endows this hatred with an element of objectivity and rectitude.

Insofar as the responsibility for this hatred is concerned, we must make a clear distinction between the Christian and the non-Christian. In the frame of merely natural morality, man is less responsible for this hatred than in the frame of Christian morality. As there is no possibility, without Christ, to avoid the alternative of indifference to the sinfulness and hatred of the sinner, hatred of the sinner is morally a lesser evil than indifference to sinfulness.

As long as the indestructible ontological value of the person is not disclosed, the extension of hatred to the sinner himself is inevitable. Notwithstanding this inevitability, hatred of the sinner remains a morally negative attitude. The inevitability of this morally negative attitude reveals to us only the limits and essential insufficiency of merely natural morality, but it does not do away with the moral wrongness of this attitude.

But for the Christian, for whom this hatred is avoidable and who knows the indestructible value of the person, who knows of the love of God for this immortal soul, who knows that Christ dies also for him on the cross, who could understand that the sin is the enemy even of the sinner—for the Christian this hatred assumes the character of a betrayal of Christ.

He betrays his original negative value-response against sin by extending it to the sinner himself. He can do so only because of the spiritual laziness in which he imparts his horror of sinfulness to this sinner and thus allows the immanent logic of his temperamental disposition to refuse to the sinner the positive value-response for which the indestructible value of his immortal soul calls. He shuns the sinfulness in the name of Christ but behaves then as if he would not know Christ. He does not take into account the revelation and commandment of Christ and sinks to the level of the non-Christian. His oversimplification is soiled with a terrible guilt because he follows Christ only halfway, and although he knows Christ and His commandment, he behaves as if he would ignore Him. He makes himself the ultimate judge and is involved in a pride that comes close to that of the Pharisee. He follows the pull of his nature and becomes thereby a slave to his concupiscence. His oversimplification severs him from Christ.

If we abstract from Christian morality, we must distinguish the following two cases.[19] A beloved person goes morally astray. A beloved son, a spouse, a friend does evil and manifests grave moral faults. In this case the mother, the loving spouse, the loving friend, if she possesses a basic value-response attitude, is indignant about the moral evil without identifying the person with this evil. Her love will enable her to distinguish between the morally negative values and the person, who is soiled by this moral wickedness. The morally negative values will present themselves to her as an objective evil for the beloved person, as her enemy, as something that is an unfaithfulness of the beloved person to herself. She will suffer because of this moral evil and fight against it, she will do anything

---

19. [The following section is an addition to the above-mentioned claim that when love of God is not the basis of morality, there is either a lack of the value-response to the sin or hatred embracing both the sinner and his sinfulness. Editor.]

in her power to bring the beloved back onto the path of virtue. Her love enables her to distinguish between the person of the beloved and the moral faults of the beloved: the image of the beloved's individuality remains lovable, endowed with potential goodness, and the moral evil she did appears to the loving person as something transitory and, as such, alien to the beloved.

Secondly, a man who is as such indifferent to us goes morally astray. His meanness and moral depravity make us indignant. He will appear to us as a mean and wicked man, and we will identify him with his moral depravity. As no individual love is at stake, there is no force that counteracts the extending of our indignation and our hatred of the moral wickedness to a hatred of the person. As the indestructible ontological value of this immortal soul, his being destined to eternal communion with God and loved by God, is not visible for us, and as no special value of this individuality is grasped, as in the case of natural love, there is no basis for a love of the morally evil man, no possibility of combining a value-response attitude of an indignation and the so-called hatred of the moral evil with a love for the person. Thus we may say: as long as it is not a beloved person, a person whom we loved before we are repulsed by her moral meanness and depravity, the following alternative presents itself in the realm of a merely natural morality: either the moral meanness does not affect us, leaving us more or less indifferent and thus we do not hate the evildoer, that is to say, we remain in a jovial, superficial friendliness to him, or we give a negative value-response to the moral evil. We react with a full indignation and a horror about the moral depravity and extend our horror to the person; we hate the evildoer.

Someone could object: but are there not noble pagans, such as a Socrates or a Plato, who in giving a true value-response to the moral depravity nevertheless do not hate the evildoer? Certainly, the attitude of these great moral personalities is a special one, but nevertheless they also do not fully escape the aforementioned alternative.

Their indignation and "hatred" of the moral evil has a more theoretical and cooler character, and thus they are preserved from degenerating into hatred of the evildoer. They neither love the evildoer nor hate the moral evil with this ardently affective indignation, it does not burn their heart. They manifest a reserved attitude to both: a moral condemnation of the evil rather than a full indignation, an ethos that corresponds to the ideal of a philosophical *bios* of antiquity.

In an analogous way, the attitude of the Stoics forms in this respect a special case. Their ideal of apathy and imperturbability, their identification of every affective value-response with passion, leads to a kind of affective indifference toward moral evil as well as toward the evildoing person. Because of their basic haughtiness, they are incapable of a true value-response. The Stoic would condemn the evil, but without allowing it to affect him, without experiencing a deep sorrow about moral evil.

In sum, we may say: the hatred of fanaticism and the hatred of a person because of her moral depravity form a special case among the different types of hatred. We saw how the original value-response of "hatred" of evil error and moral depravity degenerates into a real, wicked hatred of the person who errs or the moral scoundrel. It is a process of guilty oversimplification, of moral unconsciousness and falling prey to the immanent logic of fighting or of our nature.

But the situation is completely different if we consider a man who does not know Christ and His revelation or if we consider a Christian. In the frame of merely natural morality, we found two fundamental types: firstly, the primitive, more unconscious morality and, secondly, the conscious morality of the philosopher who is not a Christian in the true sense of the word.

In the primitive morality we saw that identifying the person who champions evil errors with his error, or the moral scoundrel with his moral depravity, is more or less inevitable. Only in the case of a natural love of such persons may the value-response of "hatred" of moral evil not be extended to the persons themselves. The love enables these persons to distinguish the evil from the persons and to look at it as an enemy of the beloved person. But as soon as the person in question is not dear to one, he will either remain indifferent toward the error or the moral depravity, or he will, in "hating" the error or the moral depravity, extend this hatred inevitably to the person.

In the conscious morality of the pagan philosopher, man may escape this alternative. But neither the fight against error nor the indignation about the immorality will manifest here its full character: the ardent affective note for which evil error and still more moral depravity calls. The pagan philosopher will not necessarily extend his condemnation of error and moral depravity to the person, but this is compensated by a certain element of neutrality both in the fight against error and the indignation about moral depravity, on the one hand, and in the attitude toward the person, on the other. Philosophical sobriety and distance may enable the pagan philosopher to distinguish the person from her error and moral faults, and his moral consciousness may save him from falling prey to the immanent logic of his fight or his indignation. In this case alone we can find an incomplete negative value-response directed to error and moral evil combined with an absence of hatred of the person who is a champion of error or a moral scoundrel. However, no love for him is to be found either.

A completely different picture of this problem is found, as we saw, in the frame of a Christian morality. The degeneration of indignation over sin into a hatred of the sinner is morally much worse as the true love of God engenders simultaneously the "hatred" of sin and the love of the sinner. The same reason that makes the saint hate sin forces him to love the sinner whose indestructible value as an immortal soul created for God and loved by Christ is disclosed to him. The Christian who permits, by oversimplification and spiritual laziness, the degeneration of his "hatred" of sin into hatred of the sinner betrays Christ in becoming prey to the automatism of his fallen nature and in failing to give the value-response to the sinner, which has been disclosed to him by Christ. He behaves as if Christ did not exist, though he knows Him.

As we saw before, also in these cases hatred is rooted in pride and concupiscence insofar as it is a real hatred, notwithstanding the different nuance that it has due to its origin in a value-response.

IV.ix. *The Nature of the Due Response to Moral Depravity*

In concluding this chapter about hatred, we must still briefly examine the specific nature of the obligatory negative response to moral depravity. We stated already that the indignation of the morally unconscious man is an impure one. Though certainly morally preferable to indifference, it is still mixed with elements of pride and concupiscence insofar as the morally unconscious man arrogates to himself a position of false security and—insofar as his response is rooted in his nature—penetrated with the overwhelming pull of our natural trends. In a word, it is not given out of *religio*. We will understand the impurity of this value-response that degenerates into a hatred of the sinner when we compare it with the morally perfect attitude, that is, with the attitude of the saint.

The so-called hatred of sin that is a pure and obligatory value-response refers to the sin as such and to the evil one, not to the sin of our neighbor. What is then the attitude of the saint to the moral depravity of his fellow man? Is it indignation in the full sense, or how does this holy indignation differ from the merely natural one?

In order to understand the nature of this holy indignation, we have to take into account the position of the sinner or the way in which his evildoing presents itself. When the moral depravity has a dramatic character, that is to say, when a situation is at stake that calls for an active intervention on our part, the attitude of the saint will be an active fight against the evil combined with a holy indignation. The act of a murderer throwing himself on his victim calls not only for an intervention in order to protect the victim and to frustrate the evil intention of the murderer, it also calls for a protest against his evildoing, a holy indignation about it. Or any injustice threatening someone calls equally for such a protest and resistance animated by holy indignation.

In all cases in which moral evil presents itself in an aggressive, impertinent way and in a dramatic situation, we are called to protest and to let the holy indignation fall on the evildoer even if we are not able to hinder him from accomplishing his evil intentions. Our Lord chases the merchants with a holy wrath from the temple of Solomon. Father Cristoforo summons, in Manzoni's masterwork *The Betrothed*, Don Rodrigo with a holy indignation after having tried to awaken his conscience with charity and kindness.

The flagrant, aggressive moral evil in a dramatic situation calls for a value-response of holy indignation. The same applies when the moral evildoer gives himself the appearance of a morally correct or even highly moral man. The acts and attitudes of the Pharisee calls for a holy indignation. Because of the pretention of moral rectitude, his moral depravity calls for an unmasking of his hypocrisy. Thus, we see that the Lord responds to the attitude of the Pharisees with holy indignation. But the sinfulness that is neither aggressive in a dramatic situation nor cloaked in a hypocritical rectitude engenders in the saint a deep sorrow rather than indignation.[20] And as soon as the sinner is in a weak and humiliating state, the response of the saint is exclusively merciful sorrow. Such is the attitude of our Lord to the adulteress.

We see thus that the morally perfect attitude toward the sinfulness in a particular person varies according to circumstances and according to the specific theme of the situation. Holy indignation is the adequate value-response only toward specific types of sinfulness, either conditioned by the dramatic character of the situation or by the strong position of the sinner or his hypocritical character.

This holy indignation differs completely, then, from merely natural indignation. It manifests the love of God as its basis. Its stern character is motivated exclusively by the aggressive, impertinent hypocritical character of the sinner; it is pervaded by sorrow and derives absolutely no satisfaction from the unfolding of our nature. It involves a specific standing apart from the situation, an acting out of God and not of our nature. It has a sublime purity that is completely formed by the love of God and by love for the sinner. Thus it assumes necessarily a different character

---

20. We abstract here from the sinner who repents his sins. His contrition creates a completely new situation that calls for merciful love. The case to which we refer is the sinner who shows no signs of contrition, who is involved in his sinfulness but who is neither in a powerful situation, nor aggressive and shameless, or a Pharisee.

when sinfulness presents itself in a situation that is neither dramatic nor aggressive nor again covered with hypocrisy.

The love of God and of the sinner manifests itself then in a deep loving sorrow without the stern gesture of holy indignation. The rejection of the particular sinfulness is manifest, but only in the form of the seriousness and gravity of this specific sorrow, in an atmosphere of moral sublimity that makes the sinner aware of the incompatibility of his sin with the saint. In this loving sorrow there is no element of camaraderie, of a jovial ignoring the terrible seriousness of sin, no yielding whatsoever to sin, no gesture of overlooking it. And as soon as the sinner is in a weak position, even if not yet filled with contrition, he is humiliated, and in front of his judges the sorrow assumes the specific character of merciful condescension. The saint's love of the sinner manifests itself in the unshakeable search for the lost sheep, in soliciting his conversion, in the loving invitation to turn back to the path of virtue.

It is obvious that this holy negative value-response attitude to the sinfulness implies *ab ovo* the love of the sinner and can thus never degenerate into hatred. As far as normal indignation is concerned, we now clearly see its impurity as value-response and its morally doubtful origin, which makes it possible and, in the frame of a non-Christian morality, more or less inevitable, to degenerate into a hatred of the sinner. Nevertheless, it remains true that this impure negative value-response is morally a *minus malum* in comparison with an indifference toward the moral depravity of our fellow man.

V

Overall Conclusion

THIS ANALYSIS OF THE ROOTS OF MORAL EVIL has disclosed to us that pride and concupiscence are always at the basis of all moral evil. The metaphysical question arises: how do these two morally negative centers enter into the human person? It is obvious that they do not come from God, that they are not something issuing from God's hand in creating man. Every creature of God is positive, possessing value, reflecting in some way His infinite goodness. "Nothing is evil, but the perversion of our will," says St. Augustine.[1]

Are they a result of the fall of man? Many symptoms of concupiscence and pride are certainly the sad heritage of original sin, such as the tendency of our nature to abandon the attitude of *religio* when we are confronted with the subjectively satisfying, the rebellion of our instincts against our spirit, the immanent logic of our nature: the continuous tendency of our nature to infect our good intentions by pride and many other symptoms of the mysterious rupture and disharmony in our fallen

1. [Possibly a paraphrase of *Confessions* 7.16.22. Editor.]

nature that, notwithstanding its negative character, has such a tremendous reality.

But is not the original sin due to pride and concupiscence? One may answer: pride and concupiscence are but a privation and nothing positively existing. This may be true, but it does not explain the mystery. The question arises: where does this privation come from?

We do not pretend to be able to answer this question and to explain the mysterious temptation to pride—potentially connected to the priceless privilege of free will. We restrict ourselves to stating the following two fundamental facts. Firstly, God can never be the cause of pride and concupiscence. Secondly, pride and concupiscence exist in fallen man and are the roots of all moral evil.

VI

Immanent Logic[1]

ONE OF THE GENERAL DANGERS of our fallen nature is to be absorbed by the immanent logic of any activity or situation. We have already touched several times on this phenomenon in the course of our analysis. Now we have to examine this danger as such and to inquire into its roots.

Every being, every situation as well as every activity possesses an immanent logic. We have to conform to this immanent logic if we want to act reasonably. If we construct a machine, we have to conform to the

---

1. [This material exists both as a manuscript (*Eigengesetzlichkeit*, 35 pp., Ana 544, VI, 14, 1) and a typescript (Immanent Law, 26 pp., Ana 544, VI, 14, 5). As in all other cases, the present volume follows the typescript, with the exception that title has been changed from "Immanent Law" to "Immanent Logic," which is the phrase Hildebrand uses in this chapter and in other works. Note that the typescript contains further emendations written in pencil. The present edition incorporates most of these emendations without noting them in the text. These emendations are not Hildebrand's. This is obvious both from the handwriting, which is not Hildebrand's, and from the content of some remarks in the margins that are written in the same hand. These remarks are not included in this volume both because they are not Hildebrand's and because they concern only the language, that is, the grammar and style of the text. Since the typescript includes also one German remark written in Hildebrand's hand, it is likely that Hildebrand read the typescript either before or after the emendations were made. Editor.]

laws of mechanics as well as to the immanent logic of our activity. The teleological activity directed toward a certain end has its logic concerning the use of the proper means, the order in which we have to proceed, and so on. A dangerous situation has its immanent logic that imposes on me a certain way of proceeding in order to overcome the danger. A research project has its immanent logic. We cannot proceed arbitrarily; we have to conform to the laws of the very nature of the object and the immanent laws of knowledge. The necessity of conforming to immanent logic applies to every activity. But as soon as this immanent logic absorbs us to such an extent that we no longer situate the end of our activity within the hierarchy of values, that we are no longer concerned with the place that our end holds in this hierarchy, we have fallen prey to the immanent logic of our activity, a state that, in itself, is undoubtedly morally negative and is moreover a source of many moral evils.

Let us first examine this absorption in the immanent logic in the cases in which it is not connected with any special moral evil. We are for instance doing some research work. We want to use some manuscript in which we have made some notes that would be useful for our work. We believe that it may be in a drawer and try to pull it out. But the drawer sticks. We begin to try to overcome this obstacle, and the immanent logic of this task catches us to such an extent that we waste much more time in opening the drawer than our aim of finding the manuscript deserves. We could have written the passage in question in a much shorter time. The characteristic of this attitude is that my interest in opening the drawer is no longer determined by the importance of the end that it originally was to serve, that the mere fact that I made it into my purpose endows it with a weight, and that the immanent logic of opening a drawer gets hold of me.

This being caught by the immanent logic of a subordinate activity, which now pushes me to insist on success and to become blind to the fact that the importance of the end for which opening the drawer is only a means does not justify my spending so much time on it, is a typical case of this imprisonment in the immanent logic of an activity.

Three main marks characterize this falling prey to the immanent logic of an activity: firstly, the fact that I detach this means from the end that it serves, that I isolate it and make of it an independent end. Secondly, that the teleology of my activity assumes the character of automatism whereby I lose the necessary distance from it. I am no longer the master of the situation, no longer approaching it sovereignly in order to use it, but I am dominated by this immanent teleology that pushes me forward according to its immanent logic. Thirdly, the subordinate end that borrows its importance exclusively from another, superior end receives the character of illegitimate importance exclusively through the law of gravity of my having made it into my purpose. When I yield to this law of gravity, I fall prey to the automatism of this teleological weight.

In this example, the result of my falling prey to the immanent logic of an activity has more the character of unreasonability than of immorality. But we shall immediately see that this imprisonment and frustration of our inner distance to the end is also the root of many moral evils. Firstly, this imprisonment in the automatism of our activity is in itself, apart from any accidental consequences of it, a slavery, a losing our moral freedom and as such it is immoral. Secondly, the isolation of a subordinate end, and the ignoring of the superior end to which the subordinate end is a means, may lead a man to become instrumental for an immoral end. Consider, for instance, the general who is so absorbed by the immanent logic of warfare that he no longer examines whether the war is just or not; or the statesman who falls prey to the immanent logic of politics and no longer examines whether a certain end is good or not. Thirdly, the imprisonment in the immanent logic of an activity may blind us to the moral significance of the means that we use for attaining our end. For instance, someone who has a lawsuit against another person is so captured by the immanent logic of winning this lawsuit that he agrees to use means that are immoral or, at least, is drawn into enmity toward his opponent because of the immanent logic of the lawsuit, which surpasses by far his original intention when he decided to bring the lawsuit.

We all know how easily the immanent logic of any dispute or quarrel leads us to uncharitable words and attitudes that were in no way intended when we began to contradict the other and that are quite out of proportion to the topic at stake. We all know how items of no importance may become the source of a quarrel and of offending our neighbor only because we fall prey to the immanent logic of a certain situation. If we would keep an inner distance to the situation, and realize the unimportance of the item at stake, no quarrel would come about, nor, above all, any hostile and offensive behavior toward another person.

Let us first analyze the moral danger of this imprisonment itself. As soon as we fall prey to the immanent logic of an activity or a situation, we have left the basic attitude of *religio*. We no longer live *in conspectu Dei* in the sight of God and in the awakedness toward the reign of values, because we have become slaves to the automatism of our activity or of a certain situation. It is not the shaking off of *religio*, as in the former cases of concupiscence, which were based on the craving for something subjectively satisfying or on the desire to avoid the burden of *religio* as such, as in the case of a certain laziness. It is, rather, a gliding away from the attitude of *religio*, a forgetting it, as it were, because of our fascination with the immanent logic of something else. It is not so much an indifference toward the reign of values nor a blindness to the values resulting from indifference but, rather, a forgetting of them, being cut off from them, overlooking them.

It has the character of a cramp or psychical spasm, and the antithesis to *religio* and moral awakedness has a formal instead of a qualitative character. It is therefore, as such, a more temporary departure from *religio* than in the above mentioned cases of concupiscence. But though it is in itself a more temporary departure from *religio*, and not so much a deliberate turning of one's back on it, it may last through the whole life of a man. Certainly the topics will change, the immanent logic that absorbs a man will vary in the course of his life, but the tendency to let himself always be dominated by the immanent logic of his different activities and the situations in which he finds himself will last. And this attitude repeats itself analogously on different levels. Also, the man who is absorbed by the immanent logic of the necessities of life, of his profession, no longer questions the value of all his deeds, he does not think of his eternal welfare, of his ultimate end, because the immanent logic of his daily life pushes and draws him forward from one step to the other, and he always postpones, so to speak, the concern with his eternal end. To fall prey to immanent logic is one of the fundamental tragedies in human life. It cuts us off from confronting the ends of our actions with God, it frustrates a *frui* of the great gifts of God, it hinders any contemplative attitude, and deprives us from inner moral freedom.

We saw in the chapter on "Freedom" that being swallowed by a passion forms the negative counterpart to the sublime loss of ourselves that contemplative abandonment to goods possessing high value, and in a completely new sense to Christ, implies.[2] The former is morally negative, and the latter is morally positive. In the former we become slaves; in the latter we attain the highest freedom of the children of God. Falling prey to immanent logic equally forms a negative counterpart to the sublime "loss of ourselves." It certainly differs completely from being swallowed by a passion, but it shares with it the character of imprisonment, of a loss of our moral freedom, and, as such, is equally opposed to the highest freedom that is implied by "losing ourselves" in the sense of the Gospel.

We turn now to the moral danger that results when we isolate a subordinate end and, in the process, fall prey to the immanent logic of our activity. Let us consider, for example, an employee of the state who is accomplishing his work in an assiduous, dutiful way; a totalitarian government comes to power and the principles of this government are immoral and against the natural law. The employee is so absorbed by the immanent logic of his work that he continues to serve the government without becoming aware that he is now serving something evil.

Let us presuppose that no selfish motives connected with his career or with money play a role in his attitude. The immanent logic of his activity alone preoccupies him to such an extent that he serves a completely different end with the same assiduity, the same accuracy, as he did before the change in government. He thinks no further than how he may attain

2. [This reference relates likely to a typescript "Freedom" (Ana 544, VI, 14, 8), more specifically to its section called "The Role of Our Freedom in the Spheres of Passions." This section includes a detailed analysis of passions in their relationship to the freedom of the will. Editor.]

the subordinate end that is the aim of his activity.

Many people consider a lot of things as necessary that in reality are not. They concentrate their energies in order to be able to buy a house or a car, not because either is a special object of their desire. It is the immanent logic of increasing their wealth that pushes them to go always further and to accept as self-evidently necessary the possession of things that are not objectively necessary. They no longer examine whether the possession of these things is really important, enjoyable, or useful for some other end.

We want to help another person in overcoming a fault and decide to make her aware of this fault through a fraternal correction. Our original aim is the moral improvement of our neighbor. We choose to make her aware of her fault as a mere means to this end. But by speaking with her, a subordinated end, we are caught by the immanent logic of this end. Absorbed by the task of showing her the fault clearly, we insist too much, say too many things, and say them in a way which offends her. Her way of reacting may logically engender an ever-increasing insistence and ever more drastic expressions on our part. Afterward, we realize that we have given her the impression that we are hostile to her, and that we have—precisely because of the way in which we proceeded—frustrated our ultimate end. The correct explanation of her fault has become so much an end in itself that it engendered a way of proceeding that frustrated the superior end. And above all, notwithstanding our original good intention, we acted uncharitably. We no longer grasped that the moment was not the right one, that the mood of our neighbor was not such as to predispose her to a fruitful acceptance, and all this because we were absorbed by the immanent logic of explaining the fault to her. We did not refrain from fulfilling our purpose when the first reaction of our neighbor revealed her insusceptibility, but, because of the automatism of the dispute, we continued to insist, instead of stepping back, which we would have done if the superior end of our undertaking had still been fully present to us.

Every bureaucratism is a further typical result of falling prey to the immanent logic of a subordinate end and of the detachment of this end from its character as a means to a superior end. But the most dangerous effect of this immanent logic manifests itself in the blindness concerning the means that we accept in order to attain an end. The capitalist who has fallen prey to the immanent logic of the process of rendering his business more and more profitable dismisses a worker without being aware that this may throw the man into misery.

The same capitalist may be disposed to help a poor man in a generous way, so long as this man has no connection with his factory. In his private life, where the immanent logic of his activity does not dominate him to this extent, he may have a full understanding of the disvalue of an uncharitable attitude, but as soon as his professional activity is at stake, he thinks only in terms of its immanent logic and behaves uncharitably and with much hardness. He no longer examines and confronts the objective importance of his drive for profit with the value of the fact that this worker is a human being who must find the possibility of earning his living. He lets himself be pushed by the immanent logic of the prosperity of his factory from one step to another. What matters here is to understand that the imprisonment in the immanent logic of the activity is the source of his lack of charity, and not a specific covetousness or avarice. The imprisonment is itself the root of moral evil.

A special example of choosing immoral means because of absorption by the immanent logic of an activity is the so-called Machiavellianism in the political field. I do not think here of the man who is motivated only by the lust of power and for whom the *raison d'etat* plays no role. He is not the real Machiavellian who has no real concern for the *bonum commune*, and for whom politics itself is only a means to the satisfaction of his pride. Rather, I am thinking of the man who is concerned with the *res publica* as such, with the good functioning of the state, with the security of his country, with its prosperity, its might and influence. Such is the case in a Richelieu, a Bismarck, a Colbert. But the immanent logic of their activity has absorbed them to such an extent that they use immoral means in order to attain their end. They proceed step by step and brush away everything that hinders the deployment of the immanent logic of their activity and that hinders the so-called *raison d'etat*. It may be that such statesmen have made of their activity an idol, the value and importance of which seems to them to justify any means. But this is another type, which we shall examine later on.[3]

But it may also be that they use any means because they are so much absorbed by the immanent logic that the immorality of the same means that they would grasp and refuse to accept in their private lives is not really recognized. It presents itself to them as an inevitable necessity; their fascination with the immanent logic hinders them from confronting the value of the good that they destroy with the value of the good that is their aim. The specific moral danger of this spiritual slavery reveals itself in perhaps the most obvious way when we think of those cases in which the end is a specifically moral or even religious one.

For example: someone directs a Catholic organization. The end is the religious renewal of a certain group. He devotes himself with the greatest ardor to his task and is ready to make any personal sacrifice for his task. Nevertheless, he lets himself be absorbed by the immanent logic of building up this group. He needs money for his task. And now we can observe that his preoccupation with the attainment of his end makes him, in the first place, overestimate the importance of this particular group and pushes him to consider everything disproportionately from the angle of his specific task. In the second place, he may even behave in an uncharitable manner in the interest of his group. He may file a lawsuit, acting in the interest of the group, and the immanent logic of this lawsuit may push him to uncharitable acts. Or he may develop an ungenerous attitude with respect to the salaries of his employees, because he wants to increase the money of the group. The same man is perhaps very generous in what concerns his personal money; he will be ready to give alms to the poor. But as soon as the interest of his group is in question, he will be stingy and even unjust. Hence, the moral danger of imprisonment by immanent logic is obvious. The exaggeration of the

---

3. [There is no such text in the *Nachlass* that would belong to the group "Roots of Moral Evil." Hildebrand analyzes various types of idols in his later book, *Graven Images*. Since this book was published only four years after *Ethics*, it is possible that this remark of Hildebrand refers to material published later in *Graven Images*. Editor.]

importance of this particular task is already morally imperfect; and the fact that he looks at everything from the point of view of this particular end is still more so.

He will perhaps rejoice about a political event, for instance, a change of government, though this government is as such morally bad, because one of the members of the government is a sponsor of his group and he may thus expect from this change favorable consequences for his group; or he will envy the money that other Catholic organizations receive. He may be drawn into an attitude of rivalry with other Catholic groups, although the realization of the authentic meaning and value of his group should make him aware that for the ultimate end, the *Corpus Christi Mysticum* [the Church, the mystical body of Christ] and the Kingdom of God, it little matters whether his group or another one flourishes, because all such groups work for the same ultimate end. The moral danger of falling prey to the immanent logic of an activity and its end manifests itself still more with respect to the different steps and attitudes leading to his aim, which he may develop in the course of his activity. He may behave unjustly, ungenerously, uncharitably. And he will do so with a good conscience because he does it, not in his personal interest, but in the interest of his group and because he is so sure of the value of its end. Instead of keeping an inner distance to this goal, notwithstanding his ardor and zeal for the goal, instead of seeing it always in the light of the *unum necessarium* and confronting it with other values, instead of preserving the flexibility of the saint to respond in every moment and in every situation to the call of God, whatever may be its relation to his particular end, instead of remaining *in conspectu Dei* in all phases of his activity, he becomes a slave to his activity and offends God, although he chose this end only in order to serve God.

Pope Paul IV, Carafa, is a tragic example of this; he became prisoner to the immanent logic of his zeal to destroy heresies. He finished by seeing a heretic in everyone, and though he hated nepotism, his mistrust pushed him to trust nobody but his relatives. The danger of this imprisonment lives in every human being. How often do we discover that because of the immanent logic of a situation we tell a lie, realizing afterward that the purpose at stake would never have led us to lie, if only we had kept an inner distance! We prefer, for instance, to keep something secret from another person, and the immanent logic of this intention leads us step by step until we discover that we have committed a sin, though the end of keeping something secret was of no great importance for us, even subjectively speaking. Just because we made it our purpose, we glide into the immanent logic of this purpose, and without seeing this purpose in its place, in its authentic importance, we fight for it as if it would have the utmost importance.

We have no longer to insist on the existence of this phenomenon of being dominated by the immanent logic of an activity, nor on the moral danger it implies. But the question arises: is the root of this evil concupiscence, pride, a combination of both, or something completely different?

Falling prey to the immanent logic of an activity or a situation implies always an element of unawakedness. It presupposes that we are not rooted enough in the value-response attitude and that other elements play an illegitimate role. Sometimes it is a kind of obstinacy, being dominated by the desire to succeed in our effort at any cost; this is, for instance, often the case when we insist on attaining some unimportant subordinate ends, though their usefulness is out of proportion to the effort and time dedicated to them. We mentioned above the man who wants to open the drawer in order to find something he needs and that—because the drawer resists—the opening of this drawer becomes an independent end; he insists on opening it and loses an amount of time that is disproportionate to the importance of finding the thing that is in the drawer. Here the fact that we are not able to open the drawer irritates us: that is to say, the mere fact that we are not successful with respect to something that we have undertaken, independently of the objective importance of our end. We insist because we hate the fact that something that belongs to the sphere in which we feel ourselves masters, the sphere of instruments upon which we look as being at our disposal, something that we expect to dominate, resists. The fact that we do not succeed hurts our consciousness of masterly sovereignty; we get impatient and look at the object with a kind of hostility, so to speak. We try and try again because mastering this activity has become an end in itself.

Here pride obviously intervenes. The object does not, so to speak, obey us. Our feeling of sovereignty is hurt. We are no longer at an uncramped, free distance from this subordinate object that would enable us to give up something that is of no essential importance, and to attain our real end in another way or postpone it until someone repairs the drawer in question. We become biased: our desire to open the drawer assumes the stature of our main purpose, instead of remaining a minor step toward it. This obstinacy of our attitude, this infantile insistence on success, is an outgrowth of pride, though a relatively innocent one.

Something analogous applies to those discussions into which we pour disproportionate effort and insistence into persuading other people that our opinion is right, although the topic of our discussion has no real importance.

For instance, someone tells us that one way to a certain destination is shorter than another; we disagree with him. Although the question is of no practical importance (suppose there is no need to reach the place in question quickly), we waste a lot of time in the discussion. We get excited and uncharitable toward another person because we have fallen prey to the immanent logic of this discussion. Here again the element of obstinacy, of satisfaction in being right, of proving to other persons that we are right, of winning the battle, so to speak, in a word, success as such, reveals our underlying pride.[4]

---

4. Someone could object: but are we not obliged to insist on success even concerning the means? Have we not seen that it was one of the specific outgrowths of laziness that we give up our effort to attain an end too easily, merely because there are many difficulties? Is the insistence on attaining an end that we have proposed to ourselves not a virtue, an indispensable element of perseverance? I respond: the insistence of the persevering man differs completely from the insistence that is an outgrowth of the imprisonment by the immanent logic of our activity. The persevering man, because of the ardor of his value-response, is not discouraged by difficulties and obstacles in his striving to attain an end. His insistence is supported exclusively by the authentic value of his end. Free from any obstinacy, from any interest in success for its own sake, he is directed toward his aim in a pure value-response attitude. He will never detach a subordinate end from the superior one, from which it borrows its importance, and let it become an end in itself. His insistence in overcom-

Even if in this case falling prey to the immanent logic of our activity is rooted in pride, there are many other cases in which this does not seem as obvious. For instance, the absorption by the immanent logic of an activity and the attainment of its immediate end that is characteristic of the general who does not question whether the war is just or not, who is concerned only with the immanent logic of waging war, is obviously rooted in something different from pride.

The end, the immanent logic that captivates him, is not something indifferent in itself, which takes on a meaning for him only because of other ends that it serves. It does not become important only because he has made it his purpose. The elements of obstinacy and irritation because of an obstacle, the being hurt in his feeling of sovereignty, are both absent.

We find here instead, firstly, the satisfaction in displaying his talents. Displaying talent in an activity for which we are gifted contains an immanent satisfaction that is as such legitimate. The greater the task, the more legitimate it is. But this satisfaction, as we saw before, becomes illegitimate and assumes a character of concupiscence when it becomes the motive in place of the objective importance and value of the end to which our activity is directed.[5] It can legitimately be the main and even exclusive motive only in games. In every serious activity, where an end is at stake that has a direct or indirect value, the immanent satisfaction of the activity as such has to play a subordinate role. As soon as the end becomes only an occasion to display our gifts and to enjoy our activity as such, a concupiscent egoistic attitude has arisen in us.

This form of concupiscence may be one of the roots of absorption by immanent logic. But it may also lead to a cynical disinterest in the superior end, an acceptance of its immorality, because we are not ready to give up the activity that we like. This would obviously no longer be a specific imprisonment in the immanent logic of an activity. To be fascinated by

---

ing obstacles will be the fruit exclusively of his unlimited ardor for the real value at stake, and he will never insist on something merely because he made it his purpose and hates to be unsuccessful.

5. [Cf. pages 64–69 above. Editor.]

the immanent satisfaction of our activity can be only one root among others in our case.

Another element may be a restriction to a subordinate end which derives from a false conception of obedience and duty in which we believe that it is not our business to think further than our special task. It is the basic error of believing that anything could release us from the duty of confronting any activity with God and the reign of the morally relevant values.

Specialized as my task may be, restricted as my activity and professional concerns may be, the moral character of the superior end in the attainment of which my activity is inserted remains indispensable. If it is not our business to occupy ourselves with other activities that serve the same end, if it is not the business of the general to declare war or to be concerned with political problems, the moral question whether the war is just or not is always his business and concerns him as well as any officer or soldier. The wrong conception of duty consists in the fact that the general believes that because his professional task consists only in winning the war, his conscience does not have to be concerned with the question of whether the war is just or not. But whatever may be his function as general, he is not primarily a general, but a man. As a person he has to be concerned with the moral question, and this duty has by far the primacy over his immanent professional duty as general. We touch here on a great danger. It is the absorption of the human person by a professional function. The danger is that someone restricts his conception of duty to the fulfilling of his professional tasks and forgets, so to speak, his incomparably superior duty to give the right responses to the morally relevant values and to God, so that he forgets the vocation of every man as man. The man who has crippled his existence by becoming a mere functionary, by letting his character as man be swallowed by a profession, has also deafened his conscience and believes that he acts correctly in looking no further than his professional task compels him. This is the "Prussian" type of employee, who, because of this absorption of the human person into a function, obeys man more than God. Because his professional task is specialized, he becomes a specialist also with respect to morals, believing that he has done everything required of him if only he fulfills his professional duties in a perfect manner.

The affinity of this attitude with falling prey to the immanent logic of our activity is obvious. But there also obviously exist two different stages in this process. The first is looking no further than the special task to which he is directed by his employer and feeling morally dispensed from bothering about the aims of his superior. The second stage is restricting the notion of duty to the mere immanent perfection of his task, that is to say, caring nothing for the morality of the means used to attain his end. He will be loyal to his superior, he will be honest in everything that concerns the fulfillment of his tasks; for instance, he will not enrich himself personally or omit anything that his professional duty requires. But moral considerations will not hinder him from using any and every means to attain the end that he considers his duty.

In the first stage, the general will dedicate all his energies to winning the war, without deliberating about whether the war is just or not. In the second stage, he will even use every means, whether morally legitimate or not, to win the war. The immanent logic of warfare alone will preoccupy him, and the question of whether he observes the moral law will no longer bother him as soon as something presents itself as a useful means to attain his end. He will accept the use of any cruelty or injustice against the enemy if it serves to win the war. In this second stage the imprisonment by the immanent logic of his aim is still more obvious.

We must now inquire whether this perversion is rooted in concupiscence. There is obviously an element of concupiscence in the absorption of the person by her specific task and function. To sink to the level of a mere instrument and to atrophy as a human person, to forget our primary vocation as man, is an outgrowth of concupiscence, of the spiritual laziness that we examined before. The abandonment of the basic attitude of *religio*, the fading away of a true awakedness, the identification of professional efficiency with the serious center of life, the fascination with the practically useful, all constitute a yielding to the automatic rhythm of our activity, a shunning of the spiritual *élan* that the resistance to this tendency of our fallen nature requires.[6]

But spiritual laziness underlies not only the instrumentalization of man and the wrong conception of duty—this is just one specific type among the immense variety of the forms of falling prey to immanent logic—spiritual laziness underlies every type of this perversion. It does not manifest itself at every stage of this process, but at the very beginning. To let ourselves be captured by the immanent logic of an activity, to yield to its automatism, to allow the dethronement of our power of taking a free distance to the world, and of our remaining rooted in *religio*: these are forms of spiritual laziness. That we are disposed to leave the attitude of *religio* so easily is already a symptom of the insufficient firmness of our value-response attitude. This is in part conditioned by a false security that is an outgrowth of pride. Partly it is an unawakedness, the antithesis to the awakedness of which our Lord says, "Keep watch," and of the attitude of the Psalmist when he says, "my heart is ready, O Lord"; it is a dumb trotting through life which is, as we saw, an outgrowth of concupiscence. But above all the lack of firmness in our value-response attitude is a symptom of our self-centeredness, of a concupiscent imprisonment in ourselves. Every type of pseudo-losing ourselves issues from concupiscence, whether it is being swallowed by a passion or falling prey to something subjectively satisfying, or to the immanent logic of an activity.

A special problem poses itself with respect to those activities that by their very nature seem to require us to be absorbed to a certain extent by their immanent logic. An artist cannot avoid being in a certain

---

6. But this sinking to the level of an instrument is not identical to falling prey to the immanent logic that leads to the wrong notion of duty and even using immoral means in order to attain the end. The instrumentalization as such leads to an impoverishment of human life, to an atrophy of the contemplative attitude, and above all to a desubstantialization of the religious life. It may even lead to a radical indifference toward our eternal end. But in itself it does not necessarily lead to a blindness and indifference toward moral values, nor to disinterest in the superior end, nor to an acceptance of immoral means in order to attain our immediate professional end. For falling prey to the immanent logic of our activity, on the one hand, more is needed than the shifting of the center of gravity of life from our existence as man to the efficiency of our work. On the other hand, it occurs also among men in whom this perversion has not taken place. The imprisonment in the immanent logic of our activities is rooted, firstly, in spiritual laziness; secondly in a prevalence of the immanent satisfaction.

way absorbed in the process of his creative inspiration. As Plato said in *Phaedrus*: all great things issue from "madness." The artist must be enraptured in a certain way; he must be possessed by his inspiration. Is this apparently inevitable absorption by the immanent logic of his activity also a morally imperfect attitude? Is it equally a departure from *religio*? It must be said: firstly, the very nature of the aim of this activity implies a continuous contact with values, being imbued by them, so that this absorption has a completely different character. But this absorption obviously refers only to the creative process in the strict sense. All activities of a more technical character share the same potential dangers of illegitimate absorption by the immanent logic that belongs to any activity as such. We have thus to distinguish the creative process in the strict sense from all other processes of a more technical character. The inevitability of being enraptured applies only to the creative process in the narrowest sense, that is, the inspiration and the objectification of the inspiration. Here, being absorbed by a kind of "ecstasy" differs completely from falling prey to the immanent logic of an activity. It is not a being drawn downward but an elevation above ourselves. It is a kind of natural analogue to the mystics' ecstasies. Notwithstanding the abyss that separates them, conditioned, on the one hand, by the nature of the values in question, and by the difference between the supernatural character of the latter and the merely natural character of the former, they have in common the character of being elevations above the normal state of our life, the character of an extraordinary intensity and of a certain passivity. There is, in both cases, notwithstanding all the differences, an analogous being endowed from above with a luminous intensity, and also an extraordinary expansion of our capacities that is experienced as a gift, as something that is not completely one's own. This kind of absorption presupposes a reverent value-response attitude, a true self-abandonment, a remaining under the reign of the world of values. Certainly, the absorption of the artist in no way guarantees that he possesses in general the true attitude of *religio*. But at least in this moment of creative inspiration, he must be in a reverent attitude, in a state of self-abandonment, in a gesture of looking upward, in true contact with the world of values. And above all this kind of absorption as such in no way draws him out of *religio* if his life is in general permeated by this attitude. It does not deprive him of his contact with the reign of values and of his inner awakedness. It does not tend to dethrone his inner freedom. We see thus that this kind of absorption differs completely from falling prey to the immanent logic of our activity. But this applies exclusively to the creative process in the strict sense of this term, which is to be found only in great artists, and even there only in some extraordinary moments. Apart from this the artistic activity shares with any other the danger of falling prey to the immanent logic. The artist can also be absorbed by his activity, by the prevalence of the immanent satisfaction that he finds in displaying his talents or by the direction toward various ends that his activity implies. Moreover, he can be so absorbed by his artistic production that he becomes blunted toward the morally relevant values. For instance, he may push aside in an uncharitable way everything that hinders him from concentrating on his activity, or he may use means for his end that are morally doubtful or even illegitimate. But it is by no means inevitable that he should do these things in order to produce great works of art, and it is rather prejudicial for his artistic activity; it is in an outspoken opposition to the true, creative, inspired process that we examined above and that is indispensable for great artistic achievements.

Summarizing we may say: the process of falling prey to the immanent logic of an activity is rooted in the following elements: firstly, in the lack of firmness of our basic value-response attitude, which is conditioned by pride and concupiscence; secondly, in false security, rooted in pride; thirdly, in unawakedness, rooted in concupiscence; fourthly, in yielding to the fascination of the immanent logic of an activity, which is rooted in concupiscence; fifthly, in the formal tendency to be successful with respect to everything that we have proposed to ourselves. This again is rooted partly in pride, insofar as it concerns the desire to exert a masterly sovereignty, and partly in concupiscence, insofar as it refers to the natural satisfaction that the successful deployment of the automatism of any activity implies. Many other elements may occur in single cases according to their specific nature, as, for instance, the prevalence of the immanent satisfaction that certain activities imply over and beyond the above mentioned formal satisfaction that the normal and successful deployment of any activity as such possesses.

Concupiscence and pride are thus both at the basis of this fundamental perversion that is as such immoral and leads to many other more or less grave moral faults.

Index

aesthetic values, xxxi, 22–23n6, 66, 116, 136, *see also* work (of art)
akrasia (ancient Greek, "lack of control," with regard to acting against one's better judgment), xxiv, xxviii, xxxii, *see also* self-control, moderation, will (weakness of)
Alyosha (*Brothers Karamazov*), 160
ambition, xxxviii, xlii, 8, 109, 129–130, 147, 151, 162–163
Ambrose, St., 176n11
Apology (Plato), 175
appropriation, 89, 148
Aquinas, St. Thomas, xxiv, 180n16
Aristippus, 28
Aristotle, xxiv, xxiii–xxiv, xxix 3–4, 10, 64–65, 75n23
Augustine, St., xxiv–xxvii 12, 29, 36, 61n20, 78, 101, 102, 176n11, 180, 193
ataraxia (ancient Greek, "imperturbability"), 44, 172–173, 187, *see also* Stoic school
avarice, 72, 74–77, 201

badness, *see* moral evil
Balzac, Honoré de, 20
banausos (ancient Greek pejorative, "manual laborer"), 85, 136, *see also* philistine
Beethoven, xxxin14, 90
Betrothed, The (Manzoni), 190
Bismarck, Otto von, 201
bodily agreeable, the: possible attitudes towards, 25–31; three types or levels of, 24; *see also* pleasure, subjectively satisfying
bodily displeasures: caused by disgusting food or unpleasant smells, 55–56; caused by unsatisfied urges, 52–54; as distinct from both pain and urges, 37
bodily pain: attitude of the soft concupiscent type to, xxxiv, 49–52; cursing as an expression of the hard concupiscent type to, xxxiv, 42–44; as distinct from both bodily displeasure and bodily urges, 37;

bodily pain: (*cont.*)
fear of undergoing it, 44–49; morally legitimate approach to, 36–43; no ordinary moral obligation to accept it when intense, xxxiii–xxxiv, 37–43; as a source of sexual pleasure, *see* sadism

Bolshevism, 46

Bonaventure, St., 100

bonum (Latin, "good"), 4, 12, 201

Brothers Karamazov (Dostoevsky), 20, 103, 136, 160

Cain and Abel, 1, 103, 160

Cajthaml, Martin, xv, xix, xxiv, xxvi, xxx–xxxi, xlv, 5n6, 6n7

call of values, the, xv, xxviii, xliv, 3, 12, 14, 18–19, 36n13, 39, 46–47, 54, 56, 60, 62, 68, 91, 94–96, 98, 107, 109, 120–123, 125–127, 137, 141, 158, 169, *see also* reign of values, *religio*, reverence, *sursum corda*, value–response attitude

calumny, 143

categories of importance, xxvii, 2–4, 6–7, 9, 14, 27–29, 83n29

Catherine, St., 103

centers in a person: center of concupiscence distinct from that of pride, 20; centers of concupiscence and pride *vs.* the value-responding center (also called the "humble," "reverent," or "loving" center), xiv, xxix, xli, 13–14, 18, 26, 159; center of irascibility (also called "the natural center of self-defense and vulnerability"), 168–177; free center (also called "free spiritual center" or "free moral center"), 10, 74, 169–170, 184, *see also* freedom; legitimate center to which the subjectively satisfying appeals (or which is repulsed by the subjectively dissatisfying), 13–15, 24, 26, 38, 56, 78–80, 82, 91–92; morally illegitimate center(s) (unspecified), 61; and revenge, 165–166

charity, xxxii, xli, 21, 23, 26, 38–39, 42, 44, 48–50, 56, 70–71, 74–77, 80, 84–85, 111, 117, 128, 132, 136, 138, 154, 159, 160–164, 172–175, 181, 190, 201

Christ, 26, 38, 70, 95, 97, 124–125, 127, 135, 154, 161, 171–176, 180, 184–185, 187–190, 199, 203, 209

Christian morality *vs.* natural morality, 25n8, 26, 47, 171–172, 174, 183–188, 191

De Civitate Dei (Augustine), 101n2, 102n3

Colbert, Jean-Baptiste, 201

conceit, as a form of pride, xxxix, 132–135, 139

concupiscence: basic or essential nature of, 17–20, 177, 198; in the bodily sphere, *see* bodily agreeable, bodily displeasures, bodily pain; and hatred, 164–165, 170–171, 176–177, 181–182, 188; enslavement to the immanent logic of an activity as rooted in, 204, 206, 208–210; and passion, 170–171, 177, 209; its positive indifference towards value, 18–19, 25, 45, 49–51, 60, 68, 72, 75–76, 99, 103, 138; in possession or ownership, xxxv–xxxvi 88, 90, 148; in the psychical sphere, *see* psychic pleasures; its relations with pride, xli, 19–20, 22, 44, 59, 68–69, 74, 82, 84, 96–97, 101–102, 103, 108, 137–138, 146–149, 152, 157–159, 164–165, 170–171, 176, 181–182, 188; the sphere of pure concupiscence, xxxiv–xxxv, 77–82; as superactual preoccupation with the merely subjectively satisfying, xvi, xxxi–xxxvi, 15, 18, 20, 24, 50, 98–99, 101–102; as tending to shake off the burden of *religio*, xxv, 74, 86, 92–94,

177, 182, 193, 198, 209, *see also* spiritual laziness; typical fruits of, 68
concupiscent center, *see* centers in a person
concupiscent types: the three main (the passionate, the lazy, and the soft), essentially distinguished, xxxii, 20–23; for their differing reactions to phenomena in various spheres, *see* bodily agreeable, bodily displeasures, bodily pain, psychic pleasures, money
Confessions (Augustine), xxv, 176n11, 193n1
conjugal act, 32, 37–38
conscience, 4–5, 7, 18, 75, 120–122, 181–182, 190, 203, 207
Coriolanus (Shakespeare), 110
covetousness, 76, 88
Crime and Punishment (Dostoevsky), 4
Cristoforo (*The Betrothed*), 190
Crosby, John, xi, xiii, xxii
curiosity (idle), xxxiii, 78–80
cursing, xxxiv, 42–44, 50, 176
Cynic school, 150n29

Daniel, 100
dethronement: of God or values, as sought by satanic pride, 103–105, 111, 117, 128, 131, 137, 141, 144, 160, *see also* metaphysical power of values, reign of values; of one's freedom due to the immanent logic of an activity, 209–211n7; of one's freedom due to the passions, 9–10, 74, 172, 175, 199; of the value-response attitude in the person necessarily results in the actualization of pride and concupiscence, 13–15
Diogenes the Cynic, 150
Don Rodrigo (*The Betrothed*), 190
Dostoevsky, Fyodor, 4, 20, 103, 136

dreaming about life when detached from reality as a fruit of concupiscence, 62–63, 93
Drennen, Donald A., xxxi
duty, wrong conception of, 96, 207–209
dynamic pride, xxxvii–xxxix, xlii, 106–107, 109, 129–132, 134, 137–139, 141–142, 145, 152–153, 163

egotism, 41, 44, 48–49, 88
élan, *see* spiritual *élan*
elegant man, the, xxxiv, 59
enmity, xlii, 166, 177, 184, 197
enemy of God, the, 177, 182, 184
envy, xl, 132, 134, 141–142, 144, 168, 177, 203, *see also* ressentiment
Eroica (Beethoven), xxxi
Ethics (Hildebrand), *see* Hildebrand, Dietrich von (works)
eudaimonia (ancient Greek, "happiness" or "personal flourishing") xxxiv, 43n15, 75n23
Eugénie Grandet, father of (Balzac), 20
evil: as a metaphysical privation of the good, xxiv–xxvi, 3, 194; in the moral sphere, *see* moral evil
exterior lordship, pride of, xxxviii, xli, 108–110, 112, 146–151, 153–154, 162

Fafner (*Rheingold*), 21, 72
fallen human nature, xxv–xxvi, 14, 59, 91, 98, 102, 169, 175–176, 180, 184, 188, 193–195, 208, *see also* original sin
fanaticism, xlii, 166, 177, 179–182, 183n17–184, 187, *see also* hatred
freedom and free will, xiv, xvii, xxvi, xxx, 10, 12, 18, 28–30, 32–35, 40–41, 53, 57, 70, 77, 114–115, 119, 122–124, 126–129, 171–172, 175–177, 194, 197, 199, 211n7, *see also* centers in a person ("free spiritual center"), self-control
Froelicher, Madeleine, xxii

frui (Latin, "to enjoy") or fruition *vs.*
  uti ("to use"), 61–62, 88–89, 94–95,
  97–98, 199

games, 56–58, 112–113, 206, *see also* psychic
  pleasures
Genealogy of Morals, The (Nietzsche),
  139n24
gift-giving, the act of, 89
Gilligan, Bernard, xxii
God: as Absolute Lord, 104; the
  concupiscent man's indifference
  towards, 18; cannot be the source or
  cause of moral evil, xxv–xxvi, 193–
  194; cursing as rebellion against, 44;
  error as an offense against Him, 179;
  and the fanatic, 181–182; the Father,
  97; as final judge, 124; as giver of
  freedom, 127–129, 199; glorifying
  Him by artistic practice, 66;
  gratitude towards, 126, 133; hatred of,
  103–104, 144, 159–161; love of Him
  (or Christ), xvi, 27, 29, 38–39, 46, 124,
  154, 172–175, 179–183, 185–186, 188,
  190–191; man as ordered towards, 19,
  60–61, 102, 183, 186, 199; as a means
  of self-glorification, 105; and moral
  obligation, 96, 124; and Pharasaic
  pride, 128, 151, 181; receiving
  pleasures as His gifts can change
  their category of importance, 27;
  and saints, 38, 125, 128, 173–174, 184,
  189–191; satanic pride rebels against
  and aims at the dethronement of,
  105, 128, 137, 141–142, 144, 149, 151,
  153, 160; and sexual pleasure, 32–34,
  37–38; and values, xxv, 12, 19, 29, 43,
  46, 73, 81, 91, 94, 98, 103, 106, 109, 114,
  118, 120–122, 128, 137, 141, 144, 158, 160,
  172, 179, 193, 207; as ultimate reality,
  98; various realities described as
  "God-given," 14, 32–35, 37, 93, 104

Gorgias (Plato), 175n9
Gospel, 76, 101, 117, 120, 122, 199, *see also*
  Luke, Matthew
grandeur: as an object of various forms of
  pride, xxxviii, 102–109, 111–112, 114–
  119, 125–127, 129–133, 135–137, 139–141–
  142, 144, 146–147, 149–151, 153, 161–
  162; of self-donation in marriage, 34;
  of values, *see* metaphysical power of
  values
Graven Images (Hildebrand), *see*
  Hildebrand, Dietrich von (works)

habitare secum (Latin, "dwelling with
  oneself"), 29, 94–95
hard concupiscent type, *see* concupiscent
  types
Harpagon (*The Miser*), 173
hatred: as the antithesis to love, xxv, xlii,
  159–160, 179; and the center of
  irascibility, 168–177; directed against
  acts of moral wickedness *vs.* against
  morally wicked persons, 166–167,
  182–189, 191, *see also* indignation;
  directed against errors and evil
  theories *vs.* against erring persons,
  166, 179–181, *see also* fanaticism;
  directed against God, Christ, or
  saints, xxxviii, xli, 103–104, 144,
  159–161, 172; directed against values,
  xxxviii, xl–xli, 103–104, 160, 176; and
  enmity, 166, 177, 184; its intrinsic
  disvalue or incompatibility with
  Christian charity, xli, 1, 171–172,
  175; mentioned, xx, xliv–xlv; as a
  passion, 170–172, 175–176, 182; and
  ressentiment, xl–xlii, 142; and revenge,
  166–168, 177; as rooted mainly in
  pride, xxi, xl–xlii, 103–104, 132, 134,
  141–142, 144, 157–164, 166, 168, 170,
  176–177, 181–182, 188; as rooted
  occasionally in concupiscence,

164–165, 170–171, 176–177, 181–182, 188; as rooted in something other than, or not obviously in, pride or concupiscence, xlii, 159, 166–167, *see also* enmity, revenge, fanaticism, indignation; satanic pride is the only type of pride that inevitably engenders it, xli, 104, 160; two stages of, 178–179

haughtiness, as a form of pride, 104, 110–112, 146–148, 150–154, 162, 187

hedonism, 28

heroism, *see* moral heroism

Herostratus, 176

hierarchy of values, 8, 196, *see also* value, world of values

Hildebrand, Alice von, xii, xxin6

Hildebrand, Dietrich von (biography), v, viii

Hildebrand, Dietrich von (works): *Ethics*, xv, xix–xxi, xxii, xxviii, xxix, xxxviii, xliv, 2n2, 6n7, 12n9, 17n1, 18n2, 20n3, 25n8, 27n9, 35n10, 36n13, 47n17, 53n18, 61n20, 83n29, 101n1, 112n8, 118n12, 159n3, 169n7, 202n3; *Graven Images*, xxx, 5n6, 6n7, 17n1, 18n2, 202n3; *Nachlass* (literary remains), xv, xix, xx, xxi–xxii, xliv–xlv, 53n18, 202n3; *Sittlichkeit und ethische Werterkenntnis*, xxxii, 5n6; *Transformation in Christ*, 105n5; writings and manuscripts on moral evil, xv–xvii, xix, xxi, xxix, xlviii–xlix, 202n3

holy indignation, 159, 189–191, *see also* indignation

Holy Spirit, 128

Horace, 112

Iago (*Othello*), 103

idols, xlii–xliii, 43, 75, 77, 110, 112, 136–139, 143, 153, 201–202, *see also* pseudo-values and pseudo-morality

ignorance of the good, moral evil not due to it, xv, xxii–xiii, xxviii, 2–5, 8

immanent logic (also called, less frequently, "immanent law"): of an activity, absorption in or enslavement to, xvi–xvii, xlii–xliv, 71, 85–86, 95–96, 195–211; of human nature, especially as tending to hostile, impulsive reactions to perceived offenses, 169–173, 176; of human nature, especially as tending to hatred of people who err or sin, 180–182, 184–185, 187–188; of human nature in general, xxvii, 97, 194; of vital instincts or passions, 33–34, 177

immorality, *see* moral evil

indignation, xl, xlii, 159, 166, 182–184, 186–191

inferiority complex, 137, 140, 144–145

intellectual values, xxiii, xxxvii–xxxviii, 8–9, 23, 66, 78, 93, 105, 115, 123, 126, 130, 133–134, 146

intelligence, xxxix, 69, 106, 108, 113–114, 116–117, 119–123, 125–127, 129, 132–133, 140, 143, 148

irascibility, 110, 168–169, *see also* centers in a person (center of irascibility)

jealousy, xl, 142, 144, 162, 177, *see also* envy, hatred, *ressentiment*

Kierkegaard, Søren, xvi

Kolya Krasotkin (*Brothers Karamazov*), 136

Lazarus, 76

laziness, xv–xvi, xxxvi, xliv, 90–100

lazy concupiscent type, *see* concupiscent types

legitimate center for the subjectively satisfying, *see* centers in a person

Letters (Augustine), 180n16
Lewy, Hans, 176n11
Litany of the Saints, 39n14
love, *see also* charity: basic or essential nature of, 34, 48, 93, 153, 177, 185–186; concupiscent reactions to being loved, 21; as expressed in gift-giving, 89; of God or Christ, xvi, 27, 29, 38–39, 46, 124, 154, 172–175, 179–183, 185–186, 188, 190–191; hatred as its antithesis, xxv, xl, 159–160, 179; in marriage, 32–35; of neighbor in the Christian sense, 38, 77, 154, 173–174, 180–182; prideful reactions to receiving it, 153–155; of the sinner or evildoer, 183, 185–191; of truth, 65; types of person incapable of it, 93, 153–154, 162–164; union established between persons by, 89–90
Lucifer, *see* Satan
Luke (Gospel), 76n24, 94n37, 97n39, 117n11, 122n15, 125n18

Macbeth (Shakespeare), 168
Manzoni, Alessandro, 190
Marra, William, xxii
marriage and sexual pleasure, 32–35, *see also* conjugal act
Mass, 95
master-morality, idol of, 139, 143, *see also* Nietzsche, idols
Matthew (Gospel), 120n13, 121n14, 135n22, 180n15
metaphysical power (or grandeur, or solemnity, or intrinsic beauty) of values, 96, 103, 103–105, 109, 111, 127–128, 131, 136–137, 141, 144
moderation, 28–32, *see also* akrasia, self-control
Molière, 173
money, 1, 4, 6–7, 21, 35, 56, 58, 69–78, 81, 84, 88, 92, 149–151, 168, 173–174, 199, 200, 202–203
Montagues and Capulets (*Romeo and Juliet*), 166
moral consciousness (or awakeness), xxx, 50, 94, 170–171, 174, 181, 188, 198, 204, 208–209, 210n7
moral evil (or badness, or disvalue, or immorality, or morally negative values): absorption in the immanent logic of an activity as a source of, xlii–xliv, 85n30, 196–197, 201–202, 206, 208n6–209n6, 210; ancient accounts of, xv, xxii–xxiv, xxvii, 3–4, 10, 12; and centers in a person, xvi, xxvii, 193; certain professions are obliged to protest against it, 41; due to evil will, xxiv–xxv, xxviii–xxx, 3, 12, 140, 157, 193; and examination of conscience, 121; given in experience as polar opposites of moral values, 1–2; in government, 199, 203; hatred as an embodiment of, 178, 184; Hildebrand's writings about, *see* Hildebrand, Dietrich von (works); as a loss of freedom, 199; and the metaphysical theory of evil as a privation of the good, xxiv–xxvi, 2, 193–194; and moral heroism, 47; and natural love, 186; not due exclusively to the interference of passions with practical reasoning, 9–11; not due to ignorance, xv, xxii–xxiii, xxviii, 2–5, 8; not due to preferring lower values to higher ones, 6–9; as an objective evil for the person, 173–175, 183, 185; one's response to it in others, 166, 173, 182–183, 185–190, *see also* enemy of God, indignation; the philosophical question of how they arise, 1–2, 11; punishment of, 167; as rooted in disrespect for, or lack of interest

in, morally relevant values (or, put another way, as rooted in disordered interest in the subjectively satisfying), xiii–xv, xxviii–xxxi, 3, 9, 11–13, 36n13, 39, 45–46, 72, 80, 140, 157, 193, 199; as rooted in either pride or concupiscence in all cases, xiv, xvii, xxii, xxv–xvi, xxx–xxxi, xxxiii, xxxvi, 9, 12, 15, 20, 26, 97, 99, 101, 129, 157–158, 193–194; and specific forms of concupiscence, xv, xxxiii–xxxiv, 25n8, 26, 30, 32, 35, 38, 42, 45, 50, 58, 69, 71–72, 76–78, 80–81; and specific forms of pride, xxxix, 43, 103, 114, 126, 133–135, 136, 138–141, 144; triumph of, sought by the satanic type of pride, 103, 153; the value-response attitude necessarily rejects it, 159

moral goodness, *see* moral values

moral heroism, 36, 38–39, 47, 70, 102, 175 *see also* saint, the

moral obligation, xxxiii–xxxiv, xxxviii, 19, 29, 36–41, 45–51, 70–71, 75, 77, 95–96, 122, 170, 179, 182, 184, 189

moral perfection, 25n8, 26–27, 48, 70, 108, 114, 118, 121, 125–126, 130, 134, 189–190, *see also* saint, the

moral unconsciousness, xxix, xxxv, 169–170, 174, 176, 187, 189

moral values (or goodness), *see also* morally relevant values; absence of them in one's own person will not hurt pride, 140–141; and absorption in the immanent logic of an activity, 209n6; the concupiscent man's indifference towards, 18, 50, 141; decisive differences between these and religious values and all other values of the person, 125–128; depend upon our freedom, 123–124; forms of pride indifferent towards, or incapable of understanding, them, xxxviii, 109, 111, 118, 131, 136; and the egocentrism of pride in general, 69; given in experience as polar opposites of moral disvalues, 1–2; and God, 12, 18–19, 91, 103, 118, 120–122, 124–125, 127–128, 141, 144, 160, 172; knowledge of one's own not given unless sought out by self-reflection, 120–122; legitimate interest in obtaining them for oneself, 48; metaphysical power and intrinsic beauty of, 109, 111, 136, 141; and personalities rooted in the world of values, 175; and Pharasaic pride, xxxvii, xxxix, 103, 114, 127, 134–135, 141, 161; the philosophical question of how they arise, 2; pride in one's own necessarily destroys them, 116–119, 122, 134; and pride of exterior lordship, xxxviii, 109; and the pride of haughtiness, 111; and pride of self-glorification, xxxviii, 115, 126–128; pride in them is graver than in exterior perfections, 115–116, 126–128; their provisional character and ordination to man's final end, 124–125; require the awareness that we might lose them in order for them to subsist, 122–124; require a spiritual *élan* antithetical to spiritual laziness, 97–98; require the value-response attitude in order for them to subsist, 117–118, 121, 128; and *ressentiment*, 143–144; retroactive effect of losing them, 124–125; satanic pride hates and wants to dethrone them, 103, 117, 141, 144, 151; and static pride, 130; technical self-control has none, 42–43; treated as distinct from morally relevant values, xxx–xxxi, 109, 137, 141; and value blindness, 4, 109, 111, 209n6; and the value-response attitude in general, xiii, 159 moral virtues: and absorption in the immanent logic of an activity, xliv; and the call of values, xliv; depend upon our freedom, 115; knowledge of one's own not given unless sought out by self-reflection, 120–121; and moral knowledge, xxx; and Pharasaic pride, 118; in Plato and Aristotle, xxiii–xxiv, xxix; pride in one's own necessarily destroys them, 116–119; pride in them is graver than in exterior perfections, 115–116; their provisional character and ordination to man's final end, 124–125; require the value-response attitude in order for them to subsist, xxix, xxxi, 116–119, 121; and satanic pride, 117; and superactual abandonment to God, 118, 121; and value-blindness, xxxii

morality: Christian *vs.* natural, 25n8, 26, 47, 171–172, 174, 183–188, 191; the idol of master-morality, 139, 143, *see also* idols, Nietzsche

morally negative values, *see* moral evil

morally neutral, xxxiii, xlii, 13, 76, 81–82

morally relevant values (or morally relevant good), xxx–xxxi, xxxv, xli, xliv, 2–13, 17–23, 25, 27, 29–32, 35–36, 39–48, 50–52, 54, 56, 67, 71–73, 75–78, 80–81, 88, 90–92, 94–95, 109, 117–118, 120–123, 127–128, 137–138, 141, 145–146, 158, 160, 165, 169, 174, 182, 207, 211n7, *see also* moral values

National Socialism, vii, 46, 143

natural morality *vs.* Christian morality, 25n8, 26, 47, 171–172, 174, 183–188, 191

Neoplatonism, xxiv

neutral importance, 6, 26, 45, 78, *see also* categories of importance

Nicomachean Ethics (Aristotle), xxiii–xxiv, 3, 64–65, 75n23

Nietzsche, Friedrich, 139n24, 143

nihilism, 103, 105

Ninth Symphony (Beethoven), 90

non serviam (Latin, "I will not serve"), 104

objective evil for the person, 47–48, 175, 180, 183, 185

objective good for the person, 2, 27, 48, 82–86, 116, 136, *see also* categories of importance

obligation, *see* moral obligation

original sin, xxv–xxvi, 193–194

Othello (Shakespeare), 103

pain, *see* bodily pain

passions: in competition with freedom and deliberation, 9–11, 29, 171–172, 175, 199; in cooperation with pride and concupiscence, 170–171, 177, 209; and hatred, 170, 172, 175, 182; moral evil not due exclusively to their interference with practical reasoning, 9–11; in the strict sense turns away from *religio*, 73–74, 177

Paul, St., 3

Paul IV, Pope, 203

person, indestructible value of the, 172, 181–186, 188

pettegolezzi (Italian, "indiscrete gossip"), 79

Phaedrus (Plato), xxiii

Pharasaic pride (or the Pharisee), xxxvii, xxxix, xli, 103, 105, 114–115, 117–118, 127–128, 130, 133–135, 137–141, 146, 149, 151, 160–161, 181, 185, 190

philistine, 85

Philo of Alexandria, 176n11

phlegmatic concupiscent type, *see* concupiscent types

Plato, xv, xxii–xxiv, xxvii, xxxix, 3–4, 66n22, 128, 150n29, 171, 174, 175n9, 176, 186, 210n7,

pleasure, *see also* subjectively satisfying; of

the body, *see* bodily agreeable; licit *vs.* illicit, xxxiii, 11–12; sexual: *see* sexual pleasure; in the strict sense, i.e., the outspokenly agreeable, 24; types of attitudes towards, xxv

Plotinus, xxxivn8

pop culture, *see* psychic pleasures

preference, 6–9, 76, 77

pride: basic or essential nature of, 101–102; becomes worse the more one's free collaboration is presupposed, 114–115; its character depends on the values that are its object, 114–129, 145; conceit as a form of, xxxix, 132–135, 139; in disvalues, xxi, xxxix, 135–139; enslavement to immanent logic of an activity as rooted in, 204–206, 209–210; the five types or dimensions of listed, xxxvii–xxxviii, 112; in non-existent values, xxi, xxxix, 107, 118, 132–139; of exterior lordship, xxxviii, xli, 108–110, 112, 146–151, 153–154, 162; and hatred, xxi, xl–xlii, 103–104, 132, 134, 141–142, 144, 157–164, 166, 168, 170, 176–177, 181–182, 188; haughtiness as a form of, xxxviii, xli, 104, 110–112, 146–148, 150–154, 162, 187; necessarily destroys moral and religious values and virtues, 116–119, 122–123, 134; and passion, 170, 176–177; Pharasaic form of, xxxvii, xxxix, xli, 103, 105, 114–115, 117–118, 127–128, 130, 133–135, 137–141, 146, 149, 151, 160–161, 181, 185, 190; and politics, 201; in possession or ownership, 148–149; its reaction to being loved, 153–155; its reaction to consciousness of inferiority, 142–144; as referring to the absence of one's personal values, xxxix–xl, 139–145; as referring to exterior goods, 145–149; as referring to money and wealth, 149–150; as referring to power and reputation, 150–153; its relations with concupiscence, xli, 19–20, 22, 44, 59, 68–69, 74, 82, 84, 96–97, 101–102, 103, 108, 137–138, 146–149, 152, 157–159, 164–165, 170–171, 176, 181–182, 188, 209–210; its role in the different spheres of life, 112–114; as rooted in the merely subjectively satisfying, xiv, xxxvi, 101–102; of self-glorification, xxi, xxxvii–xxxix, xli, 22, 102, 104–107, 112, 113–114, 116–118, 125–128, 132, 133, 137–140, 142, 145–149, 151–154, 161–162, 163; static *vs.* dynamic, distinction between, 106–107, 129–132, 145; satanic type of, *see* satanic pride; as a universal poison, 148; vanity as a form of, xxxvii–xxxviii, xli–xlii, 107–108, 112, 146–147, 149–154, 163

prodigality, 74, 76–77

property, xxxv–xxxvi, 4, 6–7, 73, 81, 86–90

Psalms, 122, 209

pseudo-values and pseudo-morality, 97, 104, 107, 118, 134–135, 138–141, 143, 161, 209, *see also* idols

psychic pleasures: in games, 56–58; in pop culture (e.g., light literature, music, movies), 61–64; in superficial forms of socializing, xxxiv, 58–61; in "the releasing of one's mental energies," xxxv, 64–69

punishment, 165, 167

Quo Vadis (Sienkiewicz), xxxii

Rakitin (*Brothers Karamazov*), 160

Raskolnikov (*Crime and Punishment*), 4

reign of values (or morally relevant values), the, 13–15, 18–21, 25, 29, 31, 35, 42–44, 54, 60, 62, 81, 86, 88, 92, 103, 108, 120, 128, 136–138, 144, 151, 160, 172, 174, 182, 198, 207, 210n7 *religio* (i.e., the fundamental moral attitude of reverence for, consciousness of, and obedience to values), xxv, xxx–xxxi, xxxiii, xxxvi, xliii–xliv, 13–14, 29–32, 35, 38, 42–44, 50, 57–62, 71–75, 78, 86, 88, 92–94, 127, 138, 172, 176–177, 182, 189, 193, 198, 208–209, 210n7; *see also* call of values, metaphysical power of values, reign of values, *sursum corda*, value-response attitude

religious values and virtues: decisive differences between these and moral values and all other values of the person, 126–128; depend upon our freedom, 115, 123–124; knowledge of one's own not given unless sought out by self-reflection, 120–122; and Pharasaic pride, xxxvii, 105, 114, 127, 134, 141; and pride of exterior lordship, xxxviii, 109; pride in one's own necessarily destroys them, 117–118, 134; and pride of self-glorification, xxxvii–xxxviii, 115, 126n19, 127; pride in them is graver than in exterior perfections, 115; their provisional character and ordination to man's final end, 124–125; and the religious *élan*, 95, 97–98, *see also sursum corda*; require the awareness that we might lose them in order for them to subsist, 124; retroactive effect of losing them, 124–125; satanic pride hates and wants to dethrone them, 103, 117; and the soft concupiscent type, 23; as a special gift of grace, 129; and static pride, 130; and the value-response attitude, 121, 128

Republic (Plato), xxii–xxiv, 3

ressentiment, xl–xlii, 137, 140, 142–144, 160, 162–163, *see also* hatred, satanic pride

Das Ressentiment im Aufbau der Moralen (Scheler), xl, 143n27

revenge, xxi, xlii, 1, 82, 164–168, 177

reverence, xxx, xxxii, xxxvi, xliii–xliv, 31, 43, 80, 100, 135, *see also religio, sursum corda*, value-responding attitude

Rheingold (Wagner), 21n4

Richelieu, Cardinal, 201

Romeo and Juliet (Shakespeare), 166

sadism, xxxii–xxxiii, 77–78, 81–82

saint, the: as the absolute antithesis to concupiscence and pride, 26; approach to bodily pain, 38–40; approach to money, 70; approach to the subjectively satisfying, xxxiii, 25–27, 83; charity of, 38, 128; conqueror of spiritual laziness, 90, 98; in constant readiness to respond to God's call, 203; contrasted with the normal morally good man, 140; lives in the pure value-response attitude, 173; and love of neighbor, 38; loves the sinner but hates the sin, 184, 188–191; mentioned, 109; moral heroism of, 47, *see also* moral obligation; moral perfection of, 25n8, 26, 189–190; more convinced than any other type of person of the call of moral values and one's own moral insufficiency in conforming to them, 121–122; and natural morality, 26; as an object of the Pharisee's hatred, 161; and pride of exterior lordship, 109; and *religio*, 38; and the transformation of the center of irascibility, 173–174; why moral and religious values demand that no one is canonized before death, 125

sanction and disavowal, 169–171

Satan, 20, 103, 128, 160n5

satanic pride: basic or essential nature of, xxxvii, 102–104, 117, 130, 141, 154, 160; compared with other forms of pride: xxxviii, xl, 20, 81, 104–105, 109, 110–111, 113, 118, 127–128, 131, 137, 139, 143–144, 146, 148–149, 151, 153–154; and concupiscence, 81; essentially distinguished from the immature, adolescent posturing to assert independence, 135–137; and exterior comforts and goods, 146; and hatred, xxxvii, xli, 159–161, 163; mentioned, 112; and money, 149; and ownership of property, 148–149; and power, 149; its reaction to being loved, 154; rebels against and aims at the dethronement of God and the moral order, 105, 128, 137, 141–142, 144, 149, 151, 153, 160; and reputation, 153

Scheler, Max, vii, xxvii, xxxi, xl, 25n8, 42n19, 143

self-control, formal or technical mastery of the will *vs.* that of the value-response attitude, 28–29, 31, 42–43, 46; *see also akrasia*, moderation

self-glorification, pride of, xxi, xxvii, xxxviii–xxxix, xli, 22, 102, 104–107, 112–114, 116–118, 125–128, 132–133, 137–140, 142, 145–149, 151–154, 161, 163

sensationalism, xxxii, 58, 79–80

sexual pleasure: 24, 31–35, 37–38, 54, 58, 81–82, 146, 148

Shakespeare, William, 103, 110, 166

Sickness Unto Death, The (Kierkegaard), xvi

Sienkiewicz, Henryk, xxxii

sin, 26, 39, 128, 159, 173–174, 180n16, 183–185, 188–189, 191, 193, 204, *see also* original sin

Sittlichkeit und ethische Werterkenntnis (Hildebrand), *see* Hildebrand, Dietrich von (works)

sobria ebrietas (Latin, "sober drunkenness"), 176

socializing, *see* psychic pleasures

Socrates, xxii–xxiv, xxx, xxxiii, 3–4, 26

soft concupiscent type, *see* concupiscent types

spiritual *élan*, xvi, 93–100, 208

spiritual laziness, xvi, xxxvi, xliv, 93–100, 170, 176–177, 180–182, 184–185, 188, 208–209

spousal love, *see* marriage and sexual pleasure

static pride, xxxvii, xlii, 106–107, 111, 129–133, 142, 145, 153, 163

Stoic school, xxiv, 31, 42–43, 112, 152, 171–172, 187

subjectively dissatisfying in the bodily sphere, 36–56

subjectively satisfying: in the bodily sphere, 23–35; disordered interest in as the root of all moral evil, xiv, xxxi–xxxii, xxxvi, 12–13, 101–102; as essentially contrasted with value, xiii–xiv, xxvii, xxxi, 4, 6–7, 11; as the motivating element of the passions, 10, 73–74; in the ownership of property, 86–87; in the psychic sphere, 56–77; legitimate types of that can become an object of concupiscence, 24–35, 56–77, 86–87; in the sphere of pure concupiscence, 77–82

Summa Theologiae (Aquinas), 180n16

sursum corda ("lift up your hearts"), 60, 93–97

Symposium (Plato), 66n22

technical self-control, 28–29, 31, 42–43, 46, *see also* self-control

Tractatus in Iohannem (Augustine), 78n20

Transformation in Christ (Hildebrand), *see* Hildebrand, Dietrich von (works)

unum necessarium (Latin, "the one thing necessary"), 94, 203
urges: bodily, 52–53; psychical, 64–69
useful, the, 84–85

value: xiii–211 *passim*. *See also* aesthetic values, call of values, categories of importance, idols, intellectual values, metaphysical power of values, moral and morally relevant values, moral virtue, pseudo-values and pseudo-morality, reign of values, *religio*, religious values, reverence, *sursum corda*, value blindness, value-responding center, value-response attitude, vital values, world of values; basic or essential nature of, xiii; as essentially contrasted with the merely subjectively satisfying: xiii–xiv, xxvii–xxviii, xxxi, 4, 6–7, 11; and God, xxv, 12, 18–19, 29, 43, 46, 73, 81, 91, 94, 98, 103, 106, 109, 114, 118, 120–122, 128, 137, 141, 144, 158, 160, 172, 179, 193, 207; as the heart of Hildebrand's ethics, xiii, xxvii; immorality of actions not due to preferring lower ones to higher ones, 6–9; of the person, 172, 181–186, 188; satanic pride's futile attempt to dethrone them, 103–105, 111, 117, 128, 131, 137, 141, 144, 160
value blindness, xxx–xxxi, 4–5, 17–18, 94, 103, 105, 109, 111, 113–114, 131, 196, 198, 209n6
value-responding center, *see* centers in a person
value-response attitude, the, xxxiv–xxxvi, xli, 13–14, 18, 24, 25n8, 27–29, 31, 35, 39, 43–46, 52, 57, 60, 66–76, 78, 80–81, 83, 85–86, 91, 97, 108, 112, 116–117, 122–123, 128, 134n21, 137–138, 140, 145, 148, 155, 159, 166, 169, 171, 173, 175, 179–181, 183–186, 191, 204–205, 209, *see also* call of values, centers in a person, reign of values, reverence, *religio*, *sursum corda*, world of values
vanity, xxxvii–xxxviii, xli–xlii, 107–108, 112, 129–130, 132, 142, 146–147, 149–154, 163
vice, xxix, 2, 121
virility, idol of, xxxviii–xxxix, 40–43, 110, 136–139, 153–154, *see also* haughtiness
virtue, *see* moral virtue
vital values, 115–116, 143

wealth, *see* money
will, *see also* freedom and free will; moral evil is due to its perversion, xxiv–xxv, xxviii–xxx, 3, 12, 140, 157, 193; perversion of is responsible for value blindness, xxxi, 5; weakness of, xxiii–xxiv, xxvii–xxviii, xxxi, 46, 91, *see also akrasia*, moderation, self-control
work (of art), especially authentic or great examples of, xvi, 61, 63–67, 88–89, 116–117, 190, 211n7
work (labor), xvi, xxxii, xxxvi, 57, 61–62, 66, 91–96, 98–99, 113, 196, 199, 201, 209n6
world of values, the, 19, 91, 97–98
wrath, 91, 164–165, 169, 171

Zosima (*Brothers Karamazov*), 160

www.ingramcontent.com/pod-product-compliance
Lightning Source LLC
Chambersburg PA
CBHW071737150426
43191CB00010B/1610